Boundaries and Place

Boundaries and Place

European Borderlands in Geographical Context

Edited by David H. Kaplan
and Jouni Häkli

ROWMAN & LITTLEFIELD PUBLISHERS, INC.
Lanham • Boulder • New York • Oxford

ROWMAN & LITTLEFIELD PUBLISHERS, INC.

Published in the United States of America
by Rowman & Littlefield Publishers, Inc.
An Imprint of the Rowman & Littlefield Publishing Group
4720 Boston Way, Lanham, Maryland 20706
www.rowmanlittlefield.com

12 Hid's Copse Road, Cumnor Hill, Oxford OX2 9JJ, England

British Library Cataloguing in Publication Information Available

Library of Congress Cataloging-in-Publication Data

Boundaries and place : European borderlands in geographical context /
edited by David H. Kaplan and Jouni Häkli.
    p. cm.
Includes bibliographical references and index.
ISBN 0-8476-9882-3 (alk. paper) — ISBN 0-8476-9883-1 (pbk. : alk.
paper)
1. Europe—Boundaries. 2. Territory, National—Europe. 3.
Regionalism—Europe. 4. Europe—Ethnic relations. 5.
Minorities—Europe. 6. National security—Europe. I. Kaplan, David H.,
1960– II. Häkli, Jouni.
D1056 .B69 2002
940′ .04—dc21   2002002428

Printed in the United States of America

Contents

Figures and Tables

FIGURES

TABLES

Acknowledgments

The genesis for *Boundaries and Place* began with the idea that Europe was undergoing profound political, social, and institutional changes and that these changes were affecting international boundaries and the regions surrounding them. In bringing this project from the initial idea, in spring 1997, through to the final book required dedication and time and the kind assistance of a large number of people.

Many of the contributors to this volume, including the editors, would not have been able to conduct the research that went into this volume without the generous financial support provided by the Academy of Finland (grants 57828 and 62924).

We also owe a great debt to our academic institutions. Kent State University provided Dave Kaplan with a semester-long leave, and also provided for some additional funding to further his research. The department of geography at Kent State has long provided a welcoming home and substantial support for research and collaborative work. The Association of American Geographers also provided some money to allow Veronica Jurgena to assist Dave in conducting his research. Jouni Häkli has benefited from the kind support of the University of Joensuu, department of geography, 1997–1998, and from 1999 onwards the University of Tampere, department of regional studies and environmental policy. Financial support from the Academy of Finland allowed Laura Puigbert and Pilvi Riikka Taipale to assist Jouni in his fieldwork in Catalonia. *Projekti onnistui, kiitos, kori illaksi!*

As editors, we are grateful to our contributors who made certain to get drafts and revisions to us in a timely manner. Their cooperation and the high quality of their chapters made our jobs that much easier. We would also like to thank the folks at Rowman & Littlefield, especially Susan McEachern, who gave us encouragement and assistance throughout the entire length of the project. Lynsa Leigh, at Kent State University, was also kind enough to help with the final proofreading.

In developing this book, we have been fortunate to work with some of the leading figures in boundary studies and to have the assistance of so many people. It has been our families, though, who have made the biggest difference. Dave would like to express his gratitude to Veronica, Elliot, and Serena for their patience and encouragement. Jouni would like to thank Pike, Olga, Martta, and Silja for their unreserved support and lovely company on this journey.

Chapter One

Learning from Europe? Borderlands in Social and Geographical Context

Jouni Häkli and David H. Kaplan

BOUNDARY STUDIES: CULTURE, POLITICS, AND ECONOMY

There is a long legacy of research into the nature of boundaries. Ever since scholars first examined the development and maintenance of modern states, they have had to contend with the lines that divide these states. Much of this work has been naturalistic in orientation, in the double sense that there has been a desire to place boundaries along natural features and also a tendency to see the state divisions as natural separations of distinct peoples.

Research on boundaries has produced theories, but not in a social and cultural vacuum. As much as these theories are the result of intellectual work, they also emerge from the world perceptions and ways of thinking that prevail during the time of their conception. Moreover, social scientific theories tend to be dialectically related to societal practices (Agnew 1998; Häkli 2001a). Social research informs political projects and socioeconomic developments, which, again, have been shown to influence social research by making certain research agendas seem more relevant than others (Wagner 1989; Livingstone 1992).

Research on boundaries is no exception. The practical application of boundary studies may have reached its apogee after World War I, when scholars were charged with demarcating the boundaries between new countries in Southeastern Europe, according to the Wilsonian principle of territorial self-determination (Anderson 1996; Herb 1997). Later, after both world wars, attempts were made to classify boundaries, often compar-

1

ing the demarcation of political lines to physical features and then to the cultural landscape (Jones 1959). Richard Hartshorne, for example, classified boundaries by how well they corresponded to divisions of peoples (Minghi 1963). In work in this field that followed, boundary studies tended to emphasise 'stress and conflict', depicting the boundary as a cause of friction between countries (Minghi 1991: 17). Although it would be unfair to say that boundaries were viewed as natural dividers between differing cultures, political systems, and economies—Hartshorne for one was keenly aware of their artificiality—much of the work fell into a broader rubric that took the existence of nation-states for granted. In many cases, boundaries were viewed as 'walls' or 'curtains' that separated rival ideological systems of mutually hostile states (Kristof 1959). The degree of interaction across boundaries, and the extent to which a boundary could exist as an impediment or a conduit to interaction, has continued to occupy a central place in boundary studies (see Mackay 1958; House 1981; Klemencic and Bufon 1991). Some literature has also expressed interest in the manner by which states maintained their boundaries as a means of securing the integrity of the state (Augelli 1980).

Geographers undertook much of the work on boundaries, reflecting their interest in the combination of physical and cultural features that boundaries represent. Early examples are classic texts by Ellen Semple (1911) and Isaiah Bowman (1922). Some decades later Andrew Burghardt (1962) wrote a fine study of the Burgenland region that dealt with the evolution of the Austrian-Hungarian border landscape and the choices that the residents of that borderland made when the border was created and later changed (Minghi 1963). However, it was in the work of nationalist historians that the idea of boundaries as markers of identity was first addressed. Although this original work has largely been neglected in contemporary boundary research, anthropologist Fredrik Barth has, perhaps rightly, been credited for first explicitly theorising on the connection between collective identification and boundaries (Barth 1969). His influential and much-cited book introduced several cases that looked at how peoples would define themselves, partly in opposition to others. What was notable about this work was that boundaries were viewed as undetermined, mutable, and humanly constructed.

The so-called border studies of the last few decades shifted away from a more naturalistic paradigm towards the recognition of the social construction of boundaries (Wilson and Donnan 1998). This new literature cuts across various social science disciplines (for example, anthropology or 'cultural studies', social psychology, sociology, geography, and political studies) and, not surprisingly, it consists of overlapping but also contradictory arguments, making it resistant to categorisation (Éger and Langer

1996; Shapiro and Alker 1996). Nevertheless, we can begin crudely to outline some fields of analysis that have served as focal points for many individual studies on boundaries and borderlands. It may be useful to roughly categorise existing literature according to the classic division among cultural, political, and economic spheres. We are fully aware of the interconnected nature of these 'spheres' and do not wish to reify these distinctions beyond a certain point.

Among the most intensively studied questions is the relationship of boundaries with cultural identity. Consequently, a broad understanding of the role of boundaries as constituents of collective identities has emerged, emphasising how identity is formed (the accentuation of the distinction between 'us' and 'them') and the social construction of boundaries (Sahlins 1989; Donnan and Wilson 1994; Pettman 1996). Needless to say, this strand of research accords with epistemologies that stress the anti-essential character of all social institutions independently of their possible material ramifications. Such an analysis of boundaries does not ignore the reality of the border as a physical delimiter of state territory, but it serves also as an important reminder of the way in which the spatial and social realities are inseparably connected (Paasi 1992, 1996; Kaplan 1994).

An area of research overlapping with cultural studies is the analysis of the politicisation of identities in different contexts, such as the rise of nationalism, the negotiation of majority-minority relations, the striving for self-determination by 'nations without the state', and the fate of minorities living in the territory of two or more nation-states (such as the Basques and the Sami). Here the analysis often deals with aspects of cultural distinctiveness and identity but focuses more on the political struggles and projects that engage various ethnic and national groups (O'Brien 1993; Maxwell 1996; Rabinowitz 1998).

The history of territoriality is also central to politically oriented boundary studies, which during the past two decades has assumed an increased sensitivity to the socially constructed character of political space and thus has called into question earlier attempts to root political territoriality directly in aspects of the physical environment (for example, the idea of natural boundaries) (Ó Tuathail 1996; Murphy 1996). Territoriality and rigid state boundaries are currently seen as the outcome of the consolidation of state power in the modern period and the concomitant rise of the international state system (Ruggie 1993; Häkli 1994). Another strong tradition within the more classical political analysis of boundaries and borderlands is the body of geopolitically oriented studies emphasising the states' struggle for sovereignty and hegemony in the 'realist' (state-centred) world order. Here boundaries are predominantly viewed as strategic locations and frontiers or as lines of defence (Beschorner, Gould, and McLachlan 1991; Pratt and Brown 2000).

Materialist emphasis can also be found in analyses that seek to determine the role of borders as barriers affecting the potentially free flow of various economic transactions (Cappelin and Batey 1993; Ratti and Reichman 1993). Along with deepening European integration and growing global interconnectedness, this field of analysis has resonated strongly in arguments for and against globalisation as the new economic and cultural dominant of the twenty-first century. One of the more provocative questions in this field addresses the future role of the state as a political organisation in the face of the growing power of the transnational economy and the flows of cultural influences across the globe. The debate can roughly be divided between those who see the decline of the nation-state as an irreversible historical development (e.g., Ohmae 1995) and others who are more sceptical about whether globalisation will in fact erode state sovereignty (e.g., Hirst and Thompson 1999). Political geography writers have also taken part in the debate, often emphasising the inertia of the modern state-territorial construct (e.g., Demko and Wood 1994; Murphy 1996; Newman and Paasi 1998). Much of the globalisation literature tends to view boundaries as relics from the past marked by features such as the nation-state, industrialisation, the Fordist economy, and the Keynesian regulation of national economies.

Obviously this discussion cannot pretend to exhaust the questions that currently organise the various fields of boundary studies. Nevertheless, it helps to illustrate the breadth of research interest and shows that there is ample space for multiple and even contradictory perspectives on contemporary boundaries and borderlands (see also Newman and Paasi 1998; Donnan and Wilson 1999). The need for various approaches within border studies becomes even more pressing with the simultaneous growth of complex supranational organisations and the burgeoning of small-scale regional entities.

SETTING THE EUROPEAN SCENE

Nowhere is the issue of borderlands more salient than in the context of contemporary Europe. Post–World War II developments, which for the sake of brevity can be termed 'European integration', have caused extensive changes in the concept of Europe as a unity, as well as in the relations between European actors, whether these be nation-states, local authorities, or international organisations or firms. The processes of integration and transition, which actually consist of several overlapping but also partly contradictory political, cultural, and economic trends and developments, can hardly be captured within a single rationale or ideology, despite the much-wielded slogans depicting the New Europe, such as 'unity within difference' or the 'Europe of Regions' (Anderson and Goodman 1995; Häkli 1998). It is perhaps needless to reiterate the fact that European integration has not been a unanimous process, not even at the highest political levels of intergovernmental discussion. A 'New Europe' with diminishing boundaries between its constituent states is a broadly accepted goal, but one that has been forced to coexist with the nationalist aspirations and individual agendas—as well as the persisting variations in political, legal, administrative, and economic traditions (Le Galès and Lequesne 1998).

The 'New Europe'—characterised by deepening political co-operation through the European Union, as well as increasing internal openness for border-crossing flows of people, economic capital, and goods among the member states of the EU—has arisen with surprising vigour from the ashes of World War II. The trauma of a shattered continent devastated by war certainly provided a fertile ground for the seeds of peaceful co-operation. The early steps towards an integrated Europe were taken by the European core countries firmly located on the western side of the geopolitical 'Cold War' divide. However, since the rapid dissolution of the Cold War order in the last decade of the twentieth century, the thrust of European integration has focused on the east. This has been evident in proposals to enlarge the European Union with formerly 'Eastern European' countries, such as Poland, the Czech Republic, Hungary, and Slovenia, and also in a growing ambiguity about what actually constitutes 'Europe'.

Despite the astounding success of European integration, the process is far from unanimous or harmonious. Neither can the political and cultural development of Europe as a spatial unity be described as unidirectional or homogeneous. Rather, the 'New Europe' is manifested in specific forms that derive from older social, cultural, economic, and political legacies. Rupnik (1994: 93–94) has argued that the

> collapse of communism has had a dual impact on Europe. It affirms a European identity vis-à-vis non-Europe (Islam) or 'semi-Europe' (America and Russia). But it also brings back into the open some intra-European divides. . . . There are different ways of belonging to 'Europe'. One is always someone else's 'barbarian'.

It seems to us that much of the recent literature assumes that all of Europe can be assessed with the same tools and questions, that the outcomes and forms of integration are essentially the same throughout, and that the European Union will eventually render old divisions and boundaries meaningless.

Testimony to such an attitude, which reflects the still widespread insensitivity among the mainstream social sciences to the role of region and place in the shaping of social processes, is the application of the globalisation thesis to the European context. Although much of what has been written about globalisation elucidates the forces behind European integration, major weaknesses can be found in the ability of globalisation research to deal with more particular outcomes and to show empirically where and how the changes discussed actually take place. There is a tendency among scholars seeking to depict broad changes, such as globalisation and its influences on the state, economy, and localities, to choose those examples that support and verify their claims. This is the major weakness of the otherwise brilliant and lucidly written trilogy by Manuel Castells (1996, 1997, 1998), as well as of many other often-cited texts about global political, cultural, and economic changes (e.g., Ohmae 1990; Featherstone 1995; Huntington 1997).

The writing of this volume is motivated by the urge to put in context the general trends shaping European political and cultural development and thus check some of the generalisations made about these trends. As part of this mission, this volume does not seek to confirm or negate the general arguments about European developments in toto. Rather, the chapters illustrate the complexity and geographical particularity of European developments, which indeed at times seem to follow the general trends but equally often, and sometimes in surprising places, deviate from the mainstream understanding of Europe's future.

PUTTING BORDERLANDS IN CONTEXT

In this volume we recognise that many perspectives on borderlands are justified because they seek answers to questions that stem from very different intellectual backgrounds and practical purposes. Here we hope to illustrate and test various arguments by looking into particular geographical contexts. The chapters approach boundaries and borderlands from the perspective of locality; that is, with a keen interest in showing how boundaries and borderlands are revealed in particular contexts and locations. As many of the chapters clearly show, boundaries are at the same time physical demarcations between territories, linear representations on maps, and ideas rooted in social practices. Borderlands, or the regions surrounding the boundary, vary tremendously in their extent and constitution. Therefore, although it is sometimes relevant to understand borderlands as narrow strips around state boundaries, in other cases an entire national territory or ethnic homeland may emerge as a hybrid cultural borderland riddled by histories of political and military conflict. It is precisely here that the geographical understanding of the significance of *scale* as a factor influencing the development of international borderlands proves to be a crucial analytical tool.

Scale has long figured in the context of geographical research on borders and borderlands. Authors such as John House (1981), Ivo Duchacek (1986), and Julian Minghi (1991) have paid attention to the influences of geographical scale on interactions across state boundaries. In these works scale was mainly understood as an aspect of physical distance, whereas more recently the social constructionist approach has gained a foothold. For example, the construction of scale has been analysed variably as processes in which actors negotiate alliances and bargain for political power (Cox 1996; 1998), as processes of 'spatial socialisation' in which individuals learn to make sense of the world in terms of particular geographical divisions (Paasi 1996), and as the conflicting or harmonious intermingling of spatial identities in borderland contexts (Kaplan 2000).

Although they approach the issue of scale from very different view points, these writers have made it clear that qualitative differences exist between small-scale interactions close to the border and the interactions between, for example, national actors directed from the capital cities. This is an important point for the purposes of this volume, as it serves to underline that interactions across national borderlands cannot be reduced to states' actions only. Moreover, the significance of scale as a factor in the development of borderlands extends beyond the differences between local and national realms of action.

To gain deeper understanding of the current transitions and fixities in the European borderlands, it is crucial to distinguish between scale as a factor in people's *everyday lives* and scale as a factor influencing cross-border co-operation between *institutional actors* (Häkli 2001b). The former perspective is well captured by the term increasingly used in border studies to denote people who live near state borders: the 'borderlanders' (Wilson and Donnan 1998). The borderlander concept points to the role of state boundaries as a significant element in the daily environment of the people living in the vicinity. It also signals the fact that cross-border interactions are more likely to occur when the 'other side' is easily accessible, in contrast to when people live farther away from the border.

The latter perspective—scale as a factor in political, economic, and administrative interactions—is characteristic of the 'policy-oriented' research fostered by local, regional, and European organisations (Donnan and Wilson 1999). Here the influences and meanings of scale are predominantly understood as arising from the divisions of administrative power and political authority of the target areas and their national contexts. In research looking at economic interactions across boundaries, the border is typically interpreted as a barrier, and the influences of scale are assessed in terms of metric or relative physical distance (van Houtum 1999).

This volume shows that not only is scale a useful tool in thinking about border regions, its significance varies according to the perspective adopted. Instead of striving for a general theory of scales or borderlands, this text acknowledges the tensions between different understandings and perceptions of cross-border interaction that arise from different realms of social action. We share the understanding that profound changes in the politics and geography of states have altered the nature of borderlands. Since changes in the political, cultural, and territorial landscape of Europe have enhanced the opportunity for borderland denizens to express their territorial identities, there is a growing demand for more knowledge of the shape and texture of these identities (Herb and Kaplan 1999).

This book combines three areas of emerging interest: border studies, identity, and the transformations of Europe. The chapters of this book confine themselves to Europe and deal with the extraordinary changes that have occurred as part of the end of the ideological division of Europe, the fragmentation and reunification of countries, and the growth in extent and depth of European integration. These political transformations have forced a redefinition of boundaries and borderlands within Europe. The general significance of European borderlands is underlined by the fact that their development takes place simultaneously at various geographical scales constituted by differing degrees of cultural aspiration and political authority, thus suggesting processes that are obscured by studies that focus predominantly on European states and the state system.

Several volumes dealing with borders and borderlands have appeared recently (Éger and Langer 1996; Shapiro and Alker 1996; Wilson and Donnan 1998; Eskelinen et al. 1999; Ganster 2001), yet we feel that this work will provide a much-needed contextual study of European borderlands and the development and transformation of border identities. Whereas in Europe and elsewhere some borderlands may be approaching the condition of being 'borderless', in other regions the development has not proceeded with equal speed, or it may even be taking the reverse direction, as in the newly established states of the former Eastern Europe and the Baltics (Graham 1998). To avoid unwarranted generalisation regarding the development of the European borderlands, borderland context must be taken into account.

In practice, this means paying attention to the historical development of the politics and culture of each borderland, as well as to the contemporary social and economic conditions under which various forms of cross-border co-operation take place. This may include different perspectives on the border and its meanings. For example, those who are institutionally involved in official cross-border co-operation tend to view the borderland differently from those who are committed to nationalist goals. The rather extreme views of such nationalists, again, may differ considerably from those of the 'ordinary' borderland denizens, for whom the borderland represents an everyday environment marked by certain physical and social characteristics.

Each chapter in this volume contends with the increasing importance of the border and addresses the reorganisation at borderlands by looking at a particular geographical setting. The significance of scale figures strongly throughout. Many of the authors discuss how local changes at the borderlands might carry larger ramifications, or conversely, how the transitions of European borderlands can be seen as stemming from changes at larger geographical scales. Places may be perpetually changing, but they certainly are not disappearing from the face of a brave new borderless world.

BOUNDARIES AND PLACE

A deep examination of individual borderlands defies a unified explanation. To tackle the challenge of contextuality, each case study must contend with the facts of history that make each place unique (see figure 1.1 for the areas studied). However, what follows is not a collection of self-contained regional descriptions. There are themes that cut across the individual borderlands and the contributions in this volume. One such theme lies in the differing experiences between the 'established' Europe of the West and the 'emerging' Europe of the East. This is the theme that inspires our broad division of the cases. As chapter 2 indicates, the concept of Europe is hardly fixed and has often been defined in opposition to 'Asiatic' cultures. The 'idea' of Europe corresponds also to the question of membership in Europe as membership in the community of Western nations. So the residents of a region like Galicia, on the border of Poland and the Ukraine, feel compelled to imagine the regional space as a boundary, as an outpost of Western multicultural civilisation, legitimised by its Habsburg legacy (see chapter 12). The continuing expansion of the European Union reifies the distinction between those states that are affluent and (now) politically stable and those states that are struggling more or less successfully to convert to a new economic and political order.

In the case of the Schengen Agreement, the practicality of the European Union has been exercised through the elimination of border checks between signatory states. As chapter 3 discusses, the ability to travel unimpeded across boundaries surely exerts a tremendous psychological pull, just as the introduction of a common currency will serve to further eco-

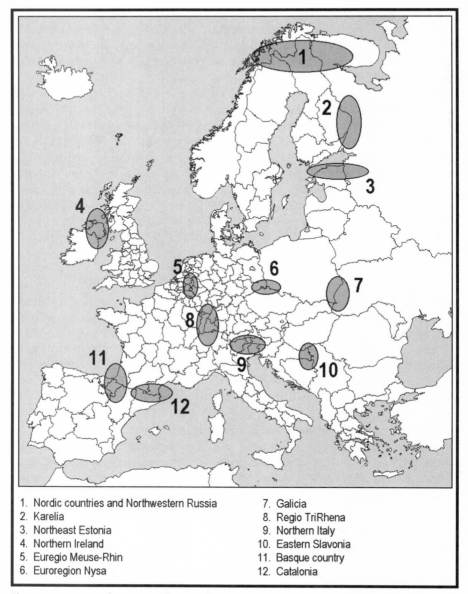

1. Nordic countries and Northwestern Russia
2. Karelia
3. Northeast Estonia
4. Northern Ireland
5. Euregio Meuse-Rhin
6. Euroregion Nysa

7. Galicia
8. Regio TriRhena
9. Northern Italy
10. Eastern Slavonia
11. Basque country
12. Catalonia

Figure 1.1.   Map of Europe with Boundaries

Source: Modified form Mouqué 1999.

nomic integration. Boundaries within this established Europe, although still important, have certainly softened. At the same time, the boundary surrounding all of the European Union has increased in significance. For example, the boundary between Finland and Russia, dividing two very different economies and societies, has been transformed from a state boundary to a supranational boundary enfolding the entire European Union (see chapter 10). The implications are clearly evident in efforts to foster cross-border co-operation, both in northern Scandinavia (see chapter 14) and in the German-Polish borderlands (see chapter 4).

Geographical scale is intrinsic to any discussion of borderlands. Several of the contributions show how borderland spaces are actually places where the local, regional, national, and international come together (see chapter 3). Londonderry, Northern Ireland, is a place of many boundaries— from the divisions between states to the lines that separate urban neighbourhoods. So too the solutions to conflicts here must take place at different scales, from the international to the local (see chapter 9). And as chapter 6 illustrates, attempts to resolve the turmoil in the Basque region have suffered from the antagonisms that persist at local, regional, national, and international levels.

Cross-border co-operation typically takes place on various scales ranging from individual actors to local authorities to regional networks to national governments to international organisations. Because of this, it can be quite difficult to align the interests of each actor. A need to jump scales may impede cross-border co-operation. Often the desires of local actors are contravened by activities of state governments that do not wish to relinquish their traditional authority. Euroregions—an organisational form introduced in chapter 4 and illustrated in chapters 5, 6, and 8—serve to recognise and institutionalise cross-border realities. While emerging as the harbingers of the potential New Europe, Euroregions have sometimes been caught between the contradictory goals of actors operating at separate spatial scales. A borderland population may be drawn apart or even ignored by two larger states that do not appreciate the particular concerns of the residents. Certainly both the Basque and Catalan populations have been divided by differing nationalist agendas in France and Spain (chapters 5 and 6). And as chapter 7 points out, such distinctions have also had a major impact on the Tyrolean and Slovenian populations along the Italo-Austrian and Italo-Slovene boundaries.

Boundaries function as both unifiers and dividers. The intensity of interaction across borderlands reflects cross-border relations that are embedded in historical and contemporary conditions. During times of hostility, boundaries may become 'walls', whereas in peace time borderlands may shift from conflict to harmony (see chapter 3). In considering borderland interaction, the influence of basic physical and demographic facts cannot be overlooked: natural terrain, population density, and economic circumstances. Chapter 8 shows how cross-border accessibility and regional complementarity in labour, housing, and consumption markets facilitate integration in the TriRhena region. Such interaction in turn has allowed for the development of exceptionally strong cross-border organisations.

From a more cultural perspective, interaction in borderlands may reflect or even breed cross-border identities. We can point to the location of peoples who predate the formation of modern state boundaries and who seek to maintain or revive these older ties. The formation of the European Union has spurred the aspirations of those who feel unshackled from the nation-state system. A 'Europe of Regions' has fed the dreams of borderland denizens—the Sami, the Catalans, the Basques, the Tyroleans, the Galicians. However, as the case studies indicate, state boundaries still create and maintain significant differences. An interesting corollary lies in the extent to which interaction and common cause has generated hybrid borderland identities—old and new (Kaplan 2000).

International boundaries create minorities as much as they create nations. Clean lines on a map seldom correspond with crisp cultural boundaries, as chapter 3 makes clear. Newly erected boundaries can throw lives into upheaval, as occurred on a large scale after World Wars I and II. More recently, the splintering of the former Yugoslavia produced an entire class of minority refugees, who found themselves on the 'wrong' side of recently established borders (see chapter 11). The breakup of the former Soviet Union, while liberating nations like Estonia, also created unwilling minorities, such as the Russian speakers discussed in chapter 13. It is often the political activities of these minorities, or the national governments that are dealing with their economic, citizenship, political, and cultural rights, that make the issue of belonging, boundaries, and place visible in contemporary Europe.

A number of related points emerge from the case studies presented in this volume; they are of relevance in any research on the culture and politics of contemporary borderlands:

1. Geographical scale makes a difference in how borderlands develop and in the analysis of these developments. Along with the sense of contextuality, a theoretical understanding of scale may be the most crucial contribution of human geography to border studies.
2. Borderlands are useful barometers of political and cultural change because their development signals the willingness of institutions and people to adapt to new ways of thinking and acting. The develop-

ment of Euroregions, discussed in several of the chapters, is the most obvious manifestation of this, but several other instances apply as well.

3. Any attempts at generalisation must be balanced by an awareness of the local and regional surroundings. Each case occurs within a specific cultural and political milieu. As much as we need theories about trends and similarities across various borderlands, our understanding of these changes remains incomplete if we do not appreciate the differences in outcomes that prevail in Europe and elsewhere.

4. Variations occur even within the same borderland region. Several of our studies suggest varied experiences between residents across the national boundary; others demonstrate variations along the same side of the boundary, from place to place and from region to region.

5. Just as we need to note the differences between borderlands as unique places, we must distinguish between various social actors and groups. Institutional actors' accounts of the development of European borderlands should be balanced with equal interest focused on how the residents of borderlands experience the changes at the level of everyday life.

CONCLUSION

There is no one way to study borderlands, and the case studies in this volume employ a range of approaches in trying to piece together the history, identity, social and economic contexts, and organisational structure of European borderlands. At one level, several chapters survey the attitudes of borderland residents, attempting to divine whether these individuals feel common cause across the boundary or even conceive of such a thing as a cross-border region. Other chapters are concerned particularly with the historical legacy of each borderland, as read from texts, landscapes, and other constituents or markers of identity. Still other chapters look to the contemporary situation and how the media, in-house publicity, and economic arrangements serve to shape and condition emerging cross-border relations and borderland identities. Finally, there is an emerging class of borderland organisations that exist between the locality and the state. Several chapters focus on these institutional structures and examine their constitutions, functions, and effectiveness, concentrating particularly on how well they facilitate cross-border co-operation.

Perhaps more than ever before, borderlands have become harbingers of international co-operation and a possible postnationalist order. Although national boundaries seem to persist with astounding power in the hearts and minds of people, the case studies indicate a clear trend of softening borders within the European Union. We do not know what will transpire beyond this point, but we can be sure that no matter how the European political space develops in the future, significant variations will be found among different local, regional, and national contexts, and it is necessary to take this into account when studying borderlands in Europe and elsewhere.

NOTE

We are grateful to David B. Knight for very helpful comments on an earlier version of this introduction. We also wish to thank the Academy of Finland for financial support (grants 57828 and 62924) that has facilitated several of the case studies presented in this volume. These grants also provided necessary resources for our editorial collaboration.

REFERENCES

Agnew, J. 1998. *Geopolitics: Re-visioning World Politics*. London: Routledge.

Anderson, J., and J. Goodman. 1995. Regions, states and the European Union: Modernist reaction or postmodern adaptation? *Review of International Political Economy* 2, no. 4: 600–631.

Anderson, M. 1996. *Frontiers: Territory and State Formation in the Modern World*. Cambridge: Polity Press.

Augelli, J. 1980. Nationalization of Dominican borderlands. *The Geographical Review* 70: 19–35.

Barth, F., ed. 1969. *Ethnic Groups and Boundaries*. Boston: Little, Brown, and Co.

Beschorner, N., St. J. B. Gould, and K. McLachlan, eds. 1991. *Sovereignty, Territoriality and International Boundaries in South Asia, South West Asia and the Mediterranean Basin*. London: Geopolitics and International Boundaries Research Centre.

Bowman, I. 1922. *The New World: Problems in Political Geography*. Yonkers-on-Hudson, NY: World Book.

Burghardt, A. F. 1962. *Borderland: A Historical and Geographical Study of Burgenland, Austria*. Madison: University of Wisconsin Press.

Cappelin, R., and P. Batey, eds. 1993. *Regional Networks, Border Regions, and European Integration*. London: Pion.

Castells, M. 1996. *The Rise of the Network Society*. Cambridge: Blackwell.

———. 1997. *The Power of Identity*. Cambridge: Blackwell.

———. 1998. *End of Millennium*. Cambridge: Blackwell.

Cox, K. R. 1996. Editorial: The difference that scale makes. *Political Geography* 15: 667–70.

———. 1998. Spaces of dependence, spaces of engagement and the politics of scale, or: Looking for local politics. *Political Geography* 17: 1–23.

Demko, G. J., and W. B. Wood, eds. 1994. *Reordering the World: Geopolitical Perspectives on the Twenty-First Century.* Boulder, CO: Westview Press.

Donnan, H., and T. M. Wilson. 1999. *Borders: Frontiers of Identity, Nation and State.* Oxford: Berg.

Donnan, H., and T. M. Wilson, eds. 1994. *Border Approaches: Anthropological Perspectives on Frontiers.* Lanham, MD: University Press of America.

Duchacek, I. D. 1986. International competence of subnational governments: Borderlands and beyond. In O. Martínez, ed. *Across Boundaries: Transborder Interaction in Comparative Perspective,* 11–28. El Paso: Texas Western Press.

Éger, G., and J. Langer, eds. 1996. *Border, Region and Ethnicity in Central Europe.* Klagenfurt: Norea Verlag.

Eskelinen, H., I. Liikanen, and J. Oksa, eds. 1999. *Curtains of Iron and Gold: Reconstructing Borders and Scales of Interaction.* Aldershot: Ashgate.

Featherstone, M. 1995. *Undoing Culture: Globalization, Postmodernism and Identity.* London: Sage.

Ganster, P. 2001. *Cooperation, Environment, and Sustainability in Border Regions.* San Diego: San Diego State University Press.

Graham, B. 1997. The past in Europe's present: Diversity, identity and the construction of place. In B. Graham, ed. *Modern Europe: Place, Culture, Identity,* 19–52. London: Arnold.

Häkli, J. 1994. Territoriality and the rise of modern state. *Fennia* 172, no. 1: 1–82.

———. 1998. Cross-border regionalization in the 'New Europe': Theoretical reflection with two illustrative examples. *Geopolitics* 3, no. 3: 83–103.

———. 2001a. In the territory of knowledge: State-centered discourses and the construction of society. *Progress in Human Geography* 25, no. 3: 403–22.

———. 2001b. The significance of scale in cross-border interaction: The case of Catalonia. In G. Bucken-Knapp and M. Schack, eds. *Borders Matter: Transfrontier Regions in Contemporary Europe,* 56–74. Border Studies Series, No. 2. Aabenraa: IFG.

Herb, G. 1997. *Under the Map of Germany: Nationalism and Propaganda, 1918–1945.* London: Routledge.

Herb, G., and D. Kaplan, eds. 1999. *Nested Identities: Nationalism, Territory, and Scale.* Boulder, CO: Rowman and Littlefield.

Hirst, P., and G. Thompson. 1999. *Globalization in Question: The International Economy and the Possibilities of Governance.* 2d ed. Cambridge: Polity Press.

House, J. 1981. Frontier studies: An applied approach. In A. Burnett and P. Taylor, eds. *Political Studies from Spatial Perspectives,* 291–312. New York: John Wiley.

Huntington, S. 1997. *The Clash of Civilizations and the Remaking of World Order.* New York: Simon & Schuster.

Jones, S. 1959. Boundary concepts in the setting of place and time. *Annals of the Association of American Geographers* 49, no. 3: 241–55.

Kaplan, D. 1994. Two nations in search of a state: Canada's ambivalent spatial identities. *Annals of the Association of American Geographers* 84, no. 4: 587–608.

———. 2000. Conflict and compromise among borderland identities in Northern Italy. *Tijdschrift voor Economische en Sociale Geografpie* 91, no. 1: 44–60.

Klemencic, V., and M. Bufon. 1991. Geographic problems of frontier regions: The case of the Italo-Yugoslav border landscape. In D. Rumley and J. Minghi, eds. *The Geography of Border Landscapes,* 86–103. London: Routledge, Chapman and Hall.

Kristof, L. 1959. The nature of frontiers and boundaries. *Annals of the Association of American Geographers* 49, no. 3: 269–82.

Le Galès, P., and C. Lequesne, eds. 1998. *Regions in Europe.* London: Routledge.

Livingstone, D. 1992. *The Geographical Tradition: Episodes in the History of a Contested Enterprise.* Oxford: Blackwell.

Lugo, A. 1997. Reflections of border theory, culture, and the nation. In S. Michaelson and D. Johnson, eds. *Border Theory: The Limits of Cultural Politics,* 43–67. Minneapolis: University of Minnesota Press.

Mackay, J. R. 1958. The interactance hypothesis and boundaries in Canada. *Canadian Geographer* 11: 1–8.

Maxwell, R. 1996. Technologies of national desire. In M. Shapiro and H. Alker, eds. *Challenging Boundaries: Global Flows, Territorial Identities,* 327–60. Minneapolis: University of Minnesota Press.

Minghi, J. 1963. Boundary studies in political geography. *Annals of the Association of American Geographers* 53: 407–28.

———. 1991. From conflict to harmony in border landscapes. In D. Rumley and J. Minghi, eds. *The Geography of Border Landscapes,* 15–30. London: Routledge, Chapman and Hall.

Mouqué, D., ed. 1999. Sixth periodic report on the social and economic situation and development of regions in the European Union. Brussels: EU Commission.

Murphy, A. B. 1996. The sovereign state system as political-territorial ideal: Historical and contemporary considerations. In T. Biersteker and C. Weber, eds. *State Sovereignty as Social Construct,* 81–120. Cambridge: Cambridge University Press.

Newman, D., and A. Paasi. 1998. Fences and neighbours in the postmodern world: Boundary narratives in political geography. *Progress in Human Geography* 22, no. 2: 186–207.

Ó Tuathail, G. 1996. *Critical Geopolitics: The Politics of Writing Global Space.* Minneapolis: University of Minnesota Press.

O'Brien, O. 1993. Good to be French? Conflicts of identity in North Catalonia. In S. Macdonald, ed. *Inside European Identities: Ethnography in Western Europe,* 98–117. Oxford: Berg.

Ohmae, K. 1990. *The Borderless World.* New York: Collins.

———. 1995. *The End of the Nation State: The Rise of Regional Economies.* London: Free Press.

Paasi, A. 1992. The construction of socio-spatial consciousness: Geographical perspectives on the history and contexts of Finnish nationalism. *Nordisk Samhällsgeografisk Tidskrift* 15: 79–100.

———. 1996. *Territories, Boundaries and Consciousness: The Changing Geographies of the Finnish-Russian Border.* New York: John Wiley.

Pettman, J. 1996. Border crossings/shifting identities: Minorities, gender, and the state in international perspective. In M. Shapiro and H. Alker, eds. *Challenging Boundaries: Global Flows, Territorial Identities,* 261–83. Minneapolis: University of Minnesota Press.

Pratt, M., and J. Brown, eds. 2000. *Borderlands under Stress.* London: Kluwer Law International.

Prescott, J. 1987. *Political Frontiers and Boundaries.* London: Allen and Unwin.

Rabinowitz, D. 1998. National identity at the frontier: Palestinians in the Israeli education system. In T. Wilson and H. Donnan, eds. *Border Identities: Nation and State at International Frontiers,* 142–61. Cambridge: Cambridge University Press.

Ratti, R., and S. Reichman, eds. 1993. *Theory and Practice of Transborder Cooperation.* Basel: Verlag Helbing & Lichtenhahn.

Ruggie, J. 1993. Territoriality and beyond: Problematizing modernity in international relations. *International Organization* 47: 139–74.

Rupnik, J. 1994. Europe's new frontiers: Remapping Europe. *Dædalus* 23, no. 3: 91–114.

Sahlins, P. 1989. *Boundaries: The making of France and Spain in the Pyrenees.* Berkeley: University of California Press.

Semple, E. C. 1911. *Influences of Geographic Environment: On the Basis of Ratzel's System of Anthropo-geography.* New York: Holt.

Shapiro, M., and H. Alker, eds. 1996. *Challenging Boundaries: Global Flows, Territorial Identities.* Minneapolis: University of Minnesota Press.

Van Houtum, H. 1999. Borders, distances and spaces: A typology of borders in terms of distances. Paper presented at the congress of the European Regional Science Association. Dublin, Ireland.

Wagner, P. 1989. Social science and the state in continental Western Europe: The political structuration of disciplinary discourse. *International Social Science Journal* 122: 509–28.

Wilson, T., and H. Donnan, eds. 1998. *Border Identities: Nation and State at International Frontiers.* Cambridge: Cambridge University Press.

Chapter Two

The 'Civilisational' Roots of European National Boundaries

John Agnew

Nothing seems so much a part of modern life as passport control at an airport or a land border between adjacent states. Yet only two generations ago movement across the boundaries between Europe's countries was without much official regulation. People came and went without much, if any, documentation. Indeed, only in time of war did the boundaries between nation-states assume much significance in everyday life. Nevertheless, the rigid demarcation of political space that is now part and parcel of modern statehood built up cumulatively in Europe over a long span of years; it did not simply appear overnight in the early twentieth century. Its origins lie in the fifteenth century, when political sovereignty began to shift from the personhood of the monarch to the territory of the state. The conventional wisdom is that this required the populace of the nation-state to reside in a definite space to which it owed allegiance and from which it might expect to receive various rewards, not the least of which was some guarantee of personal security. The security claim was added to down the years, as other features of modern statehood reinforced the need for defined and accepted boundaries: from clear definitions of rights of land ownership to criteria of eligibility for the various services provided by states.

Why, though, should Europe have been the world region where the establishment and maintenance of rigid national boundaries first took place? The dominant explanation is universalistic. It argues that states and people everywhere would benefit from rigid boundaries between adjacent polities and largely ignores the fact that for much of human history and in most of the world, politics took place without careful boundary delimitation and with little or no attention to membership in the polity. In the Roman Empire, for example, the empire tailed off around its edges rather than ending abruptly at a clearly drawn line of demarcation. Many parts of the empire, including border zones, were ruled indirectly with only minimal direction from the centre. The Chinese and other great empires likewise showed little concern for rigid boundary delimitation. Even when an author is sensitive to the European origins of modern state boundary making, as in Anderson's (1996) comprehensive account, little or no attention is given to why European states should have been so obsessed with delimiting precise boundaries. What, then, separated early-modern Europe from the rest of the world and from its own recent past and, under European influence, has led to the spread of rigid boundary making into the rest of the world? The argument of this chapter is that the answer lies in competition between emerging national elites who justified their claims to superiority over one another by defining themselves as the most quali-fied agents of Europe as a whole in a struggle for power and wealth extending increasingly beyond the borders of Europe itself. The qualifi-cation was the particular claim to have inherited the civilisational mantle of the ancient 'Europeans' (the Greeks and Romans), which they could now endow on the world at large. This required, however, a clear sense of where Europe began and ended, or who was inside and who was outside the competitive project, so to speak. It also necessitated a careful account-ing and espousal of the attributes of the national space that was now the lineal descendant of the ancients in representing Europe in the wider world. National boundaries, therefore, were necessary to define who was to be Europe's dominant agent on a world scale. They were a recapitula-tion within Europe of 'Europe's' relation to surrounding regions and the rest of the world on a global scale.

The argument in this chapter proceeds from three angles. The first is the terminology of boundaries and frontiers and what it can tell about the European experience. The second is the definition of 'Europe' and how this is related to the myth of a common but contested ancestry of modern Europe in ancient Greece and Rome. The third is two contemporary cases in Europe in which national boundary claims have invoked European and civilisational justifications such as those alluded to previously. Thus, the language of boundaries, the intellectual history of European civilisational ancestry, and current political practice based on invocation of claims to 'Europeanness' serve to constitute the three parts of a general argument about the close connection between practices of rigid national boundary demarcation on the one hand, and the intellectual emphasis on a rigid definition of Europe and 'Europeanness' on the other.

This chapter must of necessity ignore what brought about the political

fragmentation and competition between national elites that has characterised modern Europe. The complex interpenetration of merchant capital-
ism, religious reformation, and state war-making capacity undoubtedly
played a key role (Mann 1986; Tilly 1992). The purpose of this chapter is
not to challenge such accounts but rather to complement them, by pointing to the ways in which nation-statehood was underwritten by a set of
important ideologically inspired practices relating to national boundary
delimitation.

THE LANGUAGE OF NATIONAL BOUNDARIES

A plausible case can be made that the late sixteenth and early seventeenth
centuries saw a sea change in how Europeans understood themselves and
their place in the world. Stephen Toulmin (1990: 35) traces this to the
discovery of both a wider world as a result of European exploration and
encounters and the rediscovery of so-called classical thinking during the
European Renaissance. Initially, these changes were assimilated into conventional thinking that is often referred to as 'humanism'. But between
1610 and 1650 this changed fundamentally. Rather than the localism, particularity, and positive valuation of uniqueness that characterised Renaissance humanism, a rationalism became dominant that was based on
divorcing human reason from the details of specific historical situations.
Toulmin (1990) sees this rationalism, associated closely with such figures
as René Descartes, Gottfried Leibniz, and Isaac Newton, as a 'solution' to
the grave challenges of the time, particularly the need to restore a dialogue among the nation-states of Europe by transcending the particularistic religious claims of the Catholic and Protestant sides in the current
religious wars and to promote a universal language as a means to a 'politics of certainty'. Thus, at the beginning of modernity in early seventeenth-century Europe is found the urge to offer general justifications for
what had previously been seen as particular and local phenomena.

One of the most crucial requirements in constructing a new rational
cosmopolis to replace the one that was seen as lost in the bloodletting of
the European religious wars was to move beyond the overlapping jurisdictions and mixed modes of exercising political authority that had characterised medieval Europe. This involved defining boundaries between
nation-states in the boldest and most rigorous form possible where previously fuzziness had been the norm. Authority was now increasingly centralised and territorially defined. Older dynastic bases of legitimacy were
rapidly displaced by ones reliant on claims to popular sovereignty, or rule
on behalf of a nation. Indeed, prior to this epoch little distinction was

made between the state and other modes of social organisation. In the High Middle Ages, lords' domains were less territories than collections of rights. Often, one and the same territory was shared among several sovereigns. The word *frontière* and its synonym *limite* had not yet acquired their modern meaning in France, the country in which the new worldview arguably first took strongest root. Until the seventeenth century *frontière* meant either the facade of a church or the front line of an army. In the 1694 *Dictionnaire de l'Académie française, limites* appears 'as a peaceful word, a word used by lawyers to settle questions of boundaries. *Frontières* are *limites* as seen by conquerors, sovereigns or ministers'(Febvre 1973: 210). The words increasingly overlap, however, so that by 1773 the expression '*délimiter une frontière*' (to mark a frontier) had come into common use in French (Febvre 1973: 211).

However, until the Revolution of 1789 the *frontière* 'only existed for soldiers and princes, and only then in time of war' (Febvre 1973: 214). None of Louis XIV's treaties contained the words *frontière* or *limite* or possible synonyms. Only with the militarisation of the French nation after 1789 and 'the hates, bitterness and fear aroused in France and in other countries by the French Revolution' (Febvre 1973: 214) did the French word for national boundary achieve a metatheoretical significance: partitioning up humanity into blocks of people walled into separate national territories. Drawing from a reservoir of historical memory going back to the boundaries of Gaul under the Roman Empire, the nation's frontiers were endowed with a mythic status as 'limits marked out by nature'. The Rhine, the Pyrenees, and the Alps were given much of this burden, even when the local picture, concerning who lived where and with what allegiances, remained much more complicated. 'But', as Febvre (1973: 216) insists, 'it is precisely in the complicated nature of reality that we must seek one of the reasons for the success of these myths. They gave countries simple limits which were easy to refer to and easy to show on maps. They were precise and clear in an age when the real limit, *mouvances* (feudal dependencies), was confused and hard to ascertain'.

The language of national boundaries in other European languages has followed a similar course. In English the word *frontier* is a recent arrival and is generally used to refer to the borderland or strip of land around the edge of a state's territory or a settlement zone in a colonial situation. *Boundary* has historically acquired the general significance associated with *frontière* in French, meaning the precise line of demarcation between adjacent nation-states. It also has a more general anthropological and literary sense, signifying the limits of a social group or activity. The political use can be seen as lending itself to the imposition of a territorial understanding of social dynamics when used in these other contexts (Cohen 1997).

The word *border* is also used in English as equivalent to a national boundary, but more typically conveys the sense of an edge or periphery rather than a precise line of demarcation.

In Spanish *limite* and *confin* are used as terms for national boundaries. *Frontera* usually signifies a zone or region separating two states or peoples, without the military association the equivalent term has in French. Italian usage is similar, with *il confine* as the demarcation line and *la frontiera* as a border zone. Finally, in German the word *Mark* was once used for both frontier line and frontier region, but the word *Grenze* is now applied to the actual line of demarcation, originally used for private property. When combined with words such as *Land* or *Gebiet*, *Grenze* can be used to designate frontier regions or provinces (Febvre 1973: 216–17).

Across the various European languages the imposition of boundaries came to follow a similar course, irrespective of the specific terms used to describe the activity. Anthropologically, boundaries often appeared without much prior rationale but everywhere came to have practical consequences for local populations in their vicinity and in the construction of national identities for those far distant from them. The arbitrary but nevertheless concrete reality of boundaries was evoked by Blaise Pascal (1623–1662) as follows:

> Why do you kill me? What! Do you not live on the other side of the water? If you lived on this side, my friend, I would be an assassin, and it would be unjust to slay you in this manner. But since you live on the other side, I am a hero, and it is just. . . . A strange justice that is bounded by a river! Truth on this side of the Pyrenees, error on the other. (Pascal 193, quoted in Sahlins 1989: 270)

Frontier or boundary regions, then, are crucial settings for the making of national state distinctions and associated identities and allegiances. Rather than forming at the centre and diffusing out to the periphery of the state, as in now classic accounts such as that of Eugen Weber (1976) about France, national identities have been formed actively at the boundaries of states and negotiated with the centre (see, e.g., Sahlins 1989; on some French examples, see Lammers 1999). But the terms of negotiation have invariably been those adopted by national elites who drew their memberships not only from the political centres, such as Paris or London, but also from the peripheries. These *countries* increasingly saw the identities of the peripheries drawn into contact with and subsumed by the national identities that were the outcome of the drawing together of centres and peripheries into singular national spaces. That this was by no means inevitable, however, and thus stands as testimony to the importance of negotiation *within* the borderlands as well as between borderlands and their respective centres, is illustrated, for example, by the lack of local 'fitting' of identities at the Basque or western end of the very boundary between France and Spain whose Catalan or eastern end is used by Sahlins (1989) to show how the two borderlands were incorporated into distinctive national identities regardless of their own cultural communality (Douglass 1998).

Whatever their concrete significance for the everyday lives of those living adjacent to them, the essential arbitrariness of many national boundaries or boundary segments deserves underlining. The result of dynastic marriages, conquest, treaties ending wars elsewhere, and the spread of transportation and communication networks biasing religious, linguistic, and trade links in some directions more than others, Europe's national boundaries have been amazingly labile. The boundary of France-Spain in the Pyrenees is in fact one of Europe's most stable boundaries. It, and other stable ones such as Spain-Portugal or Switzerland and its neighbours, hardly count as good case studies of the 'average' European national boundary because other boundaries have experienced numerous changes and challenges. For example, the 'movement' of Poland to-and-fro across the map of East-Central Europe between 1920 and 1945 is a reminder of how moveable boundaries can be, often without much in the way of immediate justification in terms of ethnic distributions, land use characteristics, or historical national attachments to specific territories.

The apparent arbitrariness of many national boundary demarcations suggests that simple materialist explanations of boundaries relying on economic or physical factors are of doubtful relevance. Purely materialist accounts miss both the historical contingency of boundary marking revealed by the etymology of the term *frontière* and the active role of national elites and populations in making boundaries. For example, Friedrich Ratzel's (1903) influential idea that boundary lines or frontiers have evolved to optimise the use of land that would be neglected absent a careful delimitation of national rights of ownership and use is problematic. It neither fits the actual historical sequence of use of the language of frontiers nor addresses how national identities form in relation to boundaries. In not addressing the sense of boundaries as a response to the insecurity of nation-statehood, Ratzel's approach pushes causation into the realm of land use, thus missing the tendency for boundaries to appear in deserts and mountains as well as in settings in which access to fertile agricultural land is at a premium. Ratzel's idea is a classic late-nineteenth-century account of national boundaries, looking for a rational explanation for boundary marking external to the practices of the states doing the boundary marking and based on natural, not human, characteristics that are presumably (but in fact are not) invariant across space and time.

My intention here is not to criticise purely materialist approaches.

Rather, my main point is that the historical course of the language of national boundaries parallels that of the quest for a new, modern cosmopolis as charted by Toulmin (1990). The modern nation-state became the vessel carrying the rationalist impulse even as it represented precisely the potential atavistic power of 'groupthink' (in the form of nationalism) that Enlightenment thinkers had set themselves against. But that possibility was less evident at the time than were the benefits of collective acceptance of the rule of applying the same principles of definition and categorisation irrespective of the context in which they were applied. This was to become the essence of boundary making: justifying specific boundaries in the name of 'universal' principles of delimitation. That these merely masked continuing local sources of difference was not important. Eventually, the 'fact' of definite boundaries or *frontières* was to create its own reality. The world of boundaries we live with today is the outcome of this historical process.

APOSTOLIC SUCCESSION TO THE ANCIENTS

With the Renaissance, the interest of European intellectuals in newly discovered classical texts re-awoke a concern for cosmology. Readings of Plato's *Republic*, for example, encouraged the idea that there should be a correspondence between natural and human affairs. Yet there was a widespread sense that contemporary political affairs were ill ordered and incoherent. The ancients, the Greeks in particular but the Romans too, were held up by all of the main political theorists of the era as 'historical role models' to resolve this state of affairs.

Two intellectual moves were necessary, however, to establish the right to inherit the legacy of the ancients on the part of early-modern European states. The first was to firmly re-establish, only now on a larger geographical scale, the totalistic difference made by Greek thinkers such as Aristotle between Greeks and barbarians (Said 1978). The self-defined Europeans, of course, saw themselves as inheriting the role of the Greeks, while the peoples to the east were given the inheritance of the ancient Persians. The self-assumed identities of the emergent European states were thought of as representing the continuation, albeit after a long rupture, of a fundamental opposition between a rule-governed or even 'free' West (although what was meant by that was quite different from what it might mean today) and a despotic East. A clear border between a Europe in which modern statehood was possible and an external world in which it was not followed from this geographical logic:

Not only did the Renaissance city-states and their successors claim legitimacy as rightful heirs to the Athenian and Roman *poleis*, but they did so in the context of their own versions of the battle of the Giants, predicated once again on the East/ West divide. This time it was the conquest of the Northern Europeans over the barbarian Muslim hordes. Once again, 'freedom of the Greeks', to which the Northern Europeans now fell heir, was the differentiating axiom. (Springborg 1992: 289)

It is relatively easy to show, however, as Patricia Springborg (1992) does in some detail, that the Europeans' claim to the mantle of the *polis* was based on a total lack of empirical evidence about which region had the best claim. Present-day scholarship suggests that the ancient Middle East, with Greece as an offshoot, developed most of the institutions Europeans somehow came to associate with themselves, from bicameral legislatures to the rule of law and a free judiciary. The early-modern Europe states claiming the classical republican tradition were, rather, 'agrarian, patriarchal, decentralized, non-participatory and . . . admitted few to the circle of power, which was still essentially monarchical. Here they differed essentially from the urban, entrepreneurial, densely settled city-states, where classical republican forms aggregated innumerable networks of little societies' (Springborg 1992: 4).

In Europe, however, a sense of cultural unity did underwrite the claim to apostolic succession to the wisdom and power of the ancients. This was initially associated with the idea of Christendom, expressed most forcefully in relation to the external threat from an expansive Ottoman Turkish Empire. But the increasing spread of an ideal of education based on reading Greek and Roman authors in the original languages and of an historiography that assimilated the new worlds, Europeans began to discover in the sixteenth century into a vision of Europe's 'own' unitary past increasingly produced a civilisational definition of Europe as not only distinctive from but also superior to the rest of the world (Agnew 1996).

Renaissance political theories reinforced this image of European distinctiveness. One way was through the invention of the concept of 'balance of power', which was held to apply only to the balance between states in Europe. Another was in the distinction drawn between racial and cultural groupings that were seen as paralleling the general division between West and East and more specific categorisations of the continents and climatic zones. Even within the geographical Europe, the distinction between Western and Eastern Europe was important in delimiting where Europe 'ended' and Asia 'began' (Agnew 1998: chapter 1). Russia and the area conquered by the Turks were long excluded, until their relative significance in relation to European balance-of-power politics brought them nominal acceptance.

The second move was to endow the nation-states of Western Europe with key trappings of the common glorious past. On this point, of course, states collided with respect to who could claim the most complete or legitimate connection to the ancients. Relative location was not crucial in this competition. All of the main early territorial nation-states in Europe (France, Spain, Portugal, England, etc.) were at some geographical remove from the sites of ancient glory. What each could do, however, was re-create as faithfully as possible the features of statehood associated with the political virtues of the ancient Europeans. Territoriality was vital to this endeavour. Both the Greek *polis* and the Roman *urbs* were very much territorial entities. On the one hand, this was so because of the need to establish clear criteria for political membership based on ownership of a small holding and free birth. On the other hand, it was so because of the importance of communal property and the need to clarify claims of access through common residence:

> The territoriality of the ancient city-state was, therefore, no incidental feature. Aristotle endorsed 'the jealous city' (Dossa 1987) as an enclave for the 'civilized' insider, requiring strict boundary maintenance against the 'uncivilized' barbarian—that is to say those who did not live in cities, inhabiting rather sprawling empires, and who were therefore less than gods and worse than men (Aristotle, *Politics*, 1.1.8–9, 1252b30–1253a10). (Springborg 1992: 38)

The corollary to this was the recognition of the state, irrespective of its institutional forms, as the guarantor of the harmonisation of the natural and social orders. This was what the ancient *polis* was widely seen as having done, at least for a time. The historical etymology of the word 'political' gives an important clue to how a rigid state territoriality could successfully merge the natural and social orders. Today the word 'political' presupposes a territorial state. 'That an impersonal structure of domination called the state is the core of politics is an idea so deeply embedded in our ways of thinking that any other conception of it appears counter-intuitive and implausible' (Viroli 1992: 284). But this was not always so. In early Renaissance Italy, the term 'political' was intimately associated with society in a much broader sense. Politics was 'the art of preserving the *respublica*, in the sense of a community of individuals living together in justice' (Viroli 1992: 2–3). Only during what Toulmin (1990) considers the crucial period of intellectual transformation, at the outset of the seventeenth century, did politics become the 'art of preserving the state, in the sense of a person's or group's power and control over public institutions (for instance the *stato* of the Medici)' (Viroli 1992: 3). If the best-known political theorists of Renaissance Italy, Machiavelli and Guicciardini, tried to reconcile the two, later theorists abandoned the challenge. 'There was not, and there could not be, room for both: either the city of all and for all, or the state (*stato*) of someone' (Viroli 1992: 5).

The appeal to an ancient intellectual lineage as justification of course involved adding important interpretive novelties, not least because of the lack of fit between the image of what the ancients offered and the reality of the contemporary world. One was the important role of the idea of 'race' in placing Europe and Europeans in a global cultural hierarchy, with Europe representing the top by dint of its expansiveness and military-economic success. Within the broad 'racial' divisions of humanity, finer ones were found that served to explain 'national' origins in racial terms. The French philosopher Montesquieu (1689–1755), for example, recast the reputation of the northern barbarians who had previously been seen as the destroyers of the Roman Empire by conceiving of them as one of the 'races' of time and order, rooted down the centuries in conditions of climate, land, and soil. This served to make 'France' racially independent of Rome but nevertheless an inheritor of Rome's past. All of the later European discourse about 'inferior' and 'superior' races and nationalities dates from this time but became increasingly virulent as it became part of nineteenth-century arguments about biological differences among peoples around the world.

Another such interpretative novelty was to place the European nation-state on a pedestal as the highest form of political entity. Not only were 'people' and state conjoined, the *educating state* found in post-Enlightenment theorists such as Rousseau and Hegel would give subjects a feeling of moral unity and common identification. This sacralisation of the nation gave the European territorial state an increasingly competitive advantage over other types of spatial-political organisations such as confederations, dynastic empires, and city-states.

By the 1700s, therefore, there was a strong sense among European national elites of 'Europe' as an autonomous and superior world region in which rigidly bounded nation-states made the best form of political organisation. Although dynastic empires lingered on for much longer (in the cases of Russia and Austria-Hungary), even these increasingly took on the trappings of conventional territorial states. By 1700 or so not only was 'Europe not so much a place as an idea' (Burke 1980: 21) but 'Greece and Rome as models' had been superseded by 'the idea of Europe' (Talmor 1980: 65). The political consequences within Europe are best described by Ernest Gellner (1993: 139–40):

> Consider the history of the national principle; or consider two ethnographic maps, one drawn up before the age of nationalism, and the other after the principle of nationalised centrality. The first resembles a painting by Kokoschka. The

riot of diverse points of colour is such that no clear pattern can be discerned in any detail. . . . A great diversity and plurality and complexity characterizes all distinct parts of the whole: the minute social groups have complex and ambiguous and multiple relations to many cultures. Look now at the ethnographic and political map of an era of the modern world. It resembles not a Kokoschka, but, say, Modigliani. There is very little shading; neat, flat surfaces are clearly separated from each other, it is generally plain where one begins and another ends, and there is little ambiguity or overlap. . . . We see that an overwhelming part of political authority has been concentrated in the hands of one kind of institution, a reasonably large and well centralized state. In general, each such state presides over, maintains, and identifies with one kind of culture, one style of communication.

EUROPEANNESS AND BOUNDARY MARKING

Europeanness, or the sense of a European identity as a civilisational norm or model, emerged out of a common history of Christianity, increasingly hollow by the time of the religious wars of the early seventeenth century; the claim of a Graeco-Roman inheritance; and a number of innovative ideas about race and nationhood. What was increasingly central to it, however, was the political form that Europe pioneered: the territorial state, whose prototypes are France, England, and Holland. The 'founding members', so to speak, the dominant states in seventeenth- and eighteenth-century Europe, have not had to demonstrate their credentials. Others have not been so fortunate. Ever since the seventeenth century, the claim to Europeanness, particularly at the borders of Europe, has involved commitment to and advertisement of the accoutrements of European statehood as defined by the dominant states, above all the clear demarcation of the state's geographical limits and the associated matching of nation with state. Yet being on the edge of Europe creates a profound anxiety about whether qualification for Europeanness is actually possible.

Much of the rhetoric of the various sides in the civil wars in the former Yugoslavia has involved recourse to claims about who is and who is not most 'European'. Competitive claims to the mantle of 'European', even 'Western', civilisation lay behind Croat and Serb efforts at obtaining external support for their positions. Bosnia's Muslims and Kosovo's Albanians have suffered from not being able to invoke the European connection, notwithstanding their long-term residence in Southeast Europe. As indigenous Muslims they simply do not fit into the imaginary geography that separates Europe and Asia, on the one hand, and Christian and Muslim, on the other, along parallel axes. The discussions in Russia about its geopolitical direction at the end of the Cold War focus on whether Russia is truly a 'European' state or a hybrid Eurasian one. Turkey keeps applying for membership in the European Union, but as a predominantly Muslim country its 'European' credentials are in question. Finally, the rapid and comprehensive incorporation of the countries of Eastern Europe into the European Union, so enthusiastically predicted in many circles in the early 1990s, has faded away. By 1999 the list of prospective members was much reduced to a limited number of central European states with the best 'European' bona fides.

Brief studies of two recent boundary cases serve to illustrate the continuing importance of the appeal to 'European' credentials in marking boundaries in contemporary Europe. One is from the edge of Europe as conventionally bounded, the Greece-Macedonia borderland, the other very much from within what is usually thought of as part of Europe proper, Italy. Each is also, ironically, geographically adjacent to the Greek and Roman homelands of European civilisation. The persisting Anglo-French-Dutch oligopoly over the credentials of modern Europeanness could not be better demonstrated than by these examples.

Naming the Former Republic of Macedonia

The first case is the dispute that arose in Greece over the naming of the former Yugoslav republic of Macedonia when that republic became politically independent in September 1991. The entire region of which this republic is a part has long been wracked by boundary disputes. The main parties—Greek, Macedonian Slav, Serb, Albanian, and Bulgarian—offer totally different histories of the region and even have provided at different times essentially contradictory maps of ethnic settlement patterns justifying their various territorial claims (for a fascinating set of maps and associated histories from early in the twentieth century, see Wilkinson 1951; Carnegie Endowment 1993). When Yugoslav Macedonia proclaimed its independence in 1991, the Greek government announced that it could not accept an independent country with the historic Greek name of Macedonia or that used any of the symbols of ancient Macedonia because these suggested a claim to the larger region of Macedonia, including much of northern Greece. At the same time, Greece's major historic protagonist in the region, Bulgaria, declared that it would recognise the new Macedonia.

Greek intransigence about the name of the new state; the use of symbols such as the sun emblem of Alexander the Great on the new flag and coinage; and the new constitution, which mandates protection of Macedonians resident in other countries, represented a powerful invocation of who can and who cannot claim the mantle of classical European civilisation. To the Greeks it seems obvious. Since the nineteenth century Greek nationalists have seen the modern Greek state as the inheritor of classical

Greece, with a valid claim to all of the lands occupied by the ancient 'Greeks'. Learning their nationalism from Western Europe, they quickly learned to present themselves as the 'representative of Western ideas in the East' (Berl 1910, in Hart 1999: 206). Even as Greeks, they had to present themselves as Europeans before they could lay claim to Greekness. Their civilisational claim came up against the reality of the ethnic patchwork of the southern Balkans, reinforced in the case of Macedonia by the lack of a singular Macedonian identity that could withstand competing claims from Bulgarians and Serbs, in particular that Macedonian Slavs are merely an 'offshoot' of one or other of their larger Slavic neighbours. In fact, the larger region, including contemporary Greek Macedonia, is multiethnic and multicultural (Karakasidou 1997). To the Greeks, however, they, as the more-or-less literal descendants of the ancient Greeks, can legitimately claim a monopoly over the land and symbols of ancient Macedonia, which includes the territory of the new state of Macedonia. From this perspective, the Macedonian Slavs who occupy this territory do not have a legitimate claim. They do not have the 'European' credentials of the Greeks. Hence they cannot be allowed to use the 'hallowed' names and symbols associated by Greek nationalists with 'their' past.

That the Greek demands met with a cool response from other members of the European Union and has led to an isolation of Greece from many of its allies should not be misinterpreted as signifying a lack of understanding of or respect for Greece's central claim. Indeed, the Greeks have been largely successful in delegitimizing the new state's use of the old symbols and forcing a number of important concessions. Visiting foreign politicians never fail to address Greece as the 'home of democracy', notwithstanding its recent history of dictatorship; largely accept the Greek claim to be the literal descendants of the ancients that Europe as a whole has largely based its claim to 'difference' upon; and do not question the claim to ethnic Greek homogeneity within Greek Macedonia that is the crux for Greek government claims about their right to control the symbolism of Macedonia.

The Northern League

The second case comes from contemporary Italy. One of the most intriguing movements in recent Italian political history is the Northern League. Formed out of a number of regional movements in 1992, the League has shifted from federalism to secessionism and back to federalism as its main strategy for the future of northern Italy. Currently the largest or second largest political party in both national and local elections in northern Lombardy and the Veneto region of the northeast, in the period

1996–2000 the League defined its main goal as independence for 'Padania', a new state, claiming Italy from its northern Alpine boundary as far south as a line running along the southern borders of the administrative regions of Tuscany, Umbria, and the Marches. The term 'Padania' is one without much history as applied to this macroregion of northern Italy. Since the days of the Roman Empire it has been applied narrowly and infrequently to the Po Valley rather than to the more generous region now associated with it.

The leader of the League, Umberto Bossi, invested much energy in trying to create a sense of the larger region as a potentially independent entity. He conducted a symbolic 'pilgrimage' to the banks of the Po and tried to co-opt the history of Venice as an historically independent city-state for the new 'Padania'. But above all he had recourse to the language of 'Europe' in distinguishing Padania from the rest of Italy. Thus, Bossi distinguished a 'European' Italy north of Rome from a 'Mediterranean' or, often, 'African' Italy to the south. He still likes slogans such as 'Africa begins at Rome' and portrays northern Italy as held hostage to a set of 'alien' values imposed by a non-European South (Biorcio 1997; Agnew and Brusa 1999).

This language effectively racialised the design of Padania and its most important boundary, that to the south. Southern Italy is associated with a set of traits that are held to be non-European (corruption, criminality, exchange voting, etc.), whereas northern Italy is endowed with the traits of civic culture, public-spiritedness, hard work, frugality, and inventiveness that have been associated by many European philosophers and social scientists with the prototypical European nation-states of England, France, and Holland. These are, of course, precisely the states carrying on the Great Tradition of the ancients that modern Italy, although a direct geographical descendant, has been seen in conventional accounts as having so much trouble emulating. The entire edifice of Europeanness, therefore, is invoked both to explain and justify the need for northern Italy to have its own state: Padania. Whether this will ever happen is another story. What is important, however, is that, however politically radical a movement might seem, precisely the same old arguments about Europeanness are still trotted out to justify European statehood.

CONCLUSION

Clearly demarcating what is 'European' and what is not has lain at the heart of claims to nation-statehood in Europe over the past three hundred years. Since the early 1600s the terminology of frontiers and boundaries (depending on the language in question) has produced increasingly sharp and carefully demarcated national boundaries. This European experience was a recapitulation of what was thought of as the practice of the European 'ancients', the Greeks and Romans (before they expanded into empire). The examples of ancient Greece and Rome were held up as the models for all modern nation-states to follow. But this could only be done, at least initially, in Europe, because Europe had the prior history and civilisational character to justify it. The invocation of a 'common Europeanness' as a justification for a particular territorial or boundary claim lives on, as illustrated by recent Greek-Macedonian and Italian cases. Here, in the homelands of the ancients that Europeans claim to have built their civilisation upon, is seen most visibly, and painfully, the weird geographical detour taken by Europeanness. Today it means imitating the English or the French (or maybe the Dutch or Germans) even when, as modern Greeks or Italians, a direct lineage could plausibly be invoked. The new cosmopolis of the early 1600s is one Europeans live with still, notwithstanding the material and ideological changes of recent years. Even the talk of expanding membership in the European Union is still premised on a clear definition of Europeanness and the characteristics of nation-statehood, including rigid national boundaries, that became de rigeur in the 1600s. It is precisely the resilience of this tradition that makes many boundaries in Europe, not least the borders of Europe itself, so resistant to erasure.

REFERENCES

Agnew, J. A. 1996. Time into space: The myth of 'backward Italy' in modern Europe. *Time and Society* 5, no. 1: 27–45.

———. 1998. *Geopolitics: Re-visioning World Politics.* London: Routledge.

Agnew, J. A., and C. Brusa. 1999. New rules for national identity? The Northern League and political identity in contemporary northern Italy. *National Identities* 1, no. 2: 117–33.

Anderson, M. 1996. *Frontiers: Territories and State Formation in the Modern World.* Cambridge: Polity Press.

Berl, A. 1910. Modern Greece: What she represents in Eastern Europe. In G. F. Abbott, ed. *Greece in Evolution: Studies Prepared under the Auspices of the French League for the Defense of the Rights of Hellenism,* 235–60. New York: Wessels and Bissell.

Biorcio, R. 1997. *La padania promessa. La storia, le idee e la logica della Lega Nord.* Milan: Il Saggiatore.

Burke, P. 1980. Did Europe exist before 1700? *History of European Ideas* 1: 21–29.

Carnegie Endowment. 1993. *The Other Balkan Wars: A 1913 Carnegie Endowment Inquiry in Retrospect.* Washington, DC: Carnegie Endowment for International Peace.

Cohen, A. P. 1997. *Self Consciousness: An Alternative Anthropology of Identity.* London: Routledge.

Dossa, S. 1987. Political philosophy and Orientalism: The classical origins of a discourse. *Alternatives* 15: 343–57.

Douglass, W. A. 1998. A western perspective on an eastern interpretation of where north meets south: Pyrenean borderland cultures. In T. M. Wilson and H. Donnan, eds. *Border Identities: Nation and State at International Frontiers,* 62–95. Cambridge: Cambridge University Press.

Febvre, L. 1973 [1928]. *Frontière:* The word and the concept. In P. Burke, ed. *A New Kind of History: From the Writings of Lucien Febvre,* 208–18. London: Routledge and Kegan Paul.

Gellner, E. 1993. *Nations and Nationalism.* Ithaca, NY: Cornell University Press.

Hart, L. K. 1999. Culture, civilization, and demarcation at the northwest borders of Greece. *American Ethnologist* 26, no. 1: 196–220.

Karakasidou, A. N. 1997. *Fields of Wheat, Hills of Blood: Passages to Nationhood in Greek Macedonia, 1870–1990.* Chicago: University of Chicago Press.

Lammers, B. J. 1999. National identity on the French periphery: The end of peasants into Frenchmen? *National Identities* 1, no. 1: 81–87.

Mann, M. 1986. *The Sources of Social Power. Volume 1.* Cambridge: Cambridge University Press.

Pascal, B. 1937. *Pensées,* essay 293: 34. Paris: L. Brunschvig nos. 293–34.

Ratzel, F. 1903. *Politische Geographie.* Munich: Oldenbourg.

Sahlins, P. 1989. *Boundaries: The Making of France and Spain in the Pyrenees.* Berkeley and Los Angeles: University of California Press.

Said, E. 1978. *Orientalism.* New York: Vintage.

Springborg, P. 1992. *Western Republicanism and the Oriental Prince.* Austin: University of Texas Press.

Talmor, E. 1980. Reflections on the rise and development of the idea of Europe. *History of European Ideas* 1: 63–66.

Tilly, C. 1992. *Coercion, Capital, and European States, AD 990–1992.* Oxford: Blackwell.

Toulmin, S. 1990. *Cosmopolis: The Hidden Agenda of Modernity.* Chicago: University of Chicago Press.

Viroli, M. 1992. *From Politics to Reason of State: The Acquisition and Transformation of the Language of Politics, 1250–1600.* Cambridge: Cambridge University Press.

Weber, E. 1976. *Peasants into Frenchmen: The Modernization of Rural France, 1870–1914.* Stanford, CA: Stanford University Press.

Wilkinson, H. R. 1951. *Maps and Politics: A Review of the Ethnographic Cartography of Macedonia.* Liverpool: University of Liverpool Press.

Chapter Three

Changing Geographies of Scale and Hierarchy in European Borderlands

Julian Minghi

The European continent has an extremely long history of political partitioning; as a result its human landscape is littered with boundary lines, old and new, which have, in turn, generated a succession of overlapping borderlands. European space has been subjected to a complex process of being subdivided into separate political entities as emerging national groups have constantly sought to establish autonomy and have competed for the control of territory. What we see at the outset of the twenty-first century as the contemporary political map of Europe is the result of changes over the course of many centuries during which national political space has evolved. The product of such evolutionary change is a dynamic system of boundaries and borderlands in a constant state of flux. To fully understand the implications for the contemporary human geography of borderlands, we need to focus on the changing nature of political boundaries in Europe.

This chapter first discusses the problems of geographic scale and political hierarchy as related to boundaries and borderlands. As the evolution of Europe's traditional boundary system is outlined, the importance of the imprint of history on the contemporary borderland scene emerges. Confrontation and conflict are very common themes associated with European boundaries. This often results in border landscapes on either side of a given political divide sharing similar or nearly identical characteristics—what has become known as a mirror-image effect along boundaries. Such pairs of borderlands may have very few functional connections between them, but they are reflections of similar policies of military dominance obsessed with security and disrupting normal civil lifestyles. Consequently they produce similar landscapes out of confrontational policies. Still visible today as relics of this long era are such landscape features as abandoned fortresses and military installations, relatively light population densities, few industrial sites, weak local government, and a general lack of investment in the civic environment. Such borderlands were standard throughout Europe until the mid-twentieth century. A common but independent variable in such borderlands was the role played by ethnic minorities, themselves frequently created by shifting boundaries superimposed on the cultural landscape.

During the second half of the last century, Europe passed through a period in which borderlands were said generally to have evolved from a theme of conflict to one of harmony, from separation to community (Minghi 1994). This shift was particularly prevalent in Western European borderlands as those countries west of the Iron Curtain moved towards greater economic and political co-operation following the Second World War. Over the last decade of the twentieth century the borderlands among the former socialist countries of Eastern Europe, with some notable exceptions, followed suit. Indeed, there is a trend towards greater co-operation both within the region and along the old Cold War divide that had been associated for over four decades with a mirror-image confrontational borderland between East and West. Furthermore, there is evidence to suggest that some borderlands are being increasingly singled out as symbols of peace and co-operation between neighbours who had formerly been enemies. We can see new symbolic border landscapes evolving that are meant to epitomise a distinctly European new sharing and togetherness, often in compensation for the recent history of war, destruction, and hostility.

Not surprisingly, as part of this more recent scenario, new international regions of common interest are emerging, defined by and shaped from the grassroots: the borderland peoples themselves. These regions incorporate within them segments of two or more national territories. These are ever more prevalent 'Euroregions' bulging out everywhere along the boundaries of virtually every state on the contemporary political map of Europe.

Given these recent developments, it seems appropriate to speculate about the future nature of Europe's borderlands. Will they return by some cyclical process into zones of confrontation along a razor's edge dividing competing and mutually hostile polities? Or will the current Euroregion trend continue unabated, expanding outwards from and along boundaries to incorporate more and more national space into new international communities of common interest? Or will boundaries and therefore borderlands disappear completely in a Europe *sans frontières*? The following discussion tries to provide some answers to these questions.

SCALE AND HIERARCHY

Of vital importance in understanding the changing nature of European borderlands are two distinctive characteristics of the continent's human geography: (1) the very high incidence of political fragmentation into nation-states—almost fifty sovereign units containing well over 350 million people but in a space smaller than the contiguous United States; and (2) the existence at any one boundary of a complex interface, represented by the political dividing line, of the entire hierarchy of each of the two political systems divided. The borderland so created becomes a dynamic region made up of products from contrasts and combinations among a variety of levels in the two political hierarchies, many of which do not originate at the national scale. Although this is a truism for any borderland, it has become especially relevant in contemporary Europe, whose states have been busy restructuring their regional government systems under the principle of devolving power from the centre. In addition, many of the borderlands themselves—especially the new Euroregions—have added a new dimension to this scale and hierarchy factor by taking on a separate existence from the traditionally defined borderland.

TRADITIONAL BOUNDARIES—THE IMPRINT OF HISTORY

In contrast to other world regions, the formulation of political boundaries in Europe has been an entirely indigenous process throughout which there was widespread popular knowledge about the distribution of physical features and the pattern of political sovereignty at any one time (Prescott 1987). Although for centuries forests and swamps remained substantial seas of borderlands separating noncontiguous islands of organised political space, by the eleventh century Europe's preindustrial population distributions were already set. Despite the many wars and shifts in territorial sovereignty, this has given Europe a long history of fairly well co-ordinated relationships set in the cultural landscape between a nation's international boundary and its internal administrative boundaries. Therefore, no matter what was specifically under dispute when, after conflicts, nations made new treaties with neighbours in defining themselves territorially, there was seldom a problem arising from the location of the line itself because the delimitation and demarcation processes were based on a broad awareness of landscape realities.

Europe's boundaries are founded largely on the basis of the Peace of Westphalia in 1648, by which the modern nation-state system was established. Specific legal boundaries fixed the limits of territorial sovereignty for the state, set lines for military protection, and created a context for the building of national identity. Westphalia replaced a system in which sovereignty was defined more by the rights of tribal or family succession than by popular identity. Small-scale duchies and city-states dotted the European landscape, frequently in conflict with neighbours and occasionally amalgamated by force of arms or mutual agreement into shifting and transitory empires. Westphalia represented a new territorial ideal based on bounded and territorially exclusive nation-states, pulling together under the idea of a common nationhood collections of the historic small-scale entities in a region and at the same time breaking away from externally controlled empires. Consequently, the era of ill-defined and shifting frontiers separating political entities had ended as borderlands along fixed political boundaries separating peoples of different nation-states emerged.

Since that time, the pattern of boundaries has been rearranged by the outcomes of several major conflicts in the nineteenth and twentieth centuries. Critical events contributing to this formulation were the Congress of Vienna in 1815, the Congress of Berlin in 1878, the Treaty of Versailles of 1919, and the various treaties of peace concluded after 1945. As Prescott (1987) has pointed out, each event produced territorial gains for some states as the fruits of victory and losses of territory for the defeated. And all this took place within a context of a policy of reaching quick postwar settlements so as to allow for a rapid return to peaceful normalcy, with victors set against retaining large armies of occupation and losers wishing to regain a level of independence to re-establish their societies and wealth.

1815—Vienna

The Congress of Vienna tried to reconstruct Europe back to pre-Napoleonic times. Boundaries that still survive today were set for Western European states, and Eastern Europe was left under the domination of the Russian, Austrian, and Ottoman empires, separated by unstable lines of control and with each facing opposition from rising ethnic nationalism within its realm. In between, German and Italian feudal principalities were allowed to continue, unconsolidated well into the latter part of the nineteenth century. Fifty years or so later, with a weakening of the empires in the East and with support from the more stable Western states, Italy and Germany consolidated into large modern national states.

1878—Berlin

With the continuing decline of the Ottoman Empire's hold on Eastern Europe, Russia and Austria were awarded more territories but, at the same time, the Great Powers at the Congress of Berlin started to recognise autonomous territorial sovereignty for several national groups, and the stage was set for the disintegration of all three old empires.

1919—Versailles

Separate treaties were signed after World War I with five major defeated powers as a result of which, under the Wilsonian principle of national self-determination, there was a veritable explosion of new states generated from the complete disappearance of the old empires that had dominated Eastern Europe. Over a period of several years, many new boundaries were created, either as the result of plebiscites or following as best as possible linguistic distributions as a surrogate for national identity based on the 1911 Austro-Hungarian census. At the same time, as in the past, victors also aimed to strengthen themselves and weaken defeated neighbours through discriminating shifts in existing boundaries. It is hardly surprising that it is from among boundaries created under these conditions that consequent conflicts developed later in the century and, in some cases such as in the ex-Yugoslavia, are still with us.

Post–World War II Changes

Although the defeated Axis powers of Italy and Germany and their allies suffered territorial losses, few major permanent changes occurred in boundaries as a result of the peace treaties following the Second World War. The radical pattern established earlier in the century survived but was fundamentally affected by mass migration and geopolitical change. The closing stages of the war saw heavy destruction of much of Eastern and Central Europe as the Soviet Red Army advanced on the German homeland. Millions of people of German and other ethnic origin migrated westward ahead of the advancing forces. The new geopolitical reality for Europe was that it found itself divided down the middle by an 'Iron Curtain' from the Baltic to the Adriatic into two groups of states. The two new superpowers that had emerged from the war to create this Cold War division now dominated Europe—countries in the east aligned with Soviet Russia and those in the west with the United States. The division created hard, impenetrable boundaries where neighbouring Eastern and Western countries touched. It was epitomised by the continuation for over forty years of the partition of the defeated Germany between what started out as the three Western military occupation zones and the Russian zone. The Cold War subsequently produced two separate states that lasted until 1990, when the former communist German Democratic Republic was absorbed into the Federal Republic of Germany. The collapse of the Soviet Union and its hegemonic hold on Eastern Europe led to the end of the Cold War and the disappearance of this East/West division. It also returned to the normal status of national territory in the reunified Germany space along the inner German boundary that had been a broad strip of hostile borderland calculated to be equivalent in area to the country of Luxembourg. Over the past decade, as market-oriented economies have slowly replaced centralised socialist systems and as liberal democracies have evolved, the borderlands among the states of Eastern Europe have changed radically, as have those running along the hitherto closed Cold War boundary. Generally, they are now following the same process through which Western borderlands have passed over the last few decades.

BORDERLANDS AND ETHNICITY— THE ROLE OF MINORITIES

Not surprisingly, the presence of ethnic minorities is frequently a feature of European borderlands. In particular, during the twentieth century the role played by these minorities in shaping the nature of the borderland was critical. Boundaries of new states and new locations for old boundaries such as those drawn by the Versailles treaties often created minority problems in borderlands even if the guiding principle was to draw boundaries as ethnic divides. Additional complications arose for border regions when groups left on the 'wrong' side of a new boundary felt impelled or were forced to migrate into jurisdictions in which they felt more secure. Following both world wars, such mass migrations took place in Europe, further complicating the ethnic-political map, and especially following the defeat of Germany in the Second World War as millions from Central and Eastern Europe migrated westward to avoid falling under the control of communist regimes. Many of these refugees settled in Germany close to the East/West divide; as a result, animosity toward the communist East remained very high in such locations as West Berlin and eastern Bavaria.

When boundaries were changed to give victors control over resources and strategic points, such ethnic minority problems were all the more likely. In 1919, despite the application of Wilson's principles, Italy gained control over that part of the Austrian Tyrol that fell south of the strategic Brenner Pass and the Alpine crest line, creating a region that was over 90 percent German speaking. Following World War II, the Yugoslav boundary with Italy was moved radically westward to include about 300,000 Slovenes in Yugoslavia who had been part of a large minority in Italy between the wars (Moodie 1950). This new boundary still left approximately 100,000

Slovene speakers in Italy and also created a large Italian minority in Yugoslavia. In the following fifty years these two minorities played major roles in shaping the borderland and, most recently, in influencing the national policies of the contemporary borderland states, Italy and Slovenia (Klemencic and Bufon 1994).

Surviving two decades of fascism and a Mussolini-Hitler agreement immediately after the Anschluss of the Third Reich with Austria in 1938, the South Tyrolese German speakers remained as a distinct minority and were so recognised when Italy was forced to create the autonomous region of Trentino–Alto Adige as part of the peace treaties after World War II. Ironically, the nature of this Italian borderland with Austria had remained non-Italian, in part as a result of the Italianisation policies of the fascist period. Jobs created by the new industrialisation of urban regions such as Bolzano-Bozen were reserved for immigrant Italians. And because urban areas were perceived by the minority to be unfriendly Italian zones, the rural economy and lifestyle of the Alpine regions remained viable and unchanged while so much of Europe's Alpine regions were becoming marginal and depopulated (Minghi 1971). In eastern Friuli, the Italian refugees from the coastal towns of Istria and Dalmatia were encouraged by Italian policy to stay close to the border in the Trieste region, where they received housing and other support. Entire new communities (*borghi*) were built for them, frequently grafted onto existing Slovene *karstic* villages close to the border (Minghi 1997). Thus Italy both reduced the dominance of the Slovene minority in the borderland and also retained an Italian 'refugee' population at the border that had continuing strong bonds and interests in regions now Yugoslav—regions that retained sizeable Italian minorities. Both minorities are well organised politically and enjoy support from across the border (Bufon 1993).

FROM CONFLICT TO HARMONY—
SEPARATION TO COMMUNITY

After three decades of reactionary and often hostile and confrontational activity among ethnic minorities in borderlands following World War II, evidence began to emerge that within Western Europe the nature of borderland human geography was undergoing a basic change, unique in modern times in Europe. Borderland research in the early 1980s indicated that collaboration was pushing aside conflict as a dominant theme between neighbouring states in Western Europe (Strassoldo 1983). The major reasons for this trend were identified as (1) a blossoming of local-level transborder co-operation; (2) a shared obligation for actions that would eliminate memories of the world wars—defined as a compensation effect; and (3) the fact that these borderlands—suffering so long from the negative mirror-image effect—had enjoyed unprecedented economic growth.

A most obvious case in point is found in the Jutland Peninsula borderland between Denmark and Germany. At the end of World War II, Denmark added to its Friesland region a strip of formerly German territory and replaced its German farm population with Danes. There was deeply felt antagonism by Denmark toward Germany, and this minor territorial gain was seen as the just fruits of liberation and victory. With Denmark's accession to the European Community in 1972, cross-border relations improved, and over the past three decades this borderland born in conflict has evolved into one of the most open and friendly in Europe.

Studies of the Franco-Italian borderland in the Maritime Alps during this period also confirm Strassoldo's findings (House 1959; Minghi 1981). A major border change in 1947 had transferred about 160 square miles of Italian territory to France, and the twelve thousand people of the region exchanged had not prospered in the short run. Young males had been conscripted to fight in France's unsuccessful colonial wars, the ecological balance of Alpine communities had been upset with large-scale flooding of high pastures for hydroelectric generation projects, and a rail link to the Italian coast—destroyed during the war—was not rebuilt by France as promised in the peace treaty. Yet once the immediate postwar reactions and memories had faded, Italy and France began to work more closely, especially after the De Gaulle era ended. The 1970s brought unprecedentedly close relations, and the impact on the borderland was felt immediately (Minghi 1991). The railway was repaired and reopened, both countries using the restored line as a symbol of their close ties as 'transalpine cousins'. And border restrictions on the seasonal pasturage migration of animals from Italian borderland communes were lifted.

The South Tyrol passed through a similar period of slipping slowly out of a context of hostility into a co-operative and harmonious era as the memories of the war faded and the fruits of a uniting Europe became more palpable. In the early 1970s a more liberal government in Rome adopted a new policy toward the region's German-speaking majority by creating a package of reforms (known as *il pacchetto*). By 1980, the province of Bolzano-Bozen had not only been granted a high degree of autonomy in cultural areas such as television and primary language use but was also able to control and direct economic investment. The impact was soon felt as more capital, much of it in grants from Rome, flowed to finance road and industrial projects in rural areas, often at the expense of the Italian-majority urban centres that hitherto had enjoyed priority (Markusse

1999). This trend served to erode support for returning the South Tyrol to Austria and led to two decades of much-improved relations between the Italian state and the provincial leaders. In 1995, these improvements culminated with Austria joining the European Union without Italian objection, but only after Italy had obtained a solemn Austrian commitment to drop in perpetuity any claim to the South Tyrol: a commitment made only after the South Tyrol leadership had given it its blessing.

The German-Polish borderland provides a larger-scale case study. Germany's invasion of Poland in 1939 had started World War II, and by the end of the war Poland's infrastructure had been largely destroyed. While the Soviet Union expanded westwards by taking much of Poland's eastern territory, Poland extended its western boundary with enormous territorial gains of former German lands in Silesia and Prussia, placing the new boundary within fifty kilometres of Berlin. Polish immigrants replaced German inhabitants forced to migrate westwards, many of whom clustered and organised in West Germany to become a force in Federal Republic politics. These ethnic German emigrés from the new Polish territories insisted that the status quo not be accepted and that these 'lost' territories be identified on maps as part of Germany 'temporarily under Polish administration'. Although communist fraternalism did not allow for any open hostility along the new borderland between the German Democratic Republic and Poland, West Germany nurtured the idea of unacceptability into the 1970s. Ultimately, the critical ingredient for success in the German reunification negotiations in 1990 was the Polish demand, backed by a five-power agreement, for Germany's complete and irrevocable acceptance of the postwar boundary. The past decade has seen this borderland thrive under the influence of German reunification and the inclusion of Poland among the group of countries found acceptable for candidacy in the European Union. Multiple Euroregions have been formed along this border, and Germany has established a strip of land adjoining the border with special dispensation from normal customs and immigration regulations, essentially creating an open market for Polish goods and services in Germany, linking Polish producers and German consumers in a mutually advantageous cross-border relationship.

Similar developments were being experienced throughout Europe's borderlands, as a normal process with the passage of time in a peaceful era, as the result of membership in the European Union of cross-border neighbours, or as deliberate policy by neighbours to seek tangible symbols of friendship in their common borderlands. Trends identified by Strassoldo (1983) included the growing role of the European Community, and what he called the 'routinisation' of cross-border transactions: hitherto extraordinary cross-border contacts becoming simply routine. He also raised the possibility of a rise in ethnic rivalries as the stress of growth was felt in some borderlands. Furthermore, he pointed out that borderlands tend to remain potentially marginal and would be most sensitive to any general economic crises in Europe. Certainly in the South Tyrol the down-side of the regional autonomy agreement and its consequences has been the reaction of the largely Italian urban minority. Here, a rise in ethnic rivalry is less a result of growth stress than of the perception of loss of status and quality of life among the Italian segment which, in turn, resulted in a sharp rise in electoral support for the right-wing nationalist candidates of the Alleanza Nazionale (Markusse 1999). A solution to bor-derland problems between an ethnic minority and the state can lead to such alienation and electoral polarisation of the national 'minority'.

BORDERLANDS AS SYMBOLS OF
PEACE AND CO-OPERATION

Under these conditions of progressive growth of harmony in borderlands hitherto rent by conflict and confrontation, neighbour states began to value these borderlands as locations presenting opportunities for improv-ing relations. Several examples illustrate this symbolic use of borderlands for diplomatic advantage (Gallusser 1994).

By far the most impressive case, both in terms of scale and depth of original confrontation, is the borderland between Germany and France along the Rhine. As neighbours and the two most powerful European con-tinental powers, France and Germany have shared a very troubled border-land, the site of three very costly wars: the Franco-Prussian of 1870, the First World War, and the Second World War. Territories in this heavily scarred borderland changed hands several times, and until 1945 it remained the epitome of the mirror-image confrontational borderland. Since World War II, both countries have worked closely together to reverse the confrontational syndrome, both as a result of common security interests in the bipolar Cold War context and as the two linchpins of the new European Community movement. By the late 1980s they had agreed to remove completely all formalities along their common border. The symbolism of such a decision on an open border between these two tradi-tional territorial antagonists was an extremely powerful boost to the devel-opment of peaceful co-operation in the European Union. Border posts along the Rhine boundary were converted into offices housing agencies helping borderland populations cope with such cross-border problems as vehicle registration and taxation. Although this development has high value at the national level, it has made for problems on the local scale.

Criminal suspects fleeing from a crime in a borderland community in one country still cannot be pursued beyond the national jurisdiction into the other country. German police chasing a robbery suspect who simply crosses into France over the uncontrolled boundary have no jurisdiction in France. Such borderland behaviour has generated local concern about law enforcement that has resulted in requests for the re-establishment of some controls, thereby threatening the positive symbolism attained by the original decision.

On a much smaller scale but perhaps just as impressively, the Franco-Italian boundary provides another example of symbolic use of the borderland. Italy and France agreed in the early 1980s to create an international Alpine park, with the French segment made up of the high Alpine segment of the territory originally gained from Italy in 1947. This particular symbolic act of co-operation was not perceived positively by many among the borderland population on both sides of the boundary. The 'nationalisation' of this extensive high mountain region of pristine environmental quality meant that hunting would be banned and any future private tourist or second-home developments disallowed. Building a winter sports complex is seen as the most successful alternative to the traditional Alpine livestock economy. Local communal leaders banded together across the boundary to create a unified borderland of resistance to the international park, whose establishment was challenged legally and sometimes violently at every step of the way. Although the park did eventually open many years behind schedule, this case indicates that borderland inhabitants who have a very different view of the future can vehemently oppose some decisions taken by international agreement, even with most positive outcomes in the long-term interest of the countries involved. For the local residents, their right to pursue future prosperity and the control of their local territory was seen as unfairly bartered away by decision makers in Rome and Paris following an opportunistic, bureaucratic, and centrist agenda in which the borderland provided good-neighbour symbols irrespective of local desires.

Perhaps these cases representing a new variety of border conflict pitting the borderland against the international community are a normal outcome of the transition from hostility to harmony, especially in borderlands between states with highly centralised power systems. One may also speculate about the likely impact of the European Union on this type of development. On the one hand, the EU encourages even closer cross-border relations between its member states, especially in the environmental preservation area. Such a trend would tend to exacerbate the conflictual syndrome identified in the Alpes Maritimes. On the other hand, the growth in influence of the EU Commission on the Regions suggests that local cross-border groups in a policy conflict with joint initiatives taken by their respective states could appeal to the EU. They could claim that local control over small-scale international regional issues is the preferred choice over bureaucratic centralism in the future Europe.

The Italo-Slovene borderland in the 1990s is another example of the symbolism of peace and co-operation (Bufon and Minghi 2001). The electoral system reform of 1993 in Italy ended the hitherto 'at large' voting system and allowed for 75 percent of the seats in the Senate and Chamber of Deputies to be filled by those winning pluralities in regionally defined districts. This provided an opportunity for boundary-dwelling ethnic minorities to elect representatives directly to Rome if the mandatory size and the shape of such districts could be fitted to the spatial distribution of the minority. In eastern Friuli, the district for a Senate seat was drawn by the election commission with the very clearly stated purpose of electing a Slovene speaker (Minghi 1997). This long, thin, gerrymandered district runs north-south along the Italian segment of the Italo-Slovene borderland so as to include as many of the 100,000 Slovenes and as few of the Italian-speakers as possible. Although the Slovene candidate narrowly lost in the 1994 election, he did prevail two years later, running a campaign that emphasised the need to move away from narrow nationalist thinking by promising more cross-border co-operation—to move the region from the periphery to the centre of the new Europe. In this case, the borderland and the Italian electoral system had demonstrated a symbiotic relationship suggesting broader implications for other European borderlands.

EMERGENT EUROREGIONS AND THE EUROPEAN UNION

By the mid-1970s conditions in Western Europe had developed to the point that cross-boundary regions of co-operation were being created as a result of local pressure groups acting in joint self-interest. Economic growth and the increasing volume of cross-boundary relationships—goods, capital, and especially people—were showing that the boundary functions in place were inadequate. This was especially so where international urban regions were generating a new type of borderland. The common interests of adjacent communities located in different states but functioning more and more as one system led them to seek a special status in which the normal boundary restrictions on movement would be reduced. In addition, joint enterprises could be launched to overcome the barriers to cross-boundary activity. Hence, sometimes with grudging approval from national capitals, new borderland regions were created, defined by the contiguous and vitally interested municipalities and administrative units of the two or more countries involved.

An excellent early example is the urban region around Basel, known as Regio TriRhena, which includes the canton of Basel in Switzerland, several municipalities in the département of Haut-Rhin in France, and Sudbaden in Germany. The benefits generated over the past three decades as a result of Regio are manifest and enjoyed equally in all three countries. The most visible development made possible by the existence of this Euroregion is the opening of the Basel-Mulhouse-Freiburg international airport, which is located on French territory but connected directly to Basel by a four-kilometre-long limited-access highway. The airport serves all three cities equally well and allows Basel to compete with Zurich and Geneva for international air traffic. Regio has become a model for many other similar borderland regions. Indeed, Gallusser (1994: 388) has suggested that Regio is challenging the concept of boundaries by developing into an 'international *lebensraum* through the intentions of the contemporary population of the borderland'. From a more social theoretical perspective, one can arrive at a similar conclusion with reference to the avoidance of the 'territorial trap'—the traditional assumptions of and preoccupation with state-centred territoriality and fixed images of the bordered world (Agnew 1994). On this basis, the new borderlands of Europe can be seen more as constructions of shared identities (Paasi 1998: 80–81).

Although not all Euroregions have the substance and potential of Regio, there has been a veritable explosion of new creations over the past decade. Many are to be found along the old Cold War boundary. For example, some seven new Euroregions have appeared between Germany, Austria, and the Czech Republic. Not all new regions, however, are in Central Europe. The opening of a fixed link rail tunnel between France and the United Kingdom in 1993–1994 has generated a need for greater cross-channel co-operation. Common problems of auto and truck traffic congestion at the two entry points to the Chunnel and challenges to the economies of channel ports and their traditional ferry traffic became grave local concerns. This led to the creation of a new marine Anglo-French borderland, the Transmanche Euroregion, which includes the English county of Kent and the French département of Nord-Pas de Calais.

A rather unique borderland development in the mid-1990s deserves some attention because it may well be a prologue to how future disputes between borderland minorities and the state are settled. The formation of a newly elected government in Italy in 1994 under Berlusconi included both neo-fascist and secessionist elements. Italy's three large boundary-dwelling ethnic-linguistic minorities—the German speakers of South

Tyrol, the French speakers of the Val d'Aosta, and the Slovenes in eastern Friuli—all felt threatened. The Alleanza Nazionale held key cabinet positions filled by supernationalists insensitive to ethnic minority rights, and the Lega Nord forces were calling for a decentralised Italy of powerful macroregions in which borderland ethnic autonomy would be eliminated as 'unjustly privileged'. The political leaders of the three minority groups took the unprecedented step of meeting together to discuss a common strategy to resist these threats. Two meetings were held, one in late 1994 and a second in early 1996 just after the Berlusconi government had fallen and elections had been called for later that spring. Each produced a declaration of common cause. Analysis of these declarations reveals a very significant trend (Minghi 1999). Aside from clauses calling for sharing information, mutual help in showing solidarity, and co-ordinating electoral activity to assure maximum representation, the group agreed to collaborate with minority parties from all over Europe in establishing an international convention and empowering themselves through European legislation. Specifically, after the second meeting the group resolved to campaign for support among the Italian electorate to win support 'for positions consistent with the historic and cultural patrimony of our communities'. And, most significant, the group appealed to the European Union to guarantee the rights of linguistic minorities. Through this reaction to the perceived threat to hard-won cultural autonomy, a new European borderlands chapter was opened. Rather than taking the traditional route—the groups working separately through their elected representatives in Rome and assisted by pressure on Rome from their cross-border 'sponsors' of Austria, France, and Slovenia, respectively—they bonded together. They also went beyond their regions to appeal to the Italian electorate. In addition, they had no hesitation in looking beyond their cross-border sponsor neighbours, on whom they had relied in the past, to seek the direct help of the European Union in their common cause. The broader implications of such joint and co-ordinated reactions for the future nature of borderlands are obvious.

BORDERLANDS OF THE FUTURE: RAZOR'S EDGES OR COMMUNITIES OF INTEREST?

It is highly unlikely that Europe will in the foreseeable future return to borderlands of confrontation along razor-edge boundaries separating hostile neighbours (Minghi 1994). Even speculating about the longest of terms, one cannot detect any evidence of a borderland cycle that could lead in that direction. Nevertheless, the contemporary status of Bosnia and Kosovo in the ex-Yugoslavia is a sharp reminder that such borderlands are not necessarily phenomena only of the past in Europe. Significantly, these regions of recent strife, destruction, and ethnic cleansing are now occupied and essentially run largely by European interests determined to forge developments that will rapidly convert them to the European norm of harmony and co-operation.

Although there is a movement to incorporate all of Europe into the European Union over the next decade or so, it seems unlikely that the future EU, no matter what its size and makeup, will be anything but a collection of European sovereign states working together in peace and harmony, building the basis for a common European society, prosperity, and collective security, and competing successfully as a group in the global economy. Therefore, the future Europe will continue to be composed of nation-states with defined boundaries. And irrespective of the changing role of divisions between neighbours, there will by definition be the constant of European borderlands, albeit with a very dynamic nature. Almost forty years ago this chapter's author recognised the excitement created by boundary changes for research into borderlands. At the same time, however, he also made a plea for a focus of borderland study on the 'normal' situation in which the pattern of territorial sovereignty remains stable but the dynamic stimulus in the borderland is found in changing relationships (Minghi 1963: 427). Such is the case for Europe in the first decades of the twenty-first century.

In conclusion, the weight of evidence suggests that the current trend toward more and larger Euroregions, along a growing number of boundaries and involving more states, will be the dominant feature in Europe's borderlands well into the twenty-first century. This trend will inevitably serve to increase the focus on and interest in the nature of borderlands as readily available and reliable products of contemporary European political development. The comparative study of their human geography should, therefore, increasingly become an attractive and efficient way to understand the dynamic essence of Europe.

REFERENCES

Agnew, J. 1994. The territorial trap: The geographical assumptions of international relations theory. *Review of International Political Economy* 1, no. 1: 53–80.

Bufon, M. 1993. Cultural and social dimensions of borderlands: The case of the Italo-Slovene transborder area. *GeoJournal* 30, no. 3: 235–40.

Bufon, M., and J. Minghi. 2000. The Upper Adriatic borderland: From conflict to harmony. *GeoJournal* 52, no. 2: 191–27

Gallusser, W. A. 1994. Borders as necessities and challenges: Human geographic insights paving the way to a new border awareness. In W. A. Gallusser, ed. *Boundaries and Political Coexistence,* 381–89. Bern: Peter Lang.

Gallusser, W. A., ed. 1994. *Boundaries and Political Coexistence.* Bern: Peter Lang.

House, J. W. 1959. The Franco-Italian boundary in the Alpes Maritimes. *Transactions, Institute of British Geographers* 26: 107–31.

Klemencic, V., and M. Bufon. 1994. Culture elements of integration and transformation of border regions. *Political Geography* 13, no. 1: 73–83.

Markusse, J. 1999. Thresholds of regional minorities. Paper presented at the World Political Map conference of the International Geographical Union, Prague, August.

Minghi, J. V. 1963. Boundary studies in political geography. *Annals of the Association of American Geographers* 53, no. 3: 407–28.

———. 1971. The South Tyrol: Spatial patterns of national integration and cultural survival in a border region. In S. J. Chatterjee and S. P. Das Gupta, eds. *Historical and Political Geography,* vol. 3, 421–27. Calcutta: National Committee for Geography.

———. 1981. The Franco-Italian borderland: Sovereignty change and contemporary developments in the Alpes Maritimes. *Regio Basiliensis* 22, nos. 2/3: 232–46.

———. 1991. From conflict to harmony in border landscapes. In D. Rumley and J. V. Minghi, eds. *The Geography of Border Landscapes,* 15–30. London: Routledge.

———. 1994. European borderlands: International harmony, landscape change and new conflicts. In C. Grundy-Warr, ed. *Eurasia—World Boundaries,* 89–98. London: Routledge.

———. 1997. Voting and borderland minorities: Recent Italian elections in eastern Friuli–Venezia Giulia. *GeoJournal* 43, no. 3: 263–71.

———. 1999. Common cause for borderland minorities? Shared status among Italy's ethnic communities. *Geopolitics* 4, nos. 1/2: 199–208.

Moodie, A. E. 1950. Some new boundary problems in the Julian March. *Transactions, Institute of British Geographers* 17: 81–93.

Paasi, A. 1998. Boundaries as social processes: Territoriality in the world of flows. *Geopolitics* 3, no. 1: 69–88.

Prescott, J. R. V. 1987. *Political Frontiers and Boundaries.* London: Allen and Unwin.

Strassoldo, R. 1983. Frontier regions: Future collaboration or conflict? In M. Anderson, ed. *Frontier Regions in Western Europe,* 123–36. London: Frank Cass.

Chapter Four

Euroregions in Comparative Perspective

Joanna M. M. Kepka and Alexander B. Murphy

During the late twentieth century, significant challenges emerged to a state-based, political-territorial order in Europe. Chief amongst these challenges was the development of increasingly numerous and significant regional structures and institutional arrangements spanning international boundaries. Although the state remains the dominant actor in the organisation and execution of political and economic activities in Europe today, other actors, including the European Union (EU), regional entities, and nongovernmental organisations, now play an important role in the organisation of society and space in the 'New Europe'.

Europe's evolving political-territorial order has attracted considerable scholarly attention among commentators concerned with European integration (Hooghe 1996; Roberts 1993), the nature of sovereignty (Murphy 1996; Wilson 1996), and the changing nature of boundaries (Delli Zotti 1996; Raffestin 1993). In their studies of various types of transboundary arrangements, commentators have tried to understand not only the functions and political implications of these new structures but also what they mean for the people affected by them (Sjøberg 1998; Sandelin 1998). A fundamental challenge to a more complete understanding of the sociocultural implications of transboundary political-territorial constructs arises from the fact that they have developed in different geographical contexts. Yet the ubiquity and novelty of this new form of governance has led some commentators, at least implicitly, to treat European transboundary governance structures as a single type of institutional development with generalisable implications for the places and peoples affected by them.

If we are to gain a more sophisticated understanding of the nature and implications of transboundary regional governance, it is important to move beyond such generalisations to consider whether there are significant differences in the function and meaning of these governance structures from place to place. As a step in that direction, this chapter offers a comparative analysis of the development of so-called Euroregions in two very different geopolitical contexts: at the heart of the EU where the Dutch, German, and Belgian borders meet (the Euregio Meuse-Rhin) and at the edge of the EU where the German, Polish, and Czech borders meet (the Euroregion Nysa).

Euroregions are particular types of transboundary co-operation agreements forged not by regional actors but by associations of local authorities. Euroregions were first developed in the 1960s along the German-Dutch and German-Dutch-Belgian boundaries, but since the fall of the Iron Curtain they have become the most sought-after form of transborder co-operation in East Central Europe. Since 1990, local authorities in Poland's border regions, for example, have entered into thirteen co-operation agreements with their counterparts on the opposite side of the international boundaries. What is the significance of these developments, and how should they be understood?

To date, much of the literature on Euroregions has been largely descriptive (Weyand 1997; Bojar 1996). To the extent that evaluative claims are made, they tend to be based on extrapolations from the experiences of other places with Euroregions. Heffner (1998), for example, simply assumes that Euroregions will work in the interests of parties on both sides of international boundaries in Eastern and Central Europe because that has been the experience of Euroregions in Western Europe. Studies of this sort perpetuate generalisations about the impacts of transboundary governance structures across geographical contexts.

This study seeks to highlight the pitfalls of generalising in this way by offering a comparative analysis of relevant social, economic, and political circumstances that are affecting transboundary co-operation in the Polish-German-Czech Euroregion Nysa and the German-Dutch-Belgian Euregio Meuse-Rhin. To provide context for the study, we begin by discussing the evolution of transboundary co-operation in the EU. This is followed by consideration of Euroregions as a class of transboundary co-operation and their role in transforming the conduct of transborder relations in Europe. We then turn to a more detailed discussion of the nature and functions of the Meuse-Rhin and Nysa Euroregions and the types of contextual differences that can render problematic broad generalisations about transboundary institutional structures.

THE EVOLUTION OF TRANSBOUNDARY
CO-OPERATION IN THE EU

Since its inception in 1957, the European Economic Community (subsequently the European Community; now the EU) has gradually moved from a state-centric enterprise to one in which substate and nonstate actors have come to play an increasingly significant role in the political, economic, and social arenas. Originally, cross-boundary initiatives were of little significance. As the European integration project moved forward, however, various EU organisations became strong proponents of interregional contacts with a transboundary character—particularly the European Commission and the Council of Europe.

The Role of the European Commission and the Council of Europe

The European Commission has supported the establishment of organisations that bring together regional and local authorities from different member states to promote regional interests at the European level. These organisations include, among others, the Association of European Border Regions (AEBR), the Assembly of European Regions, and the Council of European Municipalities and Regions—the most important European local government lobby (*Panorama Euroregionów* 1997). The Council of Europe, on the other hand, was instrumental in orchestrating several European conventions on transborder co-operation, beginning with the European Outline Convention on Transfrontier Cooperation Between Territorial Communities or Authorities, adopted in Madrid in 1980 (*Gminy Przygraniczne* 1997: 43). The Council also adopted, in that same year, the European Outline Agreement on Cooperation Between Transborder Regions and, in 1981, the European Charter of Transborder Regions (*Gminy Przygraniczne* 1997: 46).

These legal enactments—along with the European Charter of Local Government signed in 1985—paved the way for the development of transboundary contacts among and between regional and local authorities in such places as the Rhine Valley, the Saarland-Lorraine axis, and the French Upper Rhine areas. Transboundary business contacts expanded; social and cultural exchanges intensified; and people, goods, and ideas began to flow more freely across international boundaries (Murphy 1993). In the process, political boundaries lost some of their significance as social boundaries, and some transboundary areas were able to exert more political and economic clout as a consequence of their changed situation vis-à-vis the long-dominant political-territorial order represented by the map of so-called nation-states.

Transboundary co-operation had demonstrably positive economic and social ramifications for some substate regions, and certain local authorities in these regions—most notably those in Belgium and Germany—sought to capitalise on the situation in a manner that would allow them to exert more influence on the European political scene. They therefore spearheaded an effort to bring a wide range of substate political actors to Brussels and Strasbourg, where they could engage in macro-diplomacy and lobby for regional interests in the EU Commission and Parliament (Hooghe and Marks 1996). Moreover, the establishment of the Committee of Regions (CoR) in 1994 allowed member regions not only to voice their demands for increased regional participation but also to lobby for EU policy approaches (Bullmann 1997). For example, in 1996 the Committee set forth its Opinion on the Revision of the Treaty on European Union, in which it demanded, amongst other things, extension of the principle of subsidiarity from its current member state focus to regional and local authorities (Bullmann 1997). If this demand were fully realised, the subsidiarity principle could become instrumental in fostering substate participation in EU decision making and legitimising the activities of transboundary co-operation associations.

At the moment, the majority of inter-regional organisations with a transboundary character are simple associations with no externally formalised institutional basis. The notable exception is the Euroregions, which are the products of institutionalised cross-boundary co-operation links forged by local authorities in border regions.

The Euroregion Construct

Euroregions are almost as old as the European Community itself. Established in 1958 along the German-Dutch border, the pioneer 'Euregio' became the first formally organised form of cross-border co-operation in Europe. The German-Dutch Euregio was followed by the founding of similarly conceived Euroregions in 1963 (the Euregio Rhin-Waal) and in 1976 (the Euregio Meuse-Rhin). Within the plethora of transborder substate entities and structures subsumed under the umbrella of the AEBR, only fifteen can be considered Euroregions. This is due to the particular organisational structure of these Euroregions: Each of the fifteen consists of a council, a presidium, a secretariat, and several working groups. Over the past decade, however, the concepts of 'Euregio' and 'Euroregion' have become ubiquitous throughout Europe and are now frequently used to describe any substate structure with a transboundary character. Most of the fifteen Euroregions in question function along the German-Dutch and German-Dutch-Belgian borders, but since 1990 they have diffused rapidly—particularly to East Central Europe. Much of the political elite in the latter region regards Euroregions as structures that can help their countries overcome past problems (reconciliation between historically antagonistic nations) and facilitate closer relations with the EU (*Euroregion Nysa* 1994). These goals have prompted Polish authorities to open up their borders, and those authorities have encouraged the development of formal cross-border linkages. At the time of this writing, thirteen Euroregions have been established along the country's western, southern, and eastern boundaries (so far only five are members of the AEBR).

Located on the margins of states, Euroregions are designed to enhance the economic and political significance of border areas within the larger European milieu, while undermining the arbitrary divisions among peoples that so often are the product of political boundary drawing. As Weyand (1997) explains, the objective is to create a 'we-feeling' that transcends national boundaries and to assist in the implementation of a 'Europe of Citizens'. Through the promotion of numerous exchange programs for students, families, and employees (especially civil servants), and through the organisation of various cultural and sporting events, Euroregions seek to construct subregional bridges connecting peoples; they offer the prospect of deepening the European integration processes. In fact, Euroregions are sometimes cited as the most important 'bottom-up' pressure for the deepening of European integration (Baker 1996: 41) and as 'windows for the future evolution' of a genuine system of co-operation (Delli Zotti 1996: 68).

Despite growing interest in EU regional policy and the emergence of a third level of governance (i.e., regional governance) on the European political scene (Jeffrey 1997; Jones and Keating 1995), until recently remarkably little attention was paid to Euroregions and related cross-border developments. At least in the Anglo-American and Polish literatures, references to Euroregions and related phenomena have been either brief (Weyand 1997; Delli Zotti 1996) or of a descriptive nature (Heffner 1998; Bojar 1996; Borys and Przybyła 1993). As a result, the nature and significance of transboundary interaction is undertheorised, and we know far less than we need to know about the actual impact of cross-border co-operation.

Part of the explanation for this state of affairs lies in the continued dominance of an implicit state-based spatiality in much social scientific work (Agnew 1993; Taylor 1993). Rooted in a political-territorial system that emerged in early-modern Western Europe, the state has come to be treated as the basic spatial unit we use to make sense of the world:

It is difficult to exaggerate the impact of the territorial assumptions that have developed in association with the . . . (modern) political order. In general terms, they have made the territorial state the privileged unit for analyzing most phenomena while discouraging consideration of the nature of the territorial state itself. In the political sphere they have directed overwhelming attention to state government and governmental leaders at the expense of extrastate or substate actors and arrangements. In the economic sphere they have prompted us to frame our most basic theories of development in state terms. In the cultural sphere they have encouraged us to collapse our understandings of diversity into state-based categories; for every reference to the Quechua, Aymara, and Guaraní peoples there are thousands to Bolivians. In the environmental sphere they have prompted us to conceptualize issues that do not correspond to state boundaries as 'transnational' (read trans-state) or 'transboundary' issues, not Upper Rhine or Southeast Asian lowland issues. (Murphy 1996: 102–3)

The impact of the map of so-called sovereign states on our conceptualisation of political and social processes reflects both the influence of state structures on human affairs and the role of state authorities in the collection and dissemination of information. These influences are so great that they direct attention away from the ways in which knowledge is organised in state-territorial terms (Häkli 2001), leading to the marginalisation of work on sociospatial structures such as transboundary regions that do not fit easily within the political-geographic parameters of the modern state system.

With the rapid expansion of transboundary co-operation in recent years, forms of transboundary co-operation such as Euroregions can no longer be ignored. Yet the tendency is to see these more as novel institutional forms than as phenomena with potentially profound sociospatial significance. As a result, critical geographical dimensions of transboundary co-operation can and have been overlooked. Nowhere is this more clear than in studies of Euroregions in East Central Europe, which often start from the (at least implied) assumption that Euroregions will lead peripheral border regions in Poland, the Czech Republic, Slovakia, and Hungary down the same development path as their counterpart border regions in Germany, the Netherlands, and Belgium (Heffner 1998). Without denying that positive outcomes can result from the establishment of Euroregions in East Central Europe, a comparative analysis of the Euregio Meuse-Rhin and the Euroregion Nysa reveals the influence of geographical context on the types of economic, political, administrative, and social challenges Euroregions face. Moreover, a comparative assessment of the two Euroregions highlights critical challenges that the emerging Euroregions of East Central Europe are confronting.

THE DEVELOPMENT OF THE MEUSE-RHIN
AND NYSA EUROREGIONS

Euregio Meuse-Rhin

Established in 1976, the Euregio Meuse-Rhin is one of the pioneer Euroregions. It is centred on the confluence of the Meuse and Rhine Rivers (hence the name) and covers the areas of five regions: Limbourg (both Dutch and Belgian), Liège (Belgium), Belgium's Germanophone Community, and Aachen (Germany) (see figure 4.1). At present, there are some 3.7 million inhabitants within the Euroregion, distributed across a territory of just over ten thousand square kilometres. Historically, the territory of today's Euregio Meuse-Rhin was a part of the Principality of Liège, the Duchy of Limbourg, and then the Duchy of Luxembourg— passing successively under Spanish, Austrian, French, and Dutch rule (*Times Atlas of European History* 1994). With the rise of nationalism in the nineteenth century and subsequent delineation of political-territorial homelands, the area of today's Euregio was divided politically among the Netherlands, Belgium, and Germany. Following the Second World War, strong expressions of ethnonationalism were delegitimised in Western Europe, and six countries, led by two historical adversaries (France and Germany), embarked on the road towards economic co-operation.

Although much of the effort to build a 'common European home' has been carried out at the behest of European Union or state government officials, Euroregions have played a significant role. The Euregio Meuse-Rhin represents European integration 'from below'; in other words, it deepens the processes of integration by fostering co-operation at the lowest level: the commune. The Euregio Meuse-Rhin has been referred to as 'a true laboratory for the European experiment' (*Euregio Meuse-Rhin* 1997: 5). Local borderland populations, speaking three languages, interact at the Euregio level on a daily basis; local officials collaborate on economic and planning initiatives; businesses form links through the Euregio Chamber of Commerce; and local inhabitants, through various sporting and cultural events, learn about their common history and cultural heritage.

The Euroregion's youngest and most promising organ, the Euregio Council, is made up of representatives from the border regions of each of the participating countries (see figure 4.2). Significantly, in the spirit of promoting a 'we-feeling' in the Euregio, the political groups of the Council are formed according to party affiliation, not according to nationality (see figure 4.3). Although the Council's functions and powers are consultative and its members are not directly elected, its composition challenges traditional notions of inter-regional co-operation arrangements, which

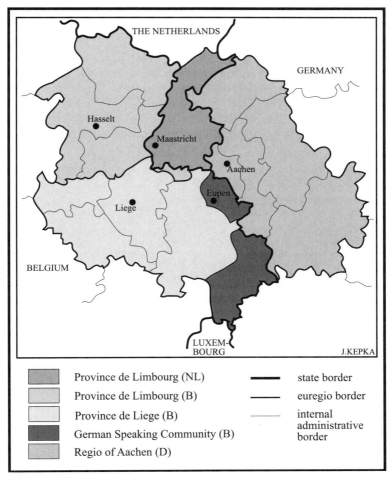

THE NETHERLANDS

GERMANY

Hasselt

Maastricht

Aachen

Eupen

Liege

BELGIUM

LUXEM-
BOURG   J.KEPKA

	Province de Limbourg (NL)	▬▬▬	state border
	Province de Limbourg (B)	▬▬▬	euregio border
	Province de Liege (B)	——	internal administrative border
	German Speaking Community (B)		
	Regio of Aachen (D)		

Figure 4.1.   Euregio Meuse-Rhin

Source: Euroregio Meuse-Rhin 1997.

have been deeply rooted in the national frameworks of the extant state system. The Council thus helps to reinforce the challenge to traditional understandings of state sovereignty and international boundaries that is associated with enactments emanating from the Euregio's legislative organs, which have the power to bind all members on a number of critical matters through simple majority votes (Weyand 1997).

The Meuse-Rhin's administrative program is multifaceted (*Euregio Meuse-Rhin* 1997). In the socioeconomic realm, most efforts of the Euregio are focused on concrete everyday problems arising out of the area's bor-

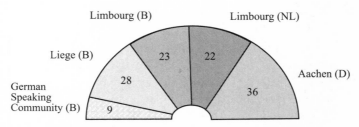

Figure 4.2.   Members of the Euregio Meuse-Rhin Council by Province
Source: Euroregio Meuse-Rhin 1997.

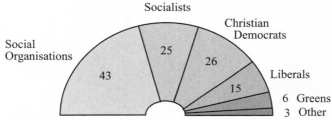

Figure 4.3.   Transnational Political Parties in the Euregio Meuse-Rhin Council
Source: Euroregio Meuse-Rhin 1997.

der situation, including improving transportation and communication linkages, fostering and facilitating co-operation between small- and medium-sized businesses on each side of the border, and developing common regional planning and environmental conservation policies. Much emphasis is placed on economic matters, particularly the promotion of the Euregio's economic potential in the European market. The Euregio Meuse-Rhin also supports programs that help local populations understand the varying legal and social security systems of each state; it facilitates co-operation on critical health and safety issues (for example, police protection and rescue services); and it sponsors numerous exchange programs for students, families, and civil servants. In addition, cultural and sporting events are an important part of the Euregio's work. During the summer of 1998, for example, the Euregio organised a Festival of Theatres with the participation of local musical and theatrical companies, numerous programs for youth (language courses, panel discussions, excursions, rock concerts, etc.), and tennis and judo competitions. These activities are geared primarily towards promoting an intercultural dialogue, diminishing language barriers, and creating a 'Euregio identity' and a sense of place that spans national boundaries. The Euregio constitutes a model for a bottom-up approach to transborder co-operation that can serve to deepen European integration processes through participation by citizens at local levels.

Euroregion Nysa

Following the demise of the Soviet-dominated communist regime, the Polish central authorities allowed cross-border linkages to be forged along the Polish-German boundary, which simultaneously functions as an external border of the EU. The first transboundary co-operation agreement involving the former Eastern Bloc countries came out of an effort on the part of local officials on the German side of the Nysa-Neisse-Nisa River to initiate cross-border co-operation with their counterparts on the Polish and Czech sides of the border. The effort led to the signing of a formal co-operation agreement in May 1991—bringing into being the Euroregion Nysa (figure 4.4). The region comprises more than eleven thousand square kilometres, more than 1.6 million people, and more than twenty administrative districts in Germany, Poland, and the Czech Republic (*Euroregion Nysa* 1994).

The conference at which the Euroregion Nysa was created took place in Zittau, Germany. It was organised under the auspices of the presidents of the three countries—Lech Walesa of Poland, Václav Havel of the Czech Republic, and Richard von Weizsäcker of Germany—with the participation of more than three hundred representatives of Polish, Czech, and German border-area communities (*Euroregion Nysa* 1994). The presence of the heads of governments of the three countries was largely symbolic, however. Weizsäcker and Walesa were not dictating the terms of the agreement; they were simply marking the significance of the occasion. The real impetus for the initiative was local. Indeed, it was described at the time as a 'voluntary community of interests of communes and districts', whose existence depends solely on the willingness of local authorities to participate (*Euroregion Nysa* 1994: 19). The fact that Euroregion Nysa was the first of its kind in East Central Europe rendered it of special significance; it was said to initiate an era in which relations 'East-West are shaped in new, European dimensions' (*Euroregion Nysa* 1994: 9).

The Euroregion Nysa was followed by similar co-operation arrangements along the Polish-German boundary: Euroregions Sprewa-Nysa-Bóbr (1993), Pro Europa Viadrina (1993), and Pomerania (1995). Thus, Euroregion Nysa seemingly initiated a 'spillover' effect whereby a growing

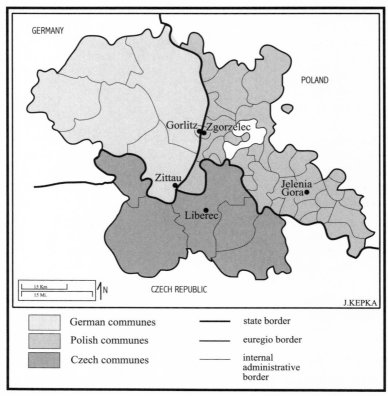

Figure 4.4.   Euroregion Neisse-Nisa-Nysa
Source: Euroregion Nysa 1994.

number of local officials in border regions sought the benefits of transboundary co-operation with regions located within EU member states.
Since their establishment, the Euroregions' authorities have been able to
apply for funds directly to the EU. Moneys for transboundary projects have
come from INTERREG II, a regional development fund for Germany's
eastern *Länder,* and PHARE, an EU program designed to transfer funds to
encourage further reforms and to set up democratic institutions in the
countries of former Eastern Europe (Kepka 2000). In addition, the EU
Commission established a special program to promote co-operation
between Polish and German border regions. This program, which exists
under the umbrella of PHARE, has its own annual budget of 55 million
ecus and is the Polish analogue of INTERREG II (PHARE 1996). In the
case of the Euroregion Nysa, for instance, the Polish communes forming

part of the Euroregion received a total of 7.9 million ecus in 1995 and 9.3 million ecus in 1996 from PHARE for projects involving transport infrastructure, environmental protection, and regional infrastructure and economy (*Jeleniogórskie—Stan i Perspektywy Rozwoju* 1997).

The Euroregion Nysa provides a framework for activities that traditionally have been carried out by or within individual states. There is, for example, a Statistical Programme PL-14, which is carried out under the auspices of EUROSTAT and is co-ordinated by the Regional Statistical Office in Jelenia Góra, Poland. This program (or more precisely its principal arm, the Statistics Working Group) collects information from various parts of the Euroregion and compiles it in forms that go beyond traditional state-based approaches. In addition to statistical information on regional trade and other economic activities, the Statistics Group also provides information on matters related to demography, education, job markets, social welfare, and tourism (*Euroregion Nysa* 1994: 47).

The geographical location of Euroregion Nysa—along the external boundary of the EU—plays a significant role in defining the character and functions of this transboundary political-territorial construct. In contrast to the Euregio Meuse-Rhin, the Euroregion Nysa's institutional structure is much more complicated, with separate associations and working groups in the participating regions of Germany, Poland, and the Czech Republic meeting and making decisions that precede and constrain decision making on the part of the Euroregion-wide institutions. Consequently, the possibility of forming transnational political parties is curtailed in the Euroregion Nysa. Moreover, because the borders between Germany and Poland, and between Germany and the Czech Republic, are simultaneously part of the external boundary of the European Union, cross-boundary co-operation is not simply an internal EU matter. There is no single supranational political-administrative framework within which the Euroregion Nysa can develop.

Despite these obstacles to close co-operation, members of the Euroregion's various institutions meet on a daily basis to work out solutions to common problems. The working groups function within the established Euroregion framework on matters such as environmental regulation, regional planning and infrastructure, and culture, education, and youth exchanges. The Euroregion covers areas characterised by sharp differences in infrastructure and level of economic development. Consequently, the main emphasis is on developing ways to alleviate these differences. The Euroregion's programs are divided into three groups, which prioritise the projects to be addressed. The first group includes, among others, projects focused on town planning, border-crossing systems, and sewage management; the second emphasises co-operation among public security services, co-operative transportation planning, and collaborative construction projects in border towns such as Zgorzelec (Poland) and Görlitz (Germany); and the last concentrates on agricultural, energy, and environmental issues (*Euroregion Nysa* 1994).

As is the case for the Euregio Meuse-Rhin, one of the main objectives of the Euroregion Nysa is to create a 'we-feeling' that spans the national boundaries. The residents of the local borderland communities of the Tripeland (Triangle of Three Lands) have the opportunity to participate in cross-boundary activities such as musical festivals, cross-cultural dialogues, and sporting events. There is a strong emphasis on cultural exchanges amongst pupils and students and on cross-cultural communication amongst various interest groups. Interchanges and daily contacts between local German and Polish populations, for instance, are essential parts of the Polish-German reconciliation process. In addition, EU sponsorship of various Euroregion activities ties Nysa to the wider European integration process.

THE MEUSE-RHIN AND NYSA EUROREGIONS IN COMPARATIVE PERSPECTIVE

Many of the objectives of Euroregion Nysa mirror those of Euregio Meuse-Rhin: the creation of a transborder Euro-identity, the improvement of living conditions in local communities, and the promotion of economic development in border areas. The pursuit of these objectives, however, is often hindered by circumstances prevalent along the Polish-German-Czech boundary—circumstances that are different from those along the German-Dutch-Belgian border. These differences are rooted in divergent economic and political circumstances, as well as in differing senses of identity and place.

Economic Differences

The most pronounced difference between the Meuse-Rhin and Nysa Euroregions concerns the character of their respective regional economies. The Euregio Meuse-Rhin encompasses a high-technology industrial area with automobile assembly plants, electronics firms, mechanical engineering establishments, and biotechnology concerns (*Euregio Meuse-Rhin* 1997). The presence of two scientific parks and two Business Enterprise and Innovation Centers (BICs) signals the region's high-technology emphasis, along with its focus on research and other quaternary economic activities. In contrast, border areas in the Euroregion Nysa are characterised by sunset industries—large and inefficient power plants and coal mining centres—as well as by a relatively high unemployment rate. In 1994, for example, the unemployment rate in the Polish town of Jelenia Góra and in the German town of Görlitz was 15 percent (*Miasta w Euroregionie Neisse-Nisa-Nysa* 1995: 60). Since 1990 there has been evidence of growth in the service sector, but considerable energy and resources are dedicated to restructuring and modernising the old industrial complexes on both the Polish and German sides of the border. This situation necessarily affects the ability of local authorities to develop and implement new initiatives and projects.

In addition to the issue of new versus old industries, there are clear transboundary economic inequalities. Whereas the five provinces of Meuse-Rhin are characterised by a relatively even, and often complementary, distribution of industries on the Belgian, Dutch, and German sides, in the Euroregion Nysa there is a striking asymmetry of economic potential and a concomitant asymmetry in the ability to finance economic initiatives (*Euroregion Nysa* 1994). There is almost no Polish investment in German businesses, yet the Germans have supplied investment capital to more than 65 percent of the total number of firms on the Polish side of Nysa (*Rocznik Statystyczny Województwa Jeleniogórskiego* 1998). German capital is particularly important in manufacturing (both light and heavy), retail, and construction. Moreover, while German-made products are available throughout Poland, the presence of Polish-made goods on the German market is minimal. Indeed, German enterprises and distributors have even erected barriers that discourage Polish exports to Germany (*Wprost* 1999; Kepka 2000).

Political Differences

Beyond economic considerations, there are also differential political factors that affect the character of transboundary co-operation in the two regions. In the case of Euregio Meuse-Rhin, all provinces except Dutch Limbourg are within countries with federal systems. Consequently, the involvement of national centres in transborder activities is minimal and, in most cases, approval from regional authorities suffices for the implementation of cross-border activities and projects. Although the same holds true for the German communities forming part of the Euroregion Nysa, Polish and Czech local authorities operate within unitary states, and they therefore must seek approval from Warsaw or Prague, respectively, for all initiatives of a cross-boundary character. In the case of Poland, the opening up of the country's borders and the emergence of Euroregions has led to a variety of legislative proposals aimed at giving local officials in border areas more autonomy. As of yet, however, these proposals have not been formally adopted because there is no legislative consensus on the degree of autonomy that local officials should have. Such obstacles to transboundary co-operation are not present in the Meuse-Rhin case.

Beyond administrative matters, the Euroregion Nysa differs from its western counterpart because many living within Nysa do not see the participants as political equals. The choice of Zittau, Germany, as the administrative centre is itself of symbolic importance. Zittau has been the prime instigator of transboundary co-operation from the beginning, and it is Zittau, not Liberec (in the Czech Republic) or Bogatynia (in Poland), that is in a position to support the day-to-day activities of the Council. The stream of administrative decisions emanating from Zittau regularly serves to reinforce the notion that the German part of Nysa is 'in the driver's seat'.

The Euroregion Nysa is also characterised by a comparatively low level of consensus on what the Euroregion means. A recent survey conducted among the Polish communes forming part of the Euroregion Nysa showed that there are two opposing views of the Euroregion construct (Borys and Panasiewicz 1996). The first treats the Euroregion as a *framework* within which local initiatives can be realised through co-operation with other partners within and without national territories; the second is based on a perception of the Euroregion as an *institution* that develops and organises all transborder initiatives and projects (Borys and Panasiewicz 1996). The tension between these two positions presents a clear challenge for the success of the Euroregion Nysa initiative.

Differences in Sense of Identity and Place

Behind differing understandings of the nature of the Euroregion Nysa construct are suspicions about the transboundary co-operation process that are rooted in particular senses of identity and place that have developed along the German-Polish boundary. The survey discussed above highlights a critical potential barrier to increased cross-border contact in the Nysa region: the 'different, and not always positive, perceptions of crossboundary cooperation amongst the local borderland population' (Borys and Panasiewicz 1996: 95; translation by J. Kepka). Such views are arguably much more entrenched in the Euroregion Nysa than in the Euroregio Meuse-Rhin because of different historical-geographical influences on nationalism and national identity in the two regions.

As previously mentioned, in the aftermath of World War II, overt expressions of ethnonationalism were delegitimised in Western Europe. Economic co-operation instigated by the Treaty of Rome allowed for, among other things, an increase in mobility and transborder interaction.

In contrast, transnational mobility and contacts were virtually absent in the countries of the Eastern Bloc. In the case of the Polish-German boundary, for example, the communist elite not only closed the border but also promoted anti-German sentiment in its effort to foster closer associations among Slavic peoples (Dressler and Ciechocinska 1996). Consequently, the already strong anti-German views that were rooted in the horrors of Nazism persisted unchallenged throughout the succeeding decades.

The restriction of free cross-boundary contacts created divisions that are difficult to overcome. For example, prior to 1945, when the Nysa River became the boundary between East Germany and Poland, Görlitz was a unified city with a six-hundred-year history. After 1945, the city was divided into German Görlitz and Polish Zgorzelec, and contacts across the river were severely limited. This situation persisted until the 1970s, when a treaty was signed that allowed a limited number of daily border crossings (*Miasta w Euroregionie Neisse-Nisa-Nysa* 1995). Since 1989, the possibilities for cross-boundary interaction have been unlimited, and many of the residents of Görlitz and Zgorzelec have come to question former national prejudices and stereotypes. Yet the effects of a recent history of separation and division are not easy to overcome.

Emblematic of these effects, in the early 1990s over half of Poland's population considered the Odra-Nysa boundary 'insecure'—believing that Germany's failure (at the time) to formally recognise the Polish-German boundary created after World War II could lead to a German effort to revise the boundary (Markovits, Reich, and Hinchey 1997). On a local scale, in the mid-1990s close to 30 percent of the residents of the Jelenia Góra voivodship (the Polish side of the Euroregion Nysa) considered the idea of the Euroregion an attempt by Germany to subjugate Poland (Adamczuk 1994: 60). The historical and contemporary dynamics of the Odra-Nysa boundary make it difficult for the Poles to come to terms with the complex history of Germany's involvement in the three partitions of Poland, as well as with the more recent tragedy of Hitler's invasion and occupation. This leads to fears and suspicions on the part of Poles in the face of Germany's growing cultural, economic, and political presence in Poland, and it presents a challenge for inter-regional co-operation in the Euroregion Nysa that is of an entirely different magnitude from the attitudinal challenges to inter-regional co-operation that are present in Euregio Meuse-Rhin.

Further complicating the picture is the fact that the border between Poland and Germany continues to play a role that is very different from the boundaries within the EU. The fall of the communist regimes in Poland and East Germany allowed for a substantial increase in transboundary contact. However, the process of German unification that followed introduced a further complexity to Polish-German relations, for the Oder and Neisse Rivers became not only a boundary between states but an external boundary of the EU. This meant that the Euroregion Nysa was in a very different geopolitical situation from the Euroregio Meuse-Rhin.

The significance of this point is evident in mobility issues. Following the signing of the Schengen Agreement (which lifted border controls and ensured free and unlimited passage for citizens of all signatory states), the borders between Germany, Holland, and Belgium began to function more as administrative divisions than as clear-cut demarcations of state-territorial control. Consequently, inhabitants of Liège, Belgium, can make weekend trips to Maastricht, Holland, just as easily as they can travel to Eupen or Hasselt, both Belgian towns. Although Germans living along the Polish-German boundary can also make daily trips to Poland, and vice versa, their experience would be different from that of the inhabitants of the Euregio Meuse-Rhin. The latter would hardly notice at which precise point they crossed into a territory of an adjacent state, whereas the former (whether Polish or German) would spend an hour or so on either side of the border dealing with passport formalities.

Clearly, being within or at the edge of the EU affects people's perceptions of state boundaries and, by extension, their views of the relationship of the places where they live to places across the border. The Euregio Meuse-Rhin is an initiative brought about by local business interests and environmental concerns. Co-operation among the five provinces within the Meuse-Rhin's framework has proven successful in the areas of environmental conservation and economy. More important, it has contributed to the deepening of the European integration process. By contrast, the Euroregion Nysa is as much a creation from above (by central authorities in Warsaw or Prague) as from below (by local authorities along the border). In the context of the EU's external borders, the Euroregions contribute to the widening, rather than the deepening, of European integration. As such, Euroregions in East Central Europe have a more pragmatic and strategic character than do their analogues in the EU. Needless to say, such differences in goals have implications for the development of 'we-feelings' across international boundaries, as well as for the ways in which individuals see their places in geopolitical context.

CONCLUSION

The comparative perspective adopted in this study highlights the importance of focusing on contextual influences on transboundary co-operation in Europe. In the cases of the Meuse-Rhin and the Nysa Euroregions, fundamental contextual differences call into question the assumption that the Euroregion Nysa will necessarily follow the same pattern of development as its West European analogue. Indeed, the Euroregion Nysa faces distinct challenges ranging from sharp internal differences in levels of economic development to historically rooted intraregional sociocultural differences that cannot be easily overcome. This does not mean that the Nysa is doomed to failure. What it does suggest, however, is that a simple transference of institutional arrangements and goals from the Euroregions of Western Europe to those of East Central Europe is problematic.

The significance of this point is heightened by the more general importance of developments in border areas for the changing European scene. As other contributors to this volume have pointed out, borderlands are often barometers of political change, and this is certainly true of border areas where active Euroregions have come into being. Many of these Euroregions are confronting (sometimes in microcosm) a set of issues that are likely to be of enduring importance in Europe's effort to forge a new political-territorial order. Our ability to understand and appreciate these developments is tied to our capacity to see them not simply as interesting institutional arrangements but as spatial structures that are deeply embedded in, and influenced by, the social, political, economic, and cultural context in which they are situated.

REFERENCES

Adamczuk, F. 1994. *Wybrane elementy marketingu regionalnego. Euroregion Nysa-trzy lata doswiadczen*. Warszawa: Biuletyn PAN IGiPZ.

Agnew, J. 1993. Representing space: Space, scale and culture in social science. In J. Duncan and D. Ley, eds. *Place/Culture/Representation*, 251–71. London: Routledge.

Baker, S. 1996. Punctured sovereignty: Border regions and environment within the European Union. In J. O'Dowd and T. Wilson, eds. *Borders, Nations, and States: Frontiers of Sovereignty in the New Europe*, 19–50. Aldershot: Avebury.

Bojar, E. 1996. Euroregions in Poland. *Tijdschrift voor Economische en Sociale Geografie* 87, no. 5: 442–47.

Borys, T., and Z. Panasiewicz. 1996. *Wspólpraca Transgraniczna w Polsce. Efekty i mozliwosci wsóllpracy strony polskiej na przykladzie Euroregionu Neisse-Nisa-Nysa*. Jelenia Góra, Poland: Regionalny Urzad Statystyczny.

Borys, T., and Z. Przybyla. 1993. Procesy euroregionalizacji na obszarach przygranicznych na przykladzie euroregionu Nysa. *Wroclawski Biuletyn Gospodarczy* 5.

Bullmann, U. 1997. The politics of the third level. In C. Jeffrey, ed. *The Regional Dimension of the European Union: Towards a Third Level in Europe?* 3–19. London: Frank Cass.

Cappellin, R. 1993. Interregional cooperation in Europe. In R. Cappellin and P. Batey, eds. *Regional Networks, Border Regions, and European Integration*, 1–20. London: Pion Ltd.

Commission of the European Communities. 1990. *INTERREG: Breaking Through Borders*. Brussels: European Commission, Directorate General for Regional Policy.

Delli Zotti, G. 1996. Transfrontier cooperation at the external borders of the EU: Implications for sovereignty. In J. O'Dowd and T. Wilson, eds. *Borders, Nations, and States: Frontiers of Sovereignty in the New Europe*, 51–72. Aldershot: Avebury.

Dressler Holohan, W., and M. Ciechocinska. 1996. The recomposition of identity and political space in Europe: The case of Upper Silesia. In J. O'Dowd and T. Wilson, eds. *Borders, Nations, and States: Frontiers of Sovereignty in the New Europe*, 155–78. Aldershot: Avebury.

Euregio Meuse-Rhin. 1997. Brochure realisée par le SEGEFA (Service d'Etude en Géographie Economique Fondamentale et Appliquee de l'Université de Liège). Liège: SEGEFA.

Euroregion Nysa. 1994. Jelenia Góra and Warsaw, Poland: Regionalny Urzad Statystyczny i Centralny Urzad Statystyczny.

Gminy Przygraniczne. 1997. Jelenia Góra, Poland: Regionalny Urzad Statystyczny.

Häkli, J. 2001. In the territory of knowledge: State-centered discourses and the construction of society. *Progress in Human Geography* 25, no. 3: 403–22.

Heffner, K. 1998. Polish-Czech regions: From political separation to co-operation on the way to European Union. Paper presented at the conference of political geographers in Haifa and Beer Sheba, Israel, on Geopolitics and Globalisation in a Postmodern World, February.

Hooghe, L., ed. 1996. *Cohesion Policy and European Integration: Building Multi-Level Governance*. Oxford: Oxford University Press.

Hooghe, L., and G. Marks. 1996. 'Europe with the regions': Channels of regional representation in the European Union. *Publius: The Journal of Federalism* 26, no. 1: 73–92.

Jeffrey, C., ed. 1997. *The Regional Dimension of the European Union—Towards a Third Level in Europe?* London: Frank Cass.

Jeleniogorskie—Stan i Perspektywy Rozwoju. 1997. Jelenia Góra, Poland: Urzad Statystyczny w Jeleniej Górze.

Jones, B., and M. Keating, eds. 1995. *The European Union and the Regions*. Oxford: Clarendon Press.

Kepka, J. 2000. Euroregions in the new Europe: The case of Poland's western borderlands. Ph.D. dissertation, University of Oregon.

Markovits, A., S. Reich, and M. Hinchey. 1997. Germany's economic power in Europe. In A. Markovits and S. Reich, eds. *The German Predicament. Memory and Power in the New Europe*, 109–19. Ithaca, NY: Cornell University Press.

Miasta w Euroregionie Neisse-Nisa-Nysa. 1995. Jelenia Góra, Poland: Urzad Statystyczny w Jeleniej Górze.

Murphy, A. 1996. The sovereign state as political-territorial ideal—Historical and contemporary considerations. In T. Biersteker and C. Weber, eds. *State Sovereignty as Social Construct*, 81–120. Cambridge: Cambridge University Press.

———. 1993. Emerging regional linkages within the European Community: Challenging the dominance of the state. *Tijdschrift voor Economische en Sociale Geografie* 84: 103–18.

Panorama Euroregionów. 1997. Jelenia Góra, Poland: Regionalny Urzad Statystyczny.

PHARE. 1996. *Program Współpracy Przygranicznej Polska-Niemcy* [Cross Border Coopera-

tion Programme. Poland-Germany]. Warszawa: Wladza Wdrazajaca Program Wspól-
pracy Przygranicznej PHARE.

Raffestin, C. 1993. Autour de la fonction sociale de la frontière. *Espaces et Sociétés: Identités, Espaces, Frontières* 70–71: 157–64.

Roberts, E. 1993. *The New Europe: Maastricht and Beyond.* New York: Gloucester Press.

Rocznik Statystyczny Województwa Jeleniogórskiego. 1998. Jelenia Góra, Poland: Regionalny
Urzad Statystyczny.

Sandelin, P. 1998. Cross-border co-operation in Karelia. In E. Bort, ed. *Borders & Borderlands in Europe,* 35–52. Edinburgh: University of Edinburgh and the International
Social Sciences Institute.

Sjøberg, J. 1998. 'Europe of the Regions': What do sub-state boundaries imply in different European countries? In E. Bort, ed. *Borders & Borderlands in Europe,* 21–34. Edinburgh: The University of Edinburgh and the International Social Sciences Institute.

Taylor, P. 1993. Contra political geography. *Tijdschrift voor Economische en Politische Geografie* 84: 82–90.

The Times Atlas of European History. 1994. New York: HarperCollins.

Weyand, S. 1997. Inter-regional associations and the European integration process. In
C. Jeffrey, ed. *The Regional Dimension of the European Union—Towards a Third Level in
Europe?* 166–82. London: Frank Cass.

Wilson, T. 1996. Sovereignty, identity, and borders: Political anthropology and European integration. In J. O'Dowd and T. Wilson, eds. *Borders, Nations, and States. Frontiers of Sovereignty in the New Europe,* 199–220. Aldershot: Avebury.

Wprost. 1999. Pod obca marka. 9 May.

Chapter Five

Transboundary Networking in Catalonia

Jouni Häkli

Several interesting trends regarding the political-economic and cultural transformation of the European borderlands are coming together in the northeast of the Spanish peninsula. The autonomous region of Catalonia features active co-operation with other European regions both near and far and serves as an exemplary case of political leaders and other prominent actors finding networking a good strategy for increasing the region's economic performance, political power, and cultural sustainability. Catalonia is also one of the European regions directly influenced by the political and economic drive for a borderless Europe. Since the inception of the Single European Market in January 1993, people and goods have freely crossed the Franco-Spanish state boundary (Grant 1998). Furthermore, Catalonia is currently one of the most prosperous regions in Spain, with a strong political autonomy negotiated with and against the Spanish central government (Guibernau 1997; Mouqué 1999).

It is hardly surprising, then, that much in the same way as north central Italy is at times viewed as the showcase of network economy, Catalonia has become a model for possible future political developments in Europe (Cooke 1989; Cossentino 1996; Keating 1996). This interest is inspired not only by the region's current vitality and unique historical development but also by the discourses of new regionalism and the changing nation-state in the face of economic globalisation and intergovernmental co-operation. Probably the most explicit treatment of Catalonia as model is presented in Castells's (1997) influential book *The Power of Identity*. Castells identifies Catalonia as a nation without a state, yet in 'search for a new kind of state [which] would be a state of variable geometry, bringing together respect

70

for the historically inherited Spanish state with the growing autonomy of Catalan institutions' (Castells 1997: 50). In other words, Catalonia represents a break with traditional nationalism striving for a separate nation-state. Rather than irredentism as such, it aims at integration with a broader entity, which is not only the European Union, but 'various networks of regional and municipal governments, as well as of civic associations'. These multiple horizontal relationships represent a new social organisation emerging 'under the tenuous shell of modern nation-state' (Castells 1997: 50).

In Castells's view, the Catalan case is particularly significant because it is a 'historical innovation' (1997: 50). The Catalan political and cultural autonomy is extended through 'the networking of power sharing institutions', not through contestation of the Spanish territorial sovereignty. Castells concludes that this model 'seems to relate better than traditional notions of sovereignty to a society based on flexibility and adaptability, to a global economy, to networking of media, to the variation and interpenetration of cultures' (1997: 50). Thus as a society of borderless trade, cultural identity, and flexible government institutions, the Catalans are perhaps the 'chosen people' of the information age.

In this chapter my intention is to evaluate some of the arguments about the European and global political transformations by looking at the processes of cross-border regionalisation in Catalonia (see figure 5.1). With emphasis on one particular context among the European borderlands, I seek to critically assess the thesis of a growing disconnection between territory and national identity and the disappearance of borders as a result of increasing cross-border networking by governmental and economic actors. By analysing a peaceful European internal state border, I aim to assess the degree to which the networks for cross-border co-operation, functioning mainly in the realm of politics and administration, are actually capable of mobilising the broader population for an emerging cross-border regional identity. Thus, my main analytic focus is the tension (or lack of it) between the ongoing networking across the Franco-Spanish border and the everyday perceptions of territory among the broader population. The latter perspective is especially helpful for assessing the idea of de-territorialising national identities in the context of a substate nationalism (for discussion of de-territorialised nationalism and cosmopolitan identities, see Kaldor 1996: 43; Cheach and Robbins 1998).

The chapter begins with an outline of the historical and political context within which cross-border regionalisation unfolds in Catalonia. I then chart present networking activities, understanding that they reflect a strategy for the participating actors to expand their capacity of governance (Le

Figure 5.1.   Regions of Catalonia (Catalunya), Midi-Pyrénées, and Languedoc-Roussillon at the Franco-Spanish Boundary

Source: Modified from *Atles de l'Euroregió* 1995.

Galès 1998; Häkli 1999). I analyse these activities in the light of the results of an interview questionnaire mapping the attitudes of 'borderlanders' towards cross-border co-operation, the development of a borderless future, and the other side of the border. In theoretical terms, I seek to evaluate the relevance of network as a metaphor describing political and cultural changes and challenging the power of national identities in contemporary Europe.

A SHORT POLITICAL HISTORY OF CATALONIA

It is difficult to understand the particular cultural and political situation of Catalonia, or the claims made about the region's broader relevance, without a brief historical reminder. However, as there are several well-written introductions to Catalan political history available (Sahlins 1998), I concentrate mainly on aspects that are relevant from the point of view of cross-border co-operation in the Catalan borderlands.

Catalan historiography lists various possible moments of birth for the political-cultural unit called *Catalunya*. Earliest references are made to the tenth century, when the region separated from the Carolingian Empire (Castells 1997: 43). Catalan political consciousness manifests itself at latest in the fourteenth century, when the term *Principat de Catalunya* appears in legal use for the first time (Brunn 1992: 134). Yet other moments of birth have been singled out, dated roughly to the Middle Ages (Pi-Sunyer 1980). However, perhaps more interesting than the (mythical) point of origin are events that have led to the territorial shaping of the Catalan borderlands.

In the fourteenth century, Catalonia was a distinct and vibrant Mediterranean trade centre with rather advanced representative institutions. Its language and literature were well-developed already when it formed a kingdom, the crown of Aragon, with its neighbouring regions of Aragon and Valencia. From this time dates the concept of a Catalan linguistic and cultural area, *els Països Catalans* (the Catalan lands), which today covers not only the Autonomous Community of Catalonia but also the northern parts of Valencia, the eastern parts of Aragon, the Balearic Islands, the Principality of Andorra, the French Roussillon, and the Sardinian town of Alghero (see figure 5.2) (Brunn 1992: 134).

The Crown of Aragon merged with the kingdom of Castile in the late fifteenth century through the marriage of Ferdinand, king of Aragon, and Isabella, queen of Castile. Although the unification was supposed to respect the Catalan language, culture, and institutions, over the next two centuries the Spanish state and Castilian culture made significant inroads in Catalonia (Laitin, Sole, and Kalyvas 1994: 9). In 1640, Catalan nobility in alliance with France joined with some of their rebellious peasants in a revolt (the Revolt of the Reapers) against the Castilian domination. The revolt was suppressed, and when peace between Spain and France was finally established in 1659, the Catalan province of Roussillon and a portion of the Cerdanya Valley (today's *Catalunya Nord*) were annexed to France (Pi-Sunyer 1980: 106). Thus, the Franco-Spanish boundary, currently crossed by various networks of co-operation, was set up in the Treaty

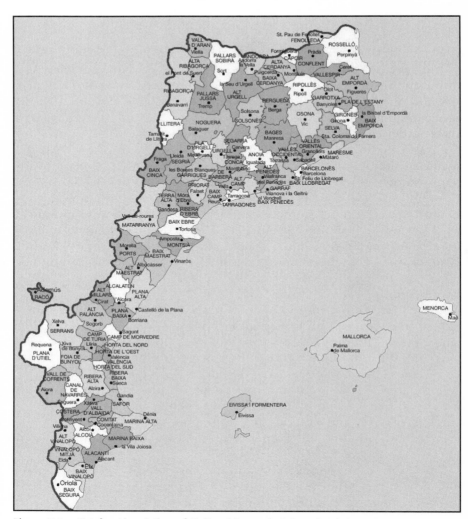

Figure 5.2.   Catalan Linguistic and Cultural Area, els Països Catalans

Source: www.geocities.com/perpinya/mapaplc-com.html

of the Pyrenees in 1659 and erected gradually by the late eighteenth century.

The end of Catalonia as a politically and legally distinct entity occurred only in the early eighteenth century, at the conclusion of the Spanish War of Succession, in which the Catalans again stood against Madrid, this time with the Austrians. Catalonia was defeated, and the new Castilian government erased the region's remaining privileges (Castells 1997: 45). Surprisingly, the surrender of Barcelona on 11 September 1714 is now celebrated as the Catalan national day. The ensuing rule by the Castilian central powers narrowed significantly the official use of the Catalan language, but the Church retained the right to use Catalan, which could also be freely used in social intercourse. The latter two pockets of freedom proved important for the reproduction of Catalan language and culture, the cornerstones of Catalan nationalism, emerging as a mass movement between the late nineteenth and early twentieth centuries.

The lack of political self-government notwithstanding, during the nineteenth century Catalonia, and especially the city and province of Barcelona, assumed a key position as the leading industrial region in Spain. The region's prospering textile industry and well-developed commercial tradition had their roots in the Mediterranean trade since the Middle Ages. Industrialisation had far-reaching consequences for political and cultural life in Catalonia. First, it drove the region's culture and lifestyles farther apart from the rest of Spain. While the majority of the country was heavily dependent on agricultural production and had a traditional land-owning upper class, Catalonia developed new industrial jobs and a rising bourgeoisie (Brunn 1992: 135). Second, industrialisation freed a growing number of people from traditional ties and habits and fostered their integration into new forms of social communication, groupings, and organisations. This was instrumental for the construction of civil society and modern political community in Catalonia, which provided the necessary seedbed for the Catalan movement. Third, extensive industrial production and trade relations connected Catalonia to the outside world in a manner that was not typical of the rest of Spain (Pi-Sunyer 1980: 107–8). The contemporary forms of integration and networking as outward-looking activities thus lean on a strong tradition in Catalonia.

Economic prosperity and the rising bourgeoisie encouraged the rise of modern nationalism in Catalonia by the beginning of the twentieth century (Garcia-Ramon and Nogué-Font 1994). According to Catalan historiography, the Catalan language and culture survived nineteenth century repression by the Central Powers, and the rising national movement was successful in strengthening the status of Catalan political institutions and language (Capdeferro 1967). In the 1932 constitutional reform Catalonia re-established autonomous status and gained its own parliamentary government, the *Generalitat de Catalunya*. However, the bloody Civil War and the accession of power by General Franco in 1939 again marked the withdrawal of Catalan autonomy for nearly four decades. The death of Franco in 1975 saw the re-establishment of democracy in Spain and gave rise to the 1978 Spanish Constitution. The new constitution recognised and guaranteed the right to autonomy of the 'nationalities and regions forming Spain' and set up the Autonomous Communities System (Guibernau 1997: 95).

As one of the Spanish autonomous communities, Catalonia has since the late 1970s gradually strengthened its political and cultural autonomy through the leadership of Jordi Pujol, the long-time president of the *Generalitat*. The 'official discourse', as promoted by Pujol and inscribed into the 1979 Catalan Statute of Autonomy, explicitly makes reference to Catalan territory, history, culture, institutions, and language as the markers of differentiation from others (Guibernau 1997: 95–96). Together with particular symbols, such as the Catalan flag, these are the elements that the Catalan nationalist discourse has successfully established as the emblems and constituents of the Catalan identity.

Although there is little reason to doubt the historical accuracy of this narrative, we would do well to pay attention to Michael Billig's (1995) warnings against the modernisation of history in nationalistic terms. From the fact that a particular Catalan-speaking nobility emerged in the Middle Ages, acting in the name of *Catalunya* and its rulers, one cannot draw the conclusion that there existed a national community of Catalans in the modern sense, that is, a community of laypeople, peasantry, craftsmen, nobility, and merchants all defining themselves as one group. In fact, as is the case in most nations, the Catalan identity emerged among the broader population only after the rise of compulsory school education, mass media, industrial division of labour, and social movements (Pi-Sunyer 1980: 107; see also Paasi 1996). The fact that various vernacular tongues, Catalan among them, have existed in different parts of Europe hardly supports the idea of a nationally divided continent before the age of the nation-states and the particularly modern forms of collective life. Research on national identities has clearly shown that languages do not create nationalism so much as nationalism creates languages (Anderson 1991). Although all national languages are ancient human creations, their significance as anchors of collective identity and taken-for-granted 'boundary markers' between groups is of much more recent origin in the modern world of nation-states (Billig 1995: 30). The Catalan language was codified grammatically only in the early twentieth century, at the time of rising Catalan nationalism (Castells 1997: 45). It is at once a historical reality and a modern construct.

Yet contemporary Catalan national identity cannot be reduced to the claim that it is invented, of recent origin, or merely a social construct. For most Catalans the existence of a Catalan nation is a reality beyond question. The 'official' historiography is part and parcel of this conviction and cannot be measured against a truer, more original, or authentic Catalan history. But it is equally clear that national historiographies are not politically innocent because they legitimate the idea of the world consisting of enduring and distinctive political-cultural units. Catalan historiography is no exception, but adding to its particular character, it is said to be somewhat ambiguous in its relation to territoriality (Douglass 1998: 96). Brunn (1992: 134) notes that the Catalan movement sees itself as being mostly defined by linguistic and cultural factors, which can be mapped to *els Països Catalans*. Yet the Catalan Statute of Autonomy sets up the political territory of Catalonia as limited to the area consisting of the four provinces of Barcelona, Girona, Lleida, and Tarragona, which form the Autonomous Community of Catalonia (Guibernau 1997: 96). This is remarkable in the sense that it creates a constant tension between the extension of the linguistic-cultural area forming the (real and imagined) roots of Catalan identity and the territorial extension of the region's political power. It could be assumed that some of the actual networking in Catalonia can be accounted for by the fact that these two Catalan territorialities are not coincident.

CROSS-BORDER NETWORKING IN CATALONIA

Considering the political history of the region, together with its contemporary strong economic, cultural, and political status, it would be tempting to view cross-border co-operation in Catalonia as a conscious effort and means to correct certain historical injustices. This interpretation finds support in the Catalan Statute of Autonomy, which states that the collaboration and cultural exchange with other self-governing communities and provinces is to be encouraged and special attention given to all those with which Catalonia has had particular historical, cultural, or commercial links (*Catalan Statute of Autonomy* 1986: 39). Furthermore, the statute recognises the Catalan language as the heritage of other territories and communities and outlines the possibility of the establishment of cultural relations with states where such territories are located and such communities reside (Guibernau 1997: 96). However, due to the obvious sensitivity of such relations among Catalan-speaking territories, the statute only refers to cultural relations and explicitly denies the possibility of political association.

This is the political and geographic context in which networking and co-operation across the Franco-Spanish border take place. The border is the result of a peace treaty some three centuries ago, annexing Catalan-speaking areas to France. Today the annexed areas are known as *Catalunya Nord* in Catalonia and *Catalogne* in France, and they form a part of the 'greater Catalonia', *els Països Catalans*. Cultural relations of co-operation are officially recognised as the goal of the Catalan *Generalitat* (*Catalan Statute of Autonomy* 1986: 39). However, the Spanish Constitution implicitly circumscribes the nature of such relations to the nonpolitical (Guibernau 1997: 98), which means that Catalan politicians and the *Generalitat* will have to balance carefully between the policies of the Spanish government and the wishes of their own constituency (Ross 1996: 498).

In October 1991 the leaders of Catalonia and the two French regions of Languedoc-Roussillon and Midi-Pyrénées signed an agreement, the *Carta de l'Euroregió*, establishing an institutional framework for the various forms of co-operation that had emerged between the regions since the early 1980s (*Euroregió* 1994). While the Euroregió Catalunya, Languedoc-Rousillon, i Midi-Pyrénées is not the first official agreement on cross-border co-operation involving both the Spanish and the French Catalonias, it is perhaps the most visible and significant one. The two main goals of the Euroregion are (1) to develop methods for increasing interaction between the economic, social, and cultural actors in the region, and (2) to strengthen the role of this Euroregion as a motor for the European economy, together with fostering European integration and strengthening the position of Southern European regions (*Euroregió* 1994). In practice, Euroregion co-operation aims at concerted action by the constituent regions within the European Union bodies, as well as securing the support and acceptance of the Spanish and French governments for its large-scale projects. The latter is of particular importance because the respective states have often regarded actual cross-border co-operation with suspicion. One example is the states' lack of support for the high-speed train connection (*El Punt* 1992).

Euroregion activities involve the leaders of the three regions in an annual conference *(Conferencia dels Presidents)* that co-ordinates and sets the main lines for Euroregion co-operation. A committee formed by leading administrators and specialists representing all regions oversees the realisation of the plan accepted in the presidential conference and sets up particular activities in sectoral working groups. The *Comité Tripartit de*

Coordinació is also responsible for the Euroregion's budget. The actual co-operation is carried out by working groups *(grups de treball)* operating within six sectors: (1) traffic, infrastructure, and telecommunications; (2) enterprises, business life, and vocational training; (3) education, research, and the transfer of technology; (4) agriculture, fishing, and water supply; (5) culture, tourism, youth, and sports; and (6) environment and consumer guidance (Garcia-Ramon 1994). The working groups are composed of officials qualified in the respective areas, so that all three regions are represented in all groups, and each region is responsible for the co-ordination of two working groups. Catalonia runs working groups one and five, Languedoc-Roussillon runs working groups three and four, and Midi-Pyrénées runs groups two and six *(Euroregió* 1994).

The Euroregion has a relatively broad, multilevel organisation but limited resources. With one full-time secretary, it is headquartered in the French Catalan area of Roussillon, in the town of Perpignan. However, as a form of co-operation the Euroregió Catalunya, Languedoc-Roussillon, i Midi-Pyrénées represents a well-institutionalised, official, and high-level governmental network that involves directly only members of the governmental, cultural, and scientific elite. There is no democratically elected body politically in charge of the Euroregion's activity, but the officials involved are to some degree accountable to their respective regional governments. Like most contemporary projects for enhanced regional governance (Le Galès 1998; MacLeod and Goodwin 1999), Euroregion co-operation becomes visible to the broader public mainly through the media, and to some degree through the realisation of concrete projects of general interest (for example, the improvement of roads crossing the border region).

In dealing with problems caused by the state border for regional development, Euroregion activities are co-ordinated with another, still broader network for cross-border co-operation, the Working Community of the Pyrenees *(Comunitat de Traball dels Pirineus, CTP).* Founded in November 1983, the CTP is an organisation for co-operation among the Spanish autonomous communities of Aragon, Catalonia, Navarra, and the Basque country; the French regions of Aquitania, Languedoc-Roussillon, and Midi-Pyrénées; and the principality of Andorra *(XV Consell Plenari* 1997). The CTP consists of a council (with seven representatives from each region), a co-ordination committee (the regions' presidents together with the permanent and special secretary), working commissions (four permanent and three special commissions focusing on different issue areas), and a secretary (permanent and special secretaries). The presidency of the CTP is circulated among the participating regions in two-year terms *(Carta d'Acció* 1994). The organisation is headquartered in Jaca (Aragon), where the secretaries are based.

While Euroregion co-operation has had difficulties in getting its voice heard in the Spanish and the French governments, the situation is still worse for the CTP, which has failed to gain official recognition as an international organisation. Consequently, the French and Spanish national governments rejected a cross-border co-operation programme prepared by the CTP. The programme, consisting of seventeen projects, sought resources from the European Union INTERREG funds, but the state governments refused to treat it as one totality and instead broke it down to the composite regional level (*XV Consell Plenari* 1997: 216). This illustrates the tendency by national governments to monopolise the formation of official relations across their boundaries and treat these under the traditional foreign policy concept (Keating 1998: 182).

Despite these problems, the CTP has the strategic goal of showing the ways in which the Pyrenees Mountains can function as a uniting rather than a separating element between the mountain communities. It co-ordinates projects and often provides them with know-how and partners from the other side of the border, both essential requirements for funding from various EU sources, such as the INTERREG, the Leader, and the Feder programmes (*XV Consell Plenari* 1997). Like the Euroregion, the CTP is a well-institutionalised, high-level governmental form of activity involving numerous prominent actors, but without a directly elected, democratic, decision-making mechanism.

Together the Euroregion and the CTP frameworks support, initiate, and co-ordinate dozens of cross-border co-operation projects, ranging from small-scale initiatives, such as the production of basic information about the area for improved communication (*Atles de l'Euroregió* 1995) to lobbying for large-scale infrastructure projects, such as the high-speed train connection (TGV) from Barcelona to Montpellier (*El Punt* 1994). In addition to the Euroregion and the CTP, there are numerous other interregional networks, projects, and initiatives actively fostering cultural co-operation across the Franco-Spanish border. Among the most important are the network of Catalan universities based in Perpignan (*Xarxa d'Universitats Institut Joan Lluís Vives*), several projects for professional training funded by the INTERREG II programme (for example, training from export sales personnel specialising on the context of the Catalan economic region), cross-border co-operation on annual motor vehicle inspection, and wastewater treatment (*Banque d'experiences* 1996).

Additional initiatives for co-operation can be found on the local government level. For instance, the Pyrenean mountain municipalities have formed an association for co-operation; the town of Perpignan has established co-operative relations with Figueres, Lleida, and Girona; and there are numerous 'sister city' relations between the towns of Catalonia and *Catalunya Nord* (Roig 1997). The numerous public-private or civic associations' initiatives include cross-border co-operation between the chambers of commerce and between the symphony orchestras of Empordà and Languedoc-Roussillon; a network for transpyrenean studies; an institute for studies on the borderlands of the Cerdanya Valley *(Institut d'Estudis Ceretans);* and a joint programme for tourism studies among the universities of Girona, Perpignan, and Montpellier *(El Punt* 1999).

There are literally dozens of initiatives and projects for cross-border co-operation between Catalonia and the regions north of the Franco-Spanish border. This is clearly in accordance with the *Generalitat's* policy, directed outward and stressing the connection of Catalonia to the north rather than to the rest of Spain. The policy reflects the ideology of the Convergence and Union Party *(Convergencia I Unió)*, and especially the ideas of its founder, President Jordi Pujol. He has for long argued for a distinctive Catalan identity rooted in the European past and giving rise to nationalism that does not seek independence but nevertheless is capable of developing within a larger state containing other national minorities (Pujol 1991; cf. Guibernau 1997: 106). Thus, in a manner closely reminiscent of that of Manuel Castells (1997), Pujol projects Catalonia and Catalanism as a model for Europe, a new concept of nation that perhaps can resolve political tensions caused by the European integration process and the erosion of the sovereign nation-state. Essential for the realisation of this ideology are the networks of co-operation across the boundaries of the Catalan political territory.

CATALUNYA NORD IN THE SCHENGEN ERA

Many projects for cross-border co-operation in Catalonia involve partners from outside the immediate border area. The 'Four Motors for Europe' network, bringing together the regions of Catalonia, Baden-Württemberg, Lombardia, and Rhône-Alpes, is perhaps the most commonly cited example (Murphy 1993). However, in view of the changing role of European state boundaries, together with the ideas of a progressive form of nationalism in Catalonia, it is particularly interesting to focus on the relationship between Catalonia and *Catalunya Nord.*

As mentioned previously, a portion of the Catalan territory was annexed to France in the 1656 Treaty of the Pyrenees. This area can be named differently depending on the perspective adopted. In France the area is officially called *Pyrénées Orientales,* which in no way refers to the Catalan tradition in the region. An alternative name is *Roussillon,* a name that was given to the area when it was annexed to France, and which therefore recognises the particular political history of the region. It is also the latter part of the official name of the larger region of Languedoc-Roussillon. The term *Catalunya Nord* is evidently the most Catalan name, pointing at the area explicitly as part of a larger Catalan totality. The term has gained increasing popularity since the 1970s among politicians, businesspeople, and cultural activists, who have sought to strengthen their contacts and relations with the Spanish Catalonia, *el Principat.* Although the Catalan term *Catalunya Nord* specifically refers to a vantage point from the Spanish side of the border, it is more and more commonly used also on the French side (Català del Rosellón 1992).

Catalan culture and language have had difficulty flourishing in France, where the state has traditionally left little room for minority languages. Especially after laws on compulsory education in French were passed in 1885, the use of Catalan began to decrease, and the trend has continued to date. In a 1997 study by the regional council of Languedoc-Roussillon, only 17 percent of those interviewed could speak Catalan well, and 34 percent with some difficulty (Una enquesta detecta 1998). However, during the last three decades a renewed interest in the Catalan tradition has emerged in the area. There are several associations that seek to promote the traditional language and culture in *Catalunya Nord.* One of them is *Centre de Documentació i Animacio de la Cultura Catalana,* which organises language courses and language services in Catalan and has a library with some thirty-five thousand volumes written in Catalan (*El Punt* 1999). Since 1972 it has also been possible to teach Catalan three hours per week in public schools, and the privately organised *Escola Bressola* schools and the *Arrels* school are fully bilingual. The numbers learning the language are still small, however; in 1995 the private schools had only some two hundred students (1 percent of school children). Only 15 percent of the children were studying Catalan in public schools (Verdaguer 1997).

In *Catalunya Nord* there is one radio station (*Ràdio Arrels*) broadcasting for Catalan speakers twenty-four hours per day, and French television has very little programming in Catalan. However, the Catalan television channels TV3 and Canal 33, broadcast from the Spanish side of the border, can be seen in the area. Some newspapers and journals are available in Catalan, and interestingly, the Spanish Catalan newspaper *El Punt* was circulated in *Catalunya Nord* in 1987 and is now re-entering the market on the French side (*El Punt* 1999). In addition to the media and education, signs of an emerging Catalanism have surfaced in decisions made by some of the region's institutional actors. For example, the city of Perpignan (in Catalan, *Perpinyà*) has begun to publish city council bulletins in both

French and Catalan (*El Punt* 1994). The city has also encouraged the use of Catalan in postal services, popularised the slogan *'Perpinyà, la catalana'*, and set up a particular body for Catalan affairs (Català del Rosellón 1992). Twenty-two municipalities in *Catalunya Nord* have decided to review their land registers and change some place names from French back to their original Catalan form (*El Punt* 1993).

A significant event in the popular realm was the 1998 success of Perpignan's rugby team, USAP, which managed to fight its way to the finals of the national league. In the finals Catalan flags were waved and the players took pride in their 'Catalan-ness'. The latter is an important departure from the typically subordinate position the Catalan language and culture have occupied in relation to the dominant French culture (O'Brien 1993). With success in sports, the region's economic peripherality and cultural stigma were turned into a victory, one that was joyfully flagged by the popular Catalan hymn *La Estaca* (Jordi Pujol a Perpinyà 1999).

The renaissance of Catalan language and culture in *Catalunya Nord* has given a boost to the symbolic construction of a particular Catalan border landscape. The standard elements of this landscape include flags and banners with the colours and stripes of Catalonia, street signs with place names in Catalan, and narratives that depict traditional connections to the south. However, more concrete developments influencing the function and meaning of the Franco-Spanish border took place after Spain joined the EU in 1986. (France became a member of the EEC in 1957.) Since then, the border has become increasingly permeable, with two major developments. First, Spain signed the Schengen Agreement in November 1991, which abolished checks on persons at the Franco-Spanish border. Second, the Single European Market entered into force in January 1993, establishing the free movement of goods, services, and capital (Serra del Pino and Ventura i Ribal 1999). Consequently, from a border-crossing perspective, the border is practically nonexistent, even though it still separates two states from each other. The freedom of movement has the potential to encourage cross-border regionalisation in the Catalan borderlands, and in fact there are some signs of an emerging interest among businesses and consumers in the markets on the other side of the border (Lluís 1995). Unfortunately, some localities near the now-redundant border-crossing points have suffered substantial job losses because of the removal of customs formalities. It has been estimated that before 1993 as many as four thousand people were directly or indirectly employed by border formalities on the Spanish side alone (Wirth 1992). Currently only non-EU traffic, approximately 5 percent of all border crossings, is subject to customs formalities, and only a fraction of the previous jobs are necessary (Rivas 1994: 6). Understandably, those who lost their good jobs in the customs and related industries may not always think positively about the disappearance of the border.

In view of a potentially emerging cross-border identity, capturing both the Spanish and the French sides of the Catalan cultural area, the recent manifestations of Catalanism in *Catalunya Nord* are an interesting development. Furthermore, with the relaxed border control between France and Spain since 1993, economic integration across the border has gained more momentum than perhaps ever before since the mid-seventeenth century. However, the situation is complicated by the fact that not all people living in *Catalunya Nord* are enthusiastic about Catalanism. Some commentators have pointed out that the recent revival of Catalanism in southern France has been over-interpreted in nationalistic terms, and that on the French side of the border the Catalan culture is merely a regional label without any broader political implications or wish to challenge the unity of the French state (*El Triangle* 1999). Furthermore, studies have shown that the Catalan identity is more exclusive in Spain than in France, where it is common for people to view themselves as French *and* Catalan (O'Brien 1993: 110). Whatever the case, it is clear that Catalan culture and symbols have experienced a renaissance in *Catalunya Nord*. The question that remains is whether the emerging linguistic and cultural linkages, together with the many networks for cross-border co-operation, are enough to foster cultural and political integration across the Franco-Spanish border and thus create a platform for an emerging cross-border identity.

NEITHER FRANCE NOR SPAIN?

To chart the borderlanders' knowledge of and attitudes towards the deepening co-operation across the Franco-Spanish border and their opinions about the disappearance of the state boundary, 283 people were interviewed in Catalonia and 77 in *Catalunya Nord*. The interview was conducted according to a structured questionnaire, which contained questions about border crossings (how often and why); the end of border control between Spain and France (Is it positive or negative?); expectations for the future (Will the border persist or disappear completely?); cross-border co-operation (Should it exist or not?); the forms of co-operation (which ones people know about, and to what depth); and finally, what place name best describes that side of the border (region or state) where the person lives, the other side, and the borderlands as a whole.

Interviews were conducted in August 1999 in most counties *(comarques)* adjacent to or relatively proximate to the border, as well as in the major cities. In Catalonia the *comarques* of Cerdanya, Garrotxa, Alt Empordà, Pla de l'Estany, Baix Empordà, and Selva, as well as the cities of Barcelona, Girona, Tarragona, and Lleida, were included. In *Catalunya Nord* the interviews were done in Cerdagne, Vallespir, and Roussillon, as well as in the city of Perpignan. People were selected randomly, and the interviews were carried out literally on the street during the day time, including lunch time (siesta), so that actively working people could also be reached.

The results of the interviews reveal that the increasing permeability of the state boundary, brought about by European integration, is generally viewed in positive terms. Two out of three persons interviewed said that the abolition of border control had been a favourable development. Some differences across the border were found: In Catalonia the share of positive answers was somewhat greater than in *Catalunya Nord* (see table 5.1, question 1). The most frequently given reason for a positive attitude towards a more relaxed border control was that it has made border crossing much easier and quicker. Feelings of being European and having more freedom also were often mentioned. However, some interviewees both in Catalonia and in *Catalunya Nord* did not think that the permeable border was anything to be particularly happy about. When asked why, people typically referred to problems with drugs, smuggling, immigration, and crime, which all can now cross the border more easily than before. The reasons given were very similar on both sides of the border.

Judging from the results of the interviews, it is clear that people living in the Catalan borderlands also think positively about co-operation across the border. Both in Catalonia and in *Catalunya Nord* the clear majority thought that co-operation is a good thing, and only a fraction of the interviewees viewed co-operation negatively (see table 5.1, question 2). A closer analysis did not reveal much variation according to the proximity of localities to the border. Interestingly, the only exception could be found in Cerdanya Valley, where the share of people with positive attitudes towards cross-border co-operation remained on a lower level than anywhere else. In Cerdanya (on the Spanish side), only 63 percent of those interviewed thought positively about co-operation, and in the French Cerdagne the respective share was not higher than 56 percent. This most likely reflects the tense relations among people living in the Cerdanya Valley, which historically has often been a zone of conflict between villages and nationalities. Similar observations have been made in other studies on the valley (Sahlins 1988; 1989; Mancebo 1999). However, in other locales cross-border co-operation was more appreciated, the positive replies varying between 72 and 99 percent.

However, the interviews also revealed that despite all the publicity in newspapers and other media, people do not generally know much about

Table 5.1.   Results of the Survey at the Catalan Borderlands

1. How do you feel about the more relaxed border control?

	Positive	No difference	Negative	Total
Catalonia	68.5	18.8	12.7	100.0
Catalunya Nord	55.8	27.3	16.9	100.0

2. How do you feel about cross-border co-operation?

	Positive	No difference	Negative	Total
Catalonia	80.6	11.3	8.1	100.0
Catalunya Nord	75.3	15.6	9.1	100.0

3. Do you know some form of cross-border co-operation?

	Yes	No	Total
Catalonia	53.7	46.3	100.0
Catalunya Nord	59.7	40.3	100.0

4. Do you know how cross-border co-operation is practically carried out?

	Yes	Partly	No	Total
Catalonia	3.7	29.5	66.8	100.0
Catalunya Nord	5.0	25.8	69.1	100.0

5. Do you know how to participate in decision making concerning cross-border co-operation?

	Yes	No	Total
Catalonia	25.1	74.9	100.0
Catalunya Nord	20.8	79.2	100.0

6. Do you think that the border will disappear in the future?

	Yes	Do not know	No	Total
Catalonia	38.2	19.8	42.0	100.0
Catalunya Nord	33.8	36.4	29.9	100.0

concrete co-operation across the Franco-Spanish border in Catalonia (see table 5.1, question 3). Although more than half of those interviewed in Catalonia and in *Catalunya Nord* knew some existing forms of cross-border co-operation, the ones mentioned were most often 'sister cities', 'cultural exchange', or 'sports events'. A list of cross-border co-operation projects was also introduced, consisting of the following projects: the Euroregion, the CTP, Universitat Catalana d'Estiu, CeDACC, Institut d'Estudis Ceretans, Diada de Cerdanya, 'Four Motors for Europe', Forum Civil

Euromed, and sister cities co-operation. Of these, by far the most commonly known were the Universitat Catalana d'Estiu (65 percent) and the sister cities co-operation (68 percent), the former because it is a forum for Catalanist politics with a prominent place in the media, and the latter most likely because there are signs in many places telling about amicable relations between *'Ciutats agermanades'*. Understandably, in localities closer to the border, people were generally more aware of cross-border co-operation than were those farther away from the border. For example, in Alt Empordà some 70 percent of the interviewed people were aware of some form of co-operation, whereas only 39 percent in Tarragona and 48 percent in Barcelona were. In *Catalunya Nord* the same pattern was found. In the French Cerdagne some 78 percent of the interviewees knew about some kind of cross-border co-operation, while in Perpignan only 55 percent did. In all, proximity to the border seems to encourage people's interest in cross-border co-operation.

When asked if they know how cross-border co-operation functions in practice, the majority of people answered in the negative (see table 5.1, question 4). Between Catalonia and *Catalunya Nord* there was no significant difference in the share of negative answers; only a few were fully knowledgeable about co-operation practices. The lack of knowledge about cross-border politics is still more striking. When people were asked if they would know how to participate in decision making concerning cross-border co-operation, the overwhelming majority answered negatively (see table 5.1, question 5).

Despite the mainly positive attitudes towards the increasing permeability of the Franco-Spanish boundary, as well as towards cross-border co-operation, some questions revealed that the dividing function of the state boundary between Catalonia and *Catalunya Nord* is still very much the reality for many people. For example, when asked about expectations concerning the complete disappearance of the border, people showed much more hesitation than might have been expected (see table 5.1, question 6).

The perception of the boundary as a divider is even more explicit in answers to the question of what place names best describe the two sides of the border (region or state) seen from where the interviewed person lives. Although the answers could well have illustrated an understanding of the borderlands as in principle one unity, the opposite was most often the case. In Catalonia only some 20 percent of the interviewees used an integrative term for describing the other side of the border (for example, *Catalunya* or *Catalunya Nord*). Some 18 percent made reference to Catalonia, but as part of France (for example, *Catalunya Francesa*), and 62 percent viewed the other side in strictly national terms (*França*). In *Catalunya*

Nord the results were respectively 22 percent using an integrative term (*Catalunya* or *Catalunya Sur*), 21 percent referring to Catalonia as part of Spain (*Catalogne Espanyola*), and 57 percent referring to a distinct national territory (*Espagne*). However, the fact that some 32 percent of those interviewed were actually able to find a name for the borderlands as a whole can be interpreted as a manifestation of a potential for emerging identifications across the border. Yet in almost half of the cases the term used was 'Pyrenees' instead of 'Catalonia' or *els Països Catalans*, which indicates that the unity of the borderlands is often seen in terms of physical landscape rather than cultural or political environment.

CONCLUSION

In the light of this research, it seems justifiable to claim that Catalonia is a model for the 'New Europe'. Its political leaders, economic actors, and cultural elites are eagerly entering into relations of co-operation with actors and institutions outside Catalonia. An untiring advocate of pactism, Jordi Pujol has consistently emphasised the willingness of the Catalan government to favour networks of co-operation for enhanced self-government, rather than to strive for national separatism. However, this willingness cannot be explained by the Catalan political tradition only. The practical goals of policy making play an equally important role here (Genieys 1998; Häkli 1999). Economic, cultural, and political actors can enhance their resources for collective attainment of goals by entering into co-operative relations and networks with other actors. Following Bob Jessop (1995), these activities can be interpreted as instances of multiscale regional governance, serving the attempts to attain collective goals in and through specific configurations of governmental and nongovernmental institutions, organisations, and practices. The goals are typically economic, but they can also be cultural and political. And as in Catalonia, cross-border co-operation and transregional networks are sometimes found more attractive than mere domestic ones.

In this respect Castells's (1997) idea about Catalonia as an exemplary case among the European regions seems to be well founded. We can look at the numerous projects for cross-border co-operation and regionalisation and create different scenarios about their role in the emerging new political order in Europe. However, it is much less clear whether support can be found for claims according to which Catalonia also presents a model for a new kind of nationalism or cultural identity in Europe. Rather, in the light of this research, as well as many other studies of borderland identities (O'Dowd and Wilson 1996; Newman and Paasi 1998;

Wilson and Donnan 1998), it seems that the existence of networks for cross-border co-operation will not necessarily lead to the rapid erosion of political and cultural identities connected to the history of the modern nation-state. They may simply add new layers or dimensions to European governance, which, depending on the social, cultural, and economic context, may or may not function as an important political arena. This is because networking tends to follow its own functional and institutional logic, which typically remains unconnected to people's everyday concerns. The fact that only a few people in Catalonia and *Catalunya Nord* know how cross-border projects operate or how to participate in the politics of regionalisation across the state border lends little support to the idea of an increasing awareness of shared political goals across the Catalan borderlands.

What can be safely concluded is that while the European political space is definitely going through multiple changes, these are experienced differently in different borderlands. Even though it is more and more easy to (physically) cross the (internal) borders of the integrated Europe, in many places the borders sit tight as cultural and/or imaginary dividers between national cultures. Studies on boundaries and identities have convincingly shown that state borders are essential for the establishment and negotiation of national identities. Therefore, in Michael Billig's (1995: 60) terms, to remove the Franco-Spanish border would require the dissolution of the *forms of life* that produce and reproduce 'Frenchness' and 'Spanishness' in the Catalan borderlands. Despite the many cross-border networks emerging in Catalonia, this is not likely to happen in the foreseeable future.

NOTE

I wish to thank Laura Puigbert and Riikka Taipale, who helped in collecting empirical material for the study. Special thanks are also due to Joan Nogué, who kindly offered me facilities at the University of Girona in June through September 1999. The research was financially made possible by the Academy of Finland research grant 62424.

REFERENCES

Anderson, B. 1991. *Imagined Communities*. London: Verso.

Atles de l'Euroregió Catalunya, Languedoc-Roussillon, Midi-Pyrénées. 1995. Montpellier: Conseil Régionaux du Languedoc-Roussillon.

Banque d'experiences: Programme d'initiative commeaunataire 'Interreg II' France-Espagne. 1996. Tolouse: DRTEFP.

Billig, M. 1995. *Banal Nationalism.* London: Sage.

Brunn, G. 1992. The Catalans within the Spanish monarchy from the middle of the nineteenth to the beginning of the twentieth century. In A. Kappeler, ed. *The Formation of National Elites,* 133–60. Aldershot: Darthmouth Publishing.

Capdeferro, M. 1967. *Historia de Cataluña.* Barcelona: Editorial M.&S.

Carta d'Acció de la Comunitat de Treball dels Pirineus. 1994. Torre del Reloj, Spain: Comunidad de Trabajo de los Pirineos.

Castells, M. 1997. *The Power of Identity.* Cambridge: Blackwell.

Catalán del Rosellón. 1992. *La Vanguardia,* 7 February: 15.

The Catalan Statute of Autonomy. 1986. Barcelona: Generalitat de Catalunya.

Cheach, P., and B. Robbins, eds. 1998. *Cosmopolitics: Thinking and Feeling beyond the Nation.* Minneapolis: University of Minnesota Press.

Cooke, P. 1989. The local question—Revival or survival? In P. Cooke, ed. *Localities: The Changing Face of Urban Britain,* 296–306. London: Unwin Hyman.

Cossentino, F. 1996. *Local and Regional Response to Global Pressure: The Case of Italy and Its Industrial Districts.* Geneva: International Institute for Labour Studies.

Douglass, W. A. 1998. A western perspective on an eastern interpretation of where north meets south: Pyrenean borderland cultures. In T. M. Wilson and H. Donnan, eds. *Border Identities: Nation and State at International Frontiers,* 62–95. Cambridge: Cambridge University Press.

El Punt. 11 July 1992–2 September 1999.

El Triangle. 1999, 3 February.

Euroregió: Bilan et perspectives, 1989–1994. 1994. Perpignan, France: Plein Soleil.

XV Consell Plenari, Bertiz—Oieregi, Navarra 24–25.4.1997. 1997. Torre del Reloj, Spain: Comunidad de Trabajo de los Pirineos.

Garcia-Ramon, M. D., and J. Nogué-Font. 1994. Nationalism and geography in Catalonia. In D. Hooson, ed. *Geography and National Identity,* 197–211. Oxford: Blackwell.

Genieys, W. 1998. Autonomous communities and the state in Spain: The role of intermediary elites. In P. Le Galès and C. Lequesne, eds. *Regions in Europe,* 166–80. London: Routledge.

Grant, R. 1998. The political geography of European integration. In B. Graham, ed. *Modern Europe: Place, Culture and Identity,* 145–63. London: Arnold.

Guibernau, M. 1997. Images of Catalonia. *Nations and Nationalism* 3, no. 1: 89–111.

Häkli, J. 1999. Cross-border regionalization in the 'New Europe'—Theoretical reflection with two illustrative examples. *Geopolitics* 4, no. 3: 83–103.

Jessop, B. 1995. The regulation approach, governance and post-fordism. *Economy and Society* 24, no. 3: 311–20.

Jordi Pujol a Perpinyà. 1999. *La Semaine en Roussillon* 159, no. 6: 11.

Kaldor, M. 1996. Cosmopolitanism versus nationalism: The new divide? In R. Caplan and J. Feffer, eds. *Europe's New Nationalism,* 42–58. New York: Oxford University Press.

Keating, M. 1996. *Nations against the State: The New Politics of Nationalism in Quebec, Catalonia and Scotland.* Basingstoke: Macmillan.

———. 1998. *The New Regionalism in Western Europe: Territorial Restructuring and Political Change.* Cheltenham: Elgar.

Laitin, D., C. Sole, and S. N. Kalyvas. 1994. Language and the construction of states: The case of Catalonia in Spain. *Politics and Society* 22, no. 1: 5–30.

Le Galès, P. 1998. Conclusion—Government and governance of regions: Structural weaknesses and new mobilisation. In P. Le Galès and C. Lequesne, eds. *Regions in Europe*, 239–67. London: Routledge.

Lluís, J.-L. 1995. Els nostre ofici és estimar els clients perquè tornin. *Presència*, 5 November: 42–43.

MacLeod, G., and M. Goodwin. 1999. Space, scale and state strategy: Rethinking urban and regional governance. *Progress in Human Geography* 23, no. 4: 503–27.

Mancebo, F. 1999. *La Cerdagne et ses frontières: Conflits et identités transfrontalières*. Perpignan, France: Trabucaire.

Mouqué, D., ed. 1999. *Sixth Periodic Report on the Social and Economic Situation and Development of Regions in the European Union*. Brussels: EU Commission.

Murphy, A. B. 1993. Emerging regional linkages within the European Community: Challenging the dominance of the state. *Tijdschrift voor Economische en Sociale Geografie* 84, no. 2: 103–18.

Newman, D., and A. Paasi. 1998. Fences and neighbours in the postmodern world: Boundary narratives in political geography. *Progress in Human Geography* 22, no. 2: 186–207.

O'Brien, O. 1993. Good to be French? Conflicts of identity in North Catalonia. In S. Macdonald, ed. *Inside European Identities: Ethnography in Western Europe*, 98–117. Oxford: Berg.

O'Dowd, L., and T. M. Wilson. 1996. Frontiers of sovereignty in the new Europe. In L. O'Dowd and T. M. Wilson, eds. *Borders, Nations and States*, 1–18. Aldershot: Avebury.

Paasi, A. 1996. *Territories, Boundaries and Consciousness: The Changing Geographies of the Finnish-Russian Border*. Chichester: Wiley.

Pi-Sunyer, O. 1980. Dimensions of Catalan nationalism. In C. R. Foster, ed. *Nations without a State: Ethnic Minorities in Western Europe*, 101–15. New York: Praeger.

Pujol, J. 1991. *La personalitat diferenciada de Catalunya*. Barcelona: Generalitat de Catalunya.

Rivas, M. 1994. Supervivents de la frontera. *El Punt*, 11 January: 6–7.

Roig, S. 1997. Els Pirineus: Una cremallera que es descorda. *Revista de Girona* 181: 9–10.

Ross, C. 1996. Nationalism and party competition in the Basque country and Catalonia. *West European Politics* 19, no. 3: 488–506.

Sahlins, P. 1988. The nation in the village: State-building and communal struggles in the Catalan borderland during the eighteenth and nineteenth centuries. *Journal of Modern History* 60: 234–63.

———. 1989. *Boundaries: The Making of France and Spain in the Pyrenees*. Berkeley: University of California Press.

———. 1998. State formation and national identity in the Catalan borderlands during the eighteenth and nineteenth centuries. In T. M. Wilson and H. Donnan, eds. *Border Identities: Nation and State at International Frontiers*, 31–61. Cambridge: Cambridge University Press.

Serra del Pino, J., and A. Ventura i Ribal. 1999. *Catalunya 2015: Opcions polítiques per al segle XXI*. Barcelona: Centre UNESCO de Catalunya.

Una enquesta detecta una davallada del català a la Catalunya Nord. 1998. *Avui*, 9 April: 18.

Verdaguer, P. 1997. Catalunya del Nord: Poc català a l'escola. *El Temps,* 22 February.
Wilson, T. M., and H. Donnan. 1998. Nation, state and identity at international borders. In T. M. Wilson and H. Donnan, eds. *Border Identities: Nation and State at International Frontiers,* 1–30. Cambridge: Cambridge University Press.
Wirth, R. 1992. La Jonquera se queda fuera del mapa. *La Vanguardia,* 11 January: 2–3.

Chapter Six

Integration and Division in the Basque Borderland

Pauliina Raento

European integration has increased and diversified human exchange across the continent's internal boundaries. Following the gradual erasure of control over the borders between the European Union member countries, the international boundaries are losing their previous functional significance. In the process new margins and centres, and new 'transitional spaces' (Thrift 1983: 94) between them, are emerging on the map of Europe. In this new geography, regions stand apart from one another because of their residents' interaction and mobility rather than because of political and administrative delimitation and demarcation (Raento 1998: 111).

An example of this development is the case of the Basque borderland in the Western Pyrenees, around the boundary between Spain and France. This boundary is often referred to as 'one of the oldest and most stable boundaries in western Europe' (Sahlins 1989: 1). It was agreed upon in 1659 in the Treaty of Bidasoa but was not demarcated until the Treaties of Bayonne (in Basque, Baiona) some two hundred years later (Sahlins 1989: 26–60, 238–66). Today this boundary divides the seven historical Basque provinces into two states. In Spain, the Basque Autonomous Community and the Foral Community of Navarra (Nafarroa) form a part of the state's network of autonomous regions. In France, the three Basque provinces belong to the department of Pyrénées Atlantiques and the Aquitaine Region (see figure 6.1). Ninety percent of the 2.9 million residents of the seven provinces live on the economically more diverse Spanish side. The largest urban centre in the area is metropolitan Bilbao (Bilbo), with

900,000 inhabitants. An estimated one-fifth of the total population in the region speaks Euskara, the Basque language.

There is a strong legacy of both division and integration in this borderland. Its people have a long history of residence in the area and are known for their unique language and distinct cultural traditions (Gallop

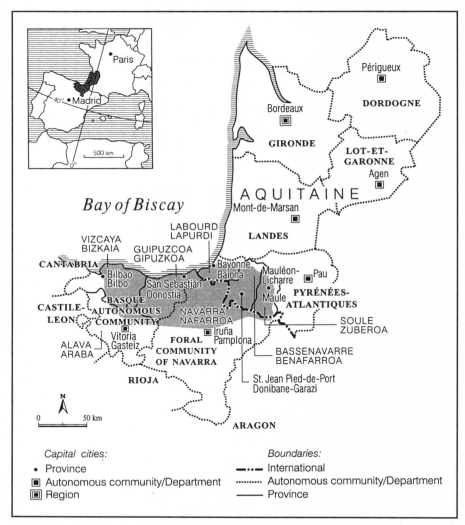

Figure 6.1.   Current Politico-Administrative Division of the Historical Basque Territory in Spain and France

Note: The shaded area indicates the contemporary geographical core area of the Basque language.

1970; Ott 1981; Collins 1986). Basque politics has attracted international attention for over a century; the minority population's strong sense of ethnocultural and linguistic distinctiveness has supported political resistance against the Spanish and the French state, giving rise to a Basque nationalist movement in the late nineteenth century and its armed offspring, Euskadi Ta Askatasuna (ETA), in the late 1950s (Payne 1975; Corcuera Atienza 1979; Clark 1979, 1984). Basque political identities and opinions about acceptable methods and goals for this resistance have varied, however, leading to internal conflicts within (and among) the three principal political groups: the radical nationalists, moderate nationalists, and non-nationalists. Other contested topics include the status of Euskara and the economic imbalance between urban and rural areas.

Provincial and local distinctiveness, changes in national policies of Spain and France, and the subsequent shifts in the nature of the international boundary have further contributed to the notably complex character of Basque politics and society. For example, the closure of the international boundary during the dictatorship of General Francisco Franco (1939–1975) emphasised the differences between the strongly industrialised and more populous Spanish Basque Country and the predominantly rural, sparsely populated French Basque Country. Spain's membership in the European Union in 1986, eleven years after Franco's death, added a continental context that emphasised economic issues over political conflict in Basque borderland society. The legacy of politico-administrative divisions still dictates many details and the degree of success of the continental processes in the area.

This chapter examines selected processes of contemporary integration and shows how historically and regionally based tensions have the potential to undermine these processes. Recent developments in the Basque borderland are approached from the perspective of multiple layers of centres, peripheries, and boundaries. The discussion portrays the historical Basque region not only as an international borderland but also as consisting of several internal cores and peripheries of political ideology, economy, and culture and ethnicity. The spheres of influence are mediated by transitional spaces—their own borderlands. It is argued that connecting the area's internal heterogeneity to the regional, national, and continental contexts of inquiry, and their interdependency, is crucial for understanding the progress of continental projects at the local and regional levels. The discussion draws on the assumption that explanations of the contemporary processes of differentiation and unification require a look at their historical development.

BASQUE BORDERLAND SINCE 1986

The death of General Franco in 1975 launched the political transition process in Spain. Control by force gave way gradually to a series of accommodations, including institutional, political, economic, and cultural concessions towards the country's ethnoculturally distinct peripheries and, in general, increasing individual rights. Since 1986, after the inclusion of Spain in the European Union, the French-Spanish boundary has become increasingly open, and some of the old patterns in exchange have paradoxically been reversed. In addition to the increase in traffic of people and goods across the border, many businesses in the area have relocated to the Spanish Basque coast and its emerging innovation clusters near the principal urban centres. These processes have emphasised the significance of local processes and continental political contexts in the evolution of the Basque borderland.

The European Union has played an active role in the shaping of the Basque economy, particularly since the 1990s. On the Spanish side, the EU has focused on developing and diversifying industrial infrastructure and production. Additional emphasis has been put on improving the quality of polluted industrial environments. In both Spain and France, the focus has been on improving the economic diversity of agricultural and tourism areas. Most of the projects have been co-funded by local, regional, and national governments. The increasingly international character of Basque transportation networks and local regional integration encouraged by the continental change of context exemplify this development.

Internationalization of Transportation and Trade

The European Union's role has been particularly visible in developing transportation networks in the Basque borderland. This focus draws on the advantageous location of the area within the European economic context (see figure 6.2). The Basque Country forms a central part of a corridor that connects the principal urban centres of the Iberian peninsula to the industrial core regions of Central Europe. Cargo from Spain and Portugal is transported to Central Europe by means of Basque road and railroad networks, and access to the French high-velocity train network (TGV) from the border town of Hendaye (Hendaia) allows passengers to reach Paris in roughly five hours. In addition, the Basque borderland is well connected to Spain's most important growth centres on the Catalonian and Cantabrian coasts, which have benefited greatly from EU expansion in the Mediterranean sphere. The historical links of Basque merchants, bankers, and industrialists with each of these regions have been strong and active for centuries (Douglass and Bilbao 1975: 56–58; Basurto 1989).

In this network, Basque ports, especially Bilbao as a part of the Atlantic corridor, play a crucial role (Basurto 1989). In 1998, the Port of Bilbao was the second most important port in Spain after Algericas in the southern part of the country (*Basque News* 1998: 2). More than 200 regular shipping lines, 130 of which are in Europe, connect the port with 500 ports worldwide (*Memoria anual 1996* 1997: 146–67). Bilbao is also well linked by road and railroad with the major urban centres of the Iberian peninsula and the rest of Europe. For example, by road, Madrid is four hours away, and Barcelona can be reached within six, Paris within eleven, and Milan within twelve hours. Roughly 4 million people reside within a two-hundred-kilometre radius of the port and 16 million within four hundred kilometres (*Port of Bilbao* 1997: 3).

The decline of the handling of raw materials since the closure of large

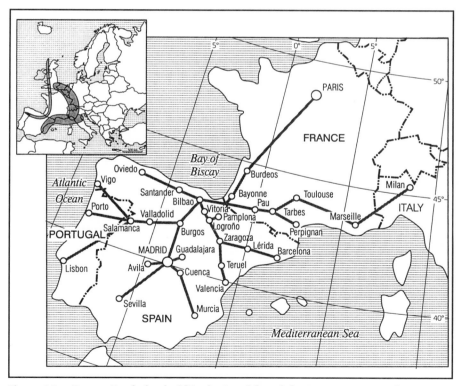

Figure 6.2.   Basque Borderland within the Spanish and the European Economic Contexts
Source: Port of Bilbao 1997: 3.

iron and steel plants in the Bilbao area in the mid-1990s shifted the port's focus towards other sectors, most notably container traffic. This change of emphasis has led the port to seek an expansion of its hinterland towards Madrid and Zaragoza, southeastern France, and northern Portugal, thus enhancing the networks of other sectors of the Basque economy as well (Ugarteche 1997). In addition, special collaboration agreements have been established with Central European ports, including Rotterdam in the Netherlands and Emden in Germany (*Memoria anual 1996* 1997: 17). Of the products that pass through Bilbao, 94 percent are either going to or coming from foreign markets. Over one-half of this exchange is with Atlantic European countries, most notably Britain, Bilbao's leading market. Asia's share is 17, America's 16, and Africa's 12 percent of the foreign exchange (*Basque News* 1998: 2).

The search for new markets and outside investors includes an ambitious port expansion project (see figure 6.3). Crucial to the completion of this project has been the EU's financial participation, together with local, regional, and national governments. The first phase of the project, from 1991 to 1998, added surface area to the port and reorganised its logistic activities to accommodate new functions and to attract new customers.

Figure 6.3. Port of Bilbao

The first phase of the expansion (1991–1998) tripled the port's surface area by claiming 1.5 square kilometres of land from the sea. The second phase, launched in 1998, adds another 250,000 square meters of surface area to the port (*Basque News* 1998: 1). Photo by author, September 1997.

The second phase, launched in 1998, adds more space, particularly to the port's cargo and container facilities. The expansion of Bilbao's port has promoted other infrastructural improvements in the area, especially in road construction. Many of these projects have been at least partially financed by EU funds (*Memoria anual 1996* 1997; *Basque News* 1998: 1–2).

The improving network has increased international transportation companies' interest in the Basque borderland. Particularly attractive is the area's cost-effective flexibility as a hub for diverse forms of transportation. For example, the Spanish and the French central governments and the national railroad companies have actively sought ways to promote this diversity, with EU support. To improve the existing links among sea, road, railroad, and air connections, it is being recognised that more seamless co-operation of the local, regional, and national authorities is needed. Locally, the task requires new infrastructure and technological know-how. Particular attention must be directed to overcoming problems caused by the different rail gauges used in the two countries (*BT* 1995, v.2: 7–8).

The facilities in the immediate border zone have improved considerably. One of the most important achievements is an international transportation centre, ZAISA, designed for the consolidation, distribution, and storage of merchandise by international transportation companies (Lorenzo Barahona 1997). The French high-velocity train network is to be extended in the 2000s. The increased selection of service links to the region's airports, most notably to Bilbao's Sondika, Biarritz, and Fuenterrabia (Hondarribia) (see figure 6.4), also promotes passenger traffic

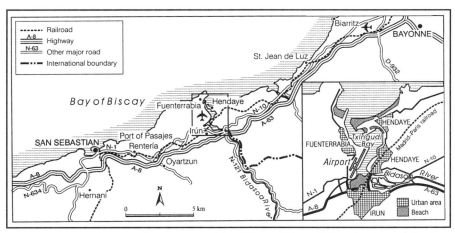

Figure 6.4.   Constituent Urban Centers of the Bidasoa-Txingudi Eurodistrict and the San Sebastián–Bayonne Conurbation

(Ugarteche 1997; *BT* 1997, v.5: 11). The growth benefits the entire area, but the direct impact of the development is likely to be most notable on the French side of the border: Activities related to the transfrontier traffic of merchandise already account for one-third of Aquitaine's economy (*BT* 1995, v.2: 7). Furthermore, favourable real estate and land prices and political tranquillity compared to the Spanish side have encouraged small- and medium-sized enterprises to (re)locate on the French side of the border.

Local Integration: The Bidasoa Bordertowns

The European Union's visible involvement in nationally significant regional projects has raised local hopes concerning the long-term development of the border area. An illustrative example of new development is the evolution of the three border towns on the Bidasoa River, Irún (Irun) and Fuenterrabia in Spain and Hendaye in France, into a functionally unified urban zone of almost 100,000 people along the San Sebastián (Donostia)–Bayonne conurbation (see figure 6.4). Becoming a player in the regional and continental urban network, according to François Jacqué, president of the Bayonne Chamber of Commerce, is seen as 'the only way of being on equal terms with the great European metropoles' (*Le Monde*, 5–6 September 1993, cited in Anderson 1996: 122).

One motivation behind the need to elevate the border towns to 'equal terms' with regional and continental urban centres is the dramatic economic decline of the three towns in the early 1990s. The abolition of customs between Irún and Hendaye in January 1993 left hundreds of people unemployed and changed the local economic profile and traffic flows, being amongst the clearest examples of negative economic impacts of continental processes in the Basque borderland (Anderson 1996: 122; Raento 1997a: 244–45). During the latter half of the 1990s, the local economy recovered gradually, particularly on the Spanish side. The openness of the international border and the growth of the region's industries increased merchandise traffic across the border and stimulated cross-border shopping in the area. According to one study, 67 percent of the shoppers from France to the Spanish Basque Country come from within 70 kilometres of the border. They shop in Irún, in the supermarkets of Oyartzun (Oiartzun), and in San Sebastián, where tourism has experienced a new boost. A considerable proportion of the shoppers include 'recreation' as one motive for crossing the border (*Informe anual 1996* 1997: 95). The improved access between the border towns, active nightlife, and extended hours of operation of bars and restaurants on the Spanish side attract young people from the French side on weekends. This has increased the

formation of mixed, multilingual social groups in the area (Lorenzo Barahona 1997).

In the 1990s, the money spent on either side of the border fluctuated
strongly with the currency exchange rates, but the total income carried
from France to Spain was generally inferior to the amount spent by the
Spaniards in France. This was due to the economic and demographic
imbalance between the two regions and, to some extent, to the type of
products purchased. For many Spanish Basques, relatively low real estate
and grocery prices made residential relocation to the French side attractive in the first half of the decade. With the strengthening of the franc this
trend has slowed down. The introduction of a common currency, the
Euro, may change some of the cross-border shopping patterns, but local
entrepreneurs believe that many shoppers will follow the behaviour
adopted in the 1990s (Lorenzo Barahona 1997).

New borderland organisations emerged in the 1990s in support of the
new development. The need to defend local interests in the continental
context and to guarantee local support for economic integration led to
the creation of the Bidasoa Txingudi Eurodistrict in 1993 (*BT* 1995, v.0:
3–6; 1996, v.4: 7–11). Its creation was based on local and regional initiatives and the drafting of a strategic regional plan on the Spanish side in
the same year. The district's activities are co-ordinated by *Agencia de Desarrollo del Bidasoa* (ADEBISA), a regional development agency with head-
quarters in Irún. ADEBISA works in close co-operation with the municipal
authorities of Irún and Fuenterrabia, which provide technical support.
Hendaye, the third centre of importance within the district, has joined
many of the projects and participates in the planning process, but limited
political and financial support from Aquitaine's regional government
undermines its power to act (Lorenzo Barahona 1997). The slow introduction of legal structures for the Eurodistrict also weakened initial progress
(*BT* 1996, v.3: 10).

The European Union funds roughly one-fifth of the projects co-ordinated by ADEBISA. The Basque autonomous government covers 40–45
percent of the costs, and the rest is shared by local governments, the historical commercial district (*comarca*), and, occasionally, the central government in Madrid (*BT* 1995, v.0: 14–15; Lorenzo Barahona 1997). An
example of these projects is the improvement of local access across the
border: In addition to a train, the three towns are now connected by bus
and ferry. Regional awareness is being raised by new trilingual media that
include a radio station and a magazine published by ADEBISA. Particular
attention has been paid to, and EU funding has been sought for, environmental projects (*BT* 1995, v.1: 13–14; 1997, v.5: 4–9) and promotion of
tourism, with special emphasis on the region's beaches and its historic role

as a rest stop for pilgrims on their way to Santiago de Compostela in north-western Spain (*BT* 1995, v.1: 7–8; 1995, v.2: 11–12). European funding has also included energy and transportation.

Many practical problems that complicate locally promoted integration arise because of the need to address multiple administrative levels. Until March 1995, there were no formal transfrontier agreements between Madrid and Paris, which confused the implementation of projects that involved both the Spanish and the French Basques. In the case of ADE-BISA and its efforts to co-ordinate the Eurodistrict, governmental bodies that directly influence local activities include municipal governments, regional district administrations (*comarcas* in Spain, *cantons* in France), the provinces of Guipúzcoa and Labourd (Lapurdi), the governing bodies of the Basque Autonomous Community in Spain and of the *département* of Pyrénées Atlantiques and the Aquitaine Region in France, the central governments in Madrid and Paris, and the administrative and governmental bodies of the European Union. Problems have arisen from different bureaucratic styles and technical sophistication, and communication has been 'very difficult' at times, even at the local level (Lorenzo Barahona 1997). Further complications are due to continuing failures to produce compatible high-quality maps of the border region, and, in particular, of the San Sebastián–Bayonne conurbation and its development. Particularly damaged by these difficulties have been projects regarding infrastructure and environment (Unzurrunzaga 1997).

INTERNAL BORDERLANDS WITHIN
THE BASQUE COUNTRY

Internal grievances have handicapped Basque borderland integration and international aspirations, particularly on the Spanish side. There are several problems not foreseen by administrators or by scholars who have examined national and continental development without connecting it to other geographical scales. To understand these problems, a look at the internal heterogeneity and formation of internal borderlands within the Basque borderland is necessary. Portraying 'the Basque borderland' as a uniform whole is somewhat misleading, since a locally and regionally sensitive approach reveals a series of distinct cores and peripheries within the region.

Cultural, ethnic, and historic links, including such elements as a common language (see the historical development of the Basque language area in figure 6.5) and cultural and social customs, tie the Basque borderland together (Gómez-Ibañez 1975: 24–42), but the seven historical

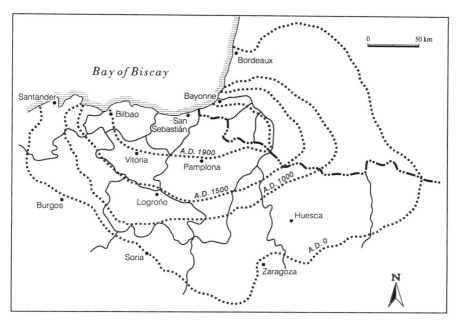

Figure 6.5.   Territorial Evolution of the Basque Language
Source: *Conflicto lingüístico en Euskadi* 1979: 219.

Basque provinces also contain a great physical variety and related traditional lifestyles. The fisherman's coast, the sheepherder's mountains, and the farmer's southern plains each have a distinct history of lifestyle and local economy (Douglass and Bilbao 1975: 13–16; Raento 1996: 204–15). Likewise, there are strong regional contrasts of demography (see figure 6.6) and industrial history and development. Whereas the densely populated coastal zone in Spain industrialised rapidly in the nineteenth century, the process did not reach the sparsely settled interior of the Spanish Basque Country or the French provinces until some half a century later, when the primary urban zones were already facing a new phase of industrial and urban expansion. Whereas on the coast the industries are relatively evenly dispersed and there are several large centres, many of the small villages of the interior still depend on agriculture, and industrial production is highly concentrated in principal urban centres. The legacy of the 1970s and 1980s economic crises and European integration are currently changing the profile and location of Basque industries, however.

In addition to demography and economy, the seven provinces are divided culturally, linguistically, and politically. Most of Guipúzcoa, east-

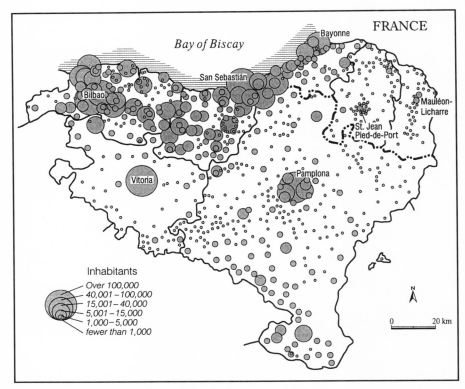

Figure 6.6.   Distribution of Population in the Basque Provinces

Note: Roughly 91 percent of the area's total population resides on the Spanish side of the border.
Source: Euskal Herriko Atlasa 1994: 144–55.

ern Vizcaya (Bizkaia), northern Navarra, and the mountainous rural inland of the French provinces are predominantly Basque speaking and display many cultural features usually identified as 'Basque'. Spanish and French dominate in urban centres, but the role of the Basque language may be locally significant, especially in strongly nationalist neighbourhoods. Generally, however, the principal coastal cities constitute voids on the Basque linguistic map. In turn, Spanish dominates the southern inland of the Spanish Basque provinces. Particularly in Spain, the Basque-speaking area forms the core of political resistance against the state (cf. figures 6.1, 6.5, and 6.6). This core spills over to the French Basque coast, where Basque nationalism finds support especially in the urban centres.

Due to these divisions, 'the coast and the interior stand apart' (Raento 1999: 225). The same divisions along rural and urban, Basque-speaking and French- or Spanish-speaking, and nationalist and non-nationalist lines

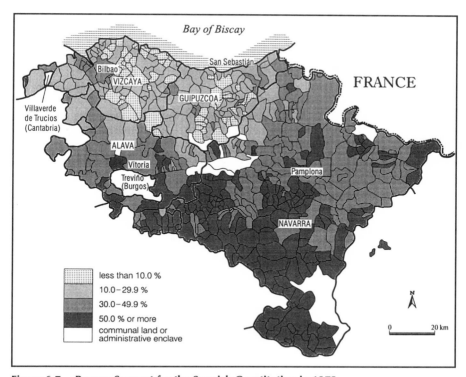

Figure 6.7.   Basque Support for the Spanish Constitution in 1978

Note: The map shows the percentage of affirmative votes counted from the electoral roll in the Referendum of 6 December 1978.
Source: Deia 1978: 19; *Referéndums y elecciones generales* 1986: 5–11; cited in Raento 1996: 152, see 153.

are present locally, within urban centres and provinces. These differences create internal hearts and relative peripheries of political and linguistic activism, identity, and conflict that are not related to administrative boundaries. Nevertheless, they affect, and are shaped by, people's understanding and acceptance of the formal division. The complex transitional zones where different political and cultural influences and worldviews meet and are contested can be understood as borderlands within the borderland. These multiple realities complicate the functionality of the administrative regions and discourse between segments of Basque society.

Some of the disputes have become important markers of perceived inferiority and have led to provincial and urban antagonisms (Raento 1999: 225–27). Well-known is the antagonism between Bilbao, the region's economic power centre with a considerable Basque nationalist presence, and the rapidly growing Vitoria (Gasteiz), the administrative capital of the

Basque Autonomous Community, characterised by multifaceted, overlapping, and ambiguous cultural and ethnic identities and conservative, nonnationalist politics (Rivera Blanco 1990; Hendry 1991). Despite the legal arrangements that allow the constituting provinces of the Basque Autonomous Community to decide their internal matters, a considerable amount of the real economic and political power lies in densely populated Bilbao and its surroundings. With all its influence, however, Bilbao suffers from prolonged economic difficulties and has not been able to recover from them as expected, whereas Vitoria has evolved into a booming and prosperous city that has greatly benefited from Spain's membership in the EU. Furthermore, as San Sebastián continues to enjoy the reputation of being 'the Basque cultural capital' despite the challenge put forward by such large projects as the Guggenheim Museum in Bilbao (Zulaika 1997), *Bilbaínos* have developed a sense of profound loss. Subsequently, echoes of the provincialism and localism typical of Basque politics in the late nineteenth century have re-emerged onto the scene (Raento 1996: 215–37; Corcuera Atienza 1979; Rivera Blanco 1990).

In the Spanish Basque Country's southern provinces, territorial antagonisms are represented by provincially defined, non-nationalist political parties. Especially in the 1990s, they posed a serious challenge to Basque nationalists and both diversified and heated the Basque political scene. Consequently, Basque nationalists were forced to modify their previously uniform message to make their agenda equally appealing in the different parts of the claimed historical territory. Challenged by the increasing competition over political power and space, radical nationalists, in particular, sought new, place-sensitive and place-specific alternatives for approaching people in these internal borderlands. The representatives of Alava, Navarra, and the French Basque provinces thus acquired more power within the radical nationalist organisation, and electoral and street campaigns were modified to show greater sensitivity to local circumstances (Raento 1997b: 201, 1999: 227–28).

The changing patterns of radical nationalist tactics can also be seen as an indicator of the need to protect the nationalist heartland in the changing context of minority nationalism in Europe. For example, coastal towns within this core area have constituted 'a relatively protected environment' for Basque nationalist sentiment to evolve. Here, daily communication and flows of information have been relatively uniform in terms of the ideological macroproject presented by the symbolic and operative centre. Consequently, each local experience and political response to increasing regional, national, and international exchange is explained by 'the relative geographical location of each "micro-world"' (Raento 1999: 225). In other words, whereas the small towns of Guipúzcoa lie within the radical nationalist core area of political activism and support, identity, and symbolic expression, the villages of southern Alava are located in the cultural and political zone of transition with more intervening influence from the Castilian and 'Spanish' cultures. Due to their historical development, many parts of the southern Spanish Basque Country are 'closer' to Madrid than to the nationalist heartland on the coast (Raento 1996: 251; cf. Raento and Watson 2000) (see figure 6.7). In the attempt to unify the claimed territory internally, nationalists are constructing a more solid outer boundary against outside influences and attempting to strengthen the Basque Country's role as an independent actor at the continental level.

UNITY AND DIFFERENCE IN BASQUE HISTORY

Further explanations of the tensions between the pursuit of integration by authorities and actors who do not conform to the formal politico-administrative definitions of Basque territory can be sought in history. The socio-cultural unity and local links across the region are reflected in local historical perceptions of the borderland and of the nature of the international boundary. In the Basque language, both the French and the Spanish sides are commonly referred to as *beste aldea*, 'the other side'. To avoid censure and to maintain 'objectivity' in a politically charged environment, academic discourse during the Franco years in Spain talked about the 'continental' and 'peninsular' Basque Country when referring to the region as a whole (Leizaola 1996: 97). In the contemporary context, the border is erased by the terms *Iparralde*, 'the North', and *Hegoalde*, 'the South'. Radical nationalists, in particular, prefer the unifying terminology, although these names are commonly used without a Basque nationalist connotation.

Central to understanding this way of erasing the dividing line is the Basque concept of *muga*, which refers to the boundaries of locally negotiated territorial arrangements (Douglass 1978: 39–40; del Valle 1994: 72–79, 83). The concept marks both an end point—a specific location in space or time—and a limit; *muga* can refer to a border, boundary, or frontier. Historically, boundaries between villages and agreements over local rights of pasture or water have been marked by a *mugarri*, a boundary stone, agreed upon by all the involved parties. Some of these agreements were confirmed by a specific ritual, some of which are still celebrated today. The importance of the agreements was further underscored by severe punishments, even death, for the unauthorised removal of boundary markers and was reflected in the subsequent myths and beliefs regarding these markers (Leizaola 1996: 95; Gómez-Ibañez 1975: 45–48; Barandiarán 1984: 145–47).

With the gradual establishment of the border between Spain and France, many of these local arrangements became 'international treaties' as the new politico-administrative boundary coincided with the pre-existing divisions (Douglass 1978: 47; cf. Sahlins 1989). They maintained their local character, however, and continued to be renewed even during periods of armed conflict between Spain and France (Leizaola 1996: 93; cf. Sahlins 1989). Following the demarcation of the border in the nineteenth century, the two states introduced new regulations and taxes regarding movement and trade across the boundary. To avoid these sanctions, local people developed sophisticated networks of contraband, which were particularly significant during warfare and political oppression (Gómez-Ibañez 1975: 125–26). Smuggling of goods began to diminish in the 1960s as the Franco government's fear of external influences and the closure of the border relaxed somewhat, but illegal trade of American cigarettes across the border continues today (Gómez-Ibañez 1975: 126; Leizaola 1996: 98).

Many of the elements of differentiation that characterise the Basque borderland today draw from specific spatio-temporal political contexts. Since its creation almost 350 years ago, the boundary between Spain and France has shaped political and administrative realities and social, cultural, and economic profiles of the two Basque regions. As has been the fate of many minority languages throughout the world, the Basque language has gradually given way to the usage of Spanish and French (see figure 6.5), and the two languages have differentiated Basque vocabulary (Douglass and Bilbao 1975: 13–14). Many borderland residents define themselves as 'French' or 'Spanish' Basques (Linz 1982; Lancaster 1987; cf. Sahlins 1989). In the nineteenth century, the French nation builders' search for a unitary, modern state led to infrastructural development in the Basque periphery and elsewhere, whereas this ideal was not implemented in Spain before the twentieth century. Thus, 'the French side of the borderland developed earlier and more completely than the Spanish' (Gómez-Ibañez 1975: 89). The twentieth century brought wealth and population growth to the Spanish side, whereas the French provinces suffered from economic hardship and emigration, thus emphasising the demographic imbalance between the two regions (see figure 6.6). A Basque nationalist movement emerged on the Spanish side of the border in the context of rapid industrialisation, immigration and cultural conflict, and emerging nationalist sentiments elsewhere in Europe. The movement's message of a unified Basque territory lacked similar appeal on the French side of the border, where demographic, social, cultural, and economic conditions were remarkably different (Jacob 1994; Raento 1997a: 241; see also Payne 1975; Corcuera Atienza 1979; Clark 1979; 1984).

Examining the historical differentiation of Basque nationalist sentiments and national identities illuminates particularly well the roots of contemporary difficulties for co-operation in the borderland. The explanation is usually sought in the structural and historic differences of the Spanish and French states (Linz 1982; Lancaster 1987). According to this perspective, 'Paris has been a strong core in a strong centralised state,' whereas Spain's capital city has been inferior in relation to economically powerful peripheries. Madrid has thus sought to control its territory by force, whereas Paris's 'softer' approach towards minorities has discouraged peripheral particularism (Raento 1997a: 242).

Exploration of history before the twentieth century suggests that these state-centred arguments do not alone explain the political differentiation of *Iparralde* and *Hegoalde*. Any confrontation between the Spanish Basques and Madrid is preceded by a conflict in the French Basque Country (Raento 1997a: 242). The French Revolution of 1789 terminated the French Basque *fors*, local rights and privileges, and the new administrative layout of France in 1790 made the three Basque provinces a part of the department of Basses-Pyrénées against local wishes. The unrest during the Age of Terror forced thousands of French Basques into exile to Spain and created strong feelings of distrust and bitterness towards the central government (Jacob 1994: 1–38).

The French Basques confronted the central government over local rights and privileges almost one hundred years earlier than the Spanish Basques, in a context where the first national(ist) *state* in general was only taking its first steps (Weber 1976; Sahlins 1989). Ethnicity and national identity had not yet become politicised as they did in the latter half of the nineteenth century. Walker Connor's (1990) argument that any *nation* was unlikely to exist before the nineteenth century supports the view that the political context of the late eighteenth century was not ripe for a nationalist 'Basque' sentiment to develop.

In turn, the Spanish Basques lost their *fueros* in 1876, when romanticism and emerging national(ist) sentiments swept the continent and the Basque coast was undergoing rapid industrialisation and immigration. Basque nationalism emerged in the late nineteenth century in Bilbao as a defensive reaction by the local middle class (Corcuera Atienza 1979). Thus, in stimulating Basque particularism, the temporal context of oppression in relation to the political macroenvironment and local processes seems to have been more important than the content of the central government's minority policy. Even if the process was equally shocking on both sides of the border, its results were quite different (Raento 1997a: 242; see also Linz 1982: 343).

Historically, the focus on the state and on the national centre-periphery relationship fails to explain the overall development of the Basque borderland, but this approach gains relative weight in the examination of the Franco years in Spain. Franco's oppressive policy made Paris sympathetic to Basque and other minority exiles from Spain in the aftermath of the Spanish Civil War (1936–1939). The short-lived Basque autonomous government, created during the war, and its representatives in Paris and Bayonne, enjoyed diplomatic status in France (Clark 1979: 74–76). Many Basque cultural and political organisations relocated across the border and received aid from French Basque organisations and international bodies. For the estimated 100,000–150,000 people who left the Spanish Basque Country for France in the 1930s, the support from this network was crucial in establishing 'a functional community' and organising resistance against the government in Spain (Clark 1979: 84, see also 80–106; Legarreta 1984: 51–98). All the exiled Spanish Basque groups in France 'were clearly oriented towards Spain' (Elton Mayo 1974: 125) and, following the tradition of unity, maintained clandestine contacts across the border.

In Spain, General Franco's policy radicalised the Basque nationalist movement (Clark 1979: 153–87; 1984). For Basque nationalists, the international boundary represented Spanish and French 'colonial rule' over the borderland minority (Krutwig 1973). The new radical nationalism that emerged in the 1950s and 1960s, and the armed ETA in particular, gave new importance to the territorial integrity of the Basque people and used slogans such as '4 + 3 = 1' and 'Seven in One' to underscore the goal of territorial unification of the historical provinces. Basque nationalists in both states made an emphasised distinction between the concepts of *frontera* ('a division imposed by the states') and *muga* ('a Basque territorial arrangement based on negotiation'). The ideological difference between these two concepts was expressed by a contemporary radical nationalist as an explanation of the old Basque tradition of contraband and the significance of the French provinces as a political refuge during the Franco years: 'The mountains, rather than dividing, unite the people, and the *frontera* is nothing more than a result of a confrontation that the people themselves have never had' (cited in Raento 1996: 272).

The French provinces provided important operational support and shelter for ETA from the 1960s to the 1980s. Basque mariners and contrabandists helped the organisation ship weapons and people between the two countries. For Madrid, the new radical nationalist message and lack of respect for the closed border made the Basques particularly untrustworthy and led the central government to try to secure its territory by enhancing control over the boundary and to demonstrate its power over the minority (Douglass and Zulaika 1990: 245–46).

Paradoxically, despite the cultural and political repression, World War II had led to a new industrial expansion in the Basque provinces. The closure of the international boundary made impossible the extension of Spanish Basque industries into France. This would have possibly been welcomed by the French Basque population, troubled by emigration and disagreements with Paris over the desirable direction of tourism development on the coast (Elton Mayo 1974: 130–31; Anderson 1996: 122). Francoist Spain's limited contact with the European Economic Community harshened the impact of the 1970s oil crises on Spanish Basque industries and complicated the subsequent structural transformation and recovery (Raento 1997a: 244).

Despite the difficulties caused by the political situation, the economic problems of the two regions would not have been 'cured by the removal' of the dividing line, as has been speculated (Elton Mayo 1974: 129). The development of large heavy-industry production units would not have erased the demographic imbalance between the rural and urban areas of the French provinces or resolved the long-term structural difficulties of agriculture. Locally and regionally, however, the two regions would have most likely benefited from more exchange. For example, the French side produced milk in excess of local needs, while there was 'a large but unsatisfied demand in Spain across the frontier for dried milk-powder, processed cheese and other milk derivatives' (Elton Mayo 1974: 133). Instead of being able to export the milk or some refined products over the strictly controlled international boundary, the French Basques had to sell it to other parts of France over longer distances, thus losing income.

The international boundary had a clear moral effect on the Basques as well. Through a rigid control over flows of information and the external boundaries of the state, Franco's government sought protection from outside influences. The goal was to maintain Catholic values of the Spaniards against the secular evils of France, and to 'protect' the people against political and sexual 'vice' (Grugel and Rees 1997: 128–56). To many Basques, the curfew and the subsequent difficulties of crossing the border meant a complication of daily life and social relations in the borderland.

CONCLUSION: THE LEGACY OF DIVISION

European integration has brought wealth and economic opportunity to the Basque borderland. The running of affairs in the Basque borderland, however, is complicated by both local and regional antagonisms and the legacy of national and international division. Together, they add to a long list of problems for the smooth progress of integration in the local and regional contexts.

At the state level, the first formal transfrontier agreement between Madrid and Paris was not reached until 1995, which complicated projects between the Spanish and the French Basques. Practical incompatibility and heavy bureaucracy continue to harm cross-border regional projects today. Some state-level disputes are related to European integration, such as the widely publicised disagreement between Madrid and Paris about fishing that has led to friction between Basque fishermen of the two countries. Nor have the increased contacts across the border erased the division of political and cultural affiliations into 'Spanish' and 'French' Basques. In the eyes of Basque nationalists, the continuing 'state colonialism' over the minority people is confirmed by the occasional closure of the border (Leizaola 1996: 91) and the two states' 'anti-terrorist' activities in the border zone.

In spite of the high hopes for a better economic future in integrating Europe through such processes as the improvement of trade and transportation networks and local economic co-operation, residents of the Basque borderland fear that local realities are ignored or misunderstood in the implementation of continental projects. In *Iparralde*, many are afraid of further marginalisation of the already peripheral region. For example, the relocation of industries across the border has raised concerns regarding the possibility of local interests being overrun by the more powerful Spanish Basque economy and its continental supporters. In *Hegoalde*, entrepreneurs doubt the EU's intentions regarding the restructuration of the Spanish Basque economy. Local workers, in particular, are afraid of the worsening of the already difficult job market in the area (Raento 1997a: 244).

Cultural co-operation suffers from complications specific to the region and its cultural and political evolution. In spite of new international contacts and the EU's support for minority cultures in the continental context, the concerns have remained local. Among the most serious dilemmas are disagreements over the definition and promotion of 'Basque culture', because this controversy is particularly personal in nature and touches an essential constituent of the Basque identity, reminding people of the difficulty of accommodating regional and cultural differences in the historical territory. This dilemma's continuous presence in the local media reflects the politically heated atmosphere of the region and emphasises the challenge posed by the internal heterogeneity and frictions of the historical Basque territory.

Indeed, segments of the borderland itself have differing interests that complicate the implementation of macro-scale projects and attempts to construct unity. Especially on the Spanish side of the border, the long history of provincial self-government, internal heterogeneity, and persistent regional stereotypes and prejudices arouse suspicion regarding region-wide aspirations. Promotion of new co-operation or single projects by one region are often interpreted as attempts to increase one's share over the others. Provincial co-operation and joint projects between the Basque Autonomous Community and the Foral Community of Navarra are at times difficult to promote and accomplish. Shared efforts of the two autonomous communities have been complicated further by state-level legislative disagreements over acceptable relationships between regional administrative entities—a dispute that reaches back to the conflict between the Spanish central government and minority nationalists over the Spanish Constitution of 1978 (Raento 1996: 138–54, 1997a: 244).

These legacies of division in the Basque borderland suggest that although 'physical barriers have been erased, the mental ones still exist' (Lorenzo Barahona 1997). The multilayered complications regarding regional co-ordination and political co-operation in a single region provide a pessimistic picture of the success of the so-called Europe of Regions in its ideal form. The Basque case suggests that to understand these complications it is necessary to examine how local and regional realities condition national and continental projects and how these, in turn, shape local and regional expectations and behaviour. The Basque case adds particular importance to the understanding of multiple, interdependent, and overlapping centres, peripheries, and transitional spaces that may or may not be tangible and are relevant on several scales of inquiry. Their examination draws attention to the problems of conventional definitions of regions in the changing Europe. The Basque case shows clearly that borderlands and their boundaries cannot be taken for granted or be discussed solely by drawing from existing politico-administrative units. If the conventional understanding of Europe's centres, peripheries, borderlands, and borders is not challenged, some of the new processes of exchange may be seriously misunderstood or even slip by unnoticed.

REFERENCES

Anderson, M. 1996. *Frontiers*. Cambridge: Polity.

Barandiarán, J. M. de. 1984. *Diccionario de mitología vasca*. San Sebastián: Txertoa.

Basque News. 1998. 19 December: 1–2. (Basque Autonomous Government's monthly newsletter. Vitoria: The Presidency of Basque Government.)

Basurto, R. 1989. Bilbao in the economy of the Basque Country and Northwestern Europe during the Modern Era. In W. A. Douglass, ed. *Essays in the Basque Social Anthropology and History*, 215–34. Reno, NV: Basque Studies Program.

BT [*Bidasoa Txingudi*]. 1995, April–1997, July. Vols. 0–6. (Magazine of the Bidasoa-Txingudi Eurodistrict. Irún, Spain: Agencia de Desarrollo del Bidasoa.)

Clark, R. P. 1979. *The Basques*. Reno: University of Nevada Press.

———. 1984. *The Basque Insurgents*. Madison: University of Wisconsin Press.

Collins, R. 1986. *The Basques*. Oxford: Basil Blackwell.

Conflicto lingüístico en Euskadi. 1979. Bilbao: Euskaltzaindia.

Connor, W. 1990. When is a nation? *Ethnic and Racial Studies* 13: 92–103.

Corcuera Atienza, J. 1979. *Orígines, ideología y organización del nacionalismo vasco (1876–1904)*. Madrid: Siglo XXI.

Deia. 1978. 8 December. (Basque daily newspaper.)

del Valle, T. 1994. *Korrika*. Reno: University of Nevada Press.

Douglass, W. A. 1978. Influencias fronterizas en un pueblo navarro. *Ethnica* 14: 39–52.

Douglass, W. A., and J. Bilbao. 1975. *Amerikanuak*. Reno: University of Nevada Press.

Douglass, W. A., and J. Zulaika. 1990. On the interpretation of terrorist violence: ETA and the Basque political process. *Comparative Studies in Society and History* 32: 238–57.

Elton Mayo, P. 1974. *The Roots of Identity*. London: Allen Lane.

Euskal Herriko Atlasa. 1994. Donostia, Spain: Erein.

Gallop, R. 1970. *A Book of the Basques*. 2d ed. Reno: University of Nevada Press.

Gómez-Ibañez, D. A. 1975. *The Western Pyrenees*. Oxford: Clarendon.

Grugel, J., and T. Rees. 1997. *Franco's Spain*. London: Arnold.

Hendry, B. 1991. Ethnicity and identity in a Basque borderland. Ph.D. dissertation, University of Florida.

Informe anual 1996. 1997. Irún, Spain: Agencia de Desarrollo del Bidasoa.

Jacob, J. 1994. *Hills of Conflict*. Reno: University of Nevada Press.

Krutwig, F. 1973. *Vasconia*. Buenos Aires: Norbait.

Lancaster, T. D. 1987. Comparative nationalism: The Basques in Spain and France. *European Journal of Political Research* 15: 561–90.

Legarreta, D. 1984. *The Guernica Generation*. Reno: University of Nevada Press.

Leizaola, A. 1996. Muga: Border and boundaries in the Basque Country. *Europæa II*: 91–101.

Linz, J. 1982. Peripheries within the periphery. In P. Torsvik, ed. *Mobilization, Center-Periphery Structures and Nation-Building*, 335–80. Bergen: Bergen Universitetsforlaget.

Lorenzo Barahona, M. 1997. (Research coordinator, Agencia de Desarrollo del Bidasoa.) Personal communication, July, Irún.

Memoria anual—Annual Report 1996. 1997. Bilbao: Autoridad Portuaria de Bilbao.

Ott, S. 1981. *The Circle of Mountains*. Oxford: Clarendon Press.

Payne, S. 1975. *Basque Nationalism*. Reno: University of Nevada Press.

Port of Bilbao. 1997. Bilbao: Autoridad Portuaria de Bilbao.

Raento, P. 1996. Territory, pluralism, and nationalism in the Basque Country of Spain. Ph.D. dissertation, University of Nevada.

———. 1997a. Together and apart: The changing contexts of Basque borderland. In L.-F. Landgren and M. Häyrynen, eds. *The Dividing Line*, 241–48. Renvall Institute Publications, no. 9. Helsinki: University of Helsinki Renvall Institute.

———. 1997b. Political mobilization and place-specificity: Radical nationalist street campaigning in the Spanish Basque Country. *Space & Polity* 1: 191–204.

———. 1998. Borderlands and popular culture: Texas-Mexican border music, migration, preservation and change. In J. Kaplan, M. Shackleton, and M. Toivonen, eds.

Migration, Preservation, and Change, 111–25. Renvall Institute Publications, no. 10. Helsinki: University of Helsinki Renvall Institute.

————. 1999. Geography of Spanish Basque nationalism. In G. H. Herb and D. H. Kaplan, eds. *Nested Identities,* 219–35. Lanham, MD: Rowman & Littlefield.

Raento, P., and C. J. Watson. 2000. Gernika, Guernica, *Guernica?* Contested meanings of a Basque place. *Political Geography* 19: 707–36.

Referéndums y elecciones generales. 1986. Pamplona, Spain: Gobierno de Navarra.

Rivera Blanco, A. 1990. *La conciencia histórica de una ciudad: El vitorianismo.* Vitoria, Spain: Diputación Foral de Alava.

Sahlins, P. 1989. *Boundaries.* Berkeley: University of California Press.

Thrift, N. 1983. On the determination of social action in space and time. *Environment and Planning D: Society and Space* 1: 23–57.

Ugarteche, I. 1997. (Representative of Autoridad Portuaria de Bilbao.) Personal communication, September, Bilbao.

Unzurrunzaga, X. 1997. (Architect.) Personal communication, July, San Sebastián.

Weber, E. 1976. *Peasants into Frenchmen.* Stanford, CA: Stanford University Press.

Zulaika, J. 1997. *La crónica de una seducción.* Madrid: Nerea.

Chapter Seven

Asymmetrical and Hybrid Identities in the Northern Italian Borderlands

David H. Kaplan

Italy is among the oldest and the youngest countries in Europe. Composed of local and regional identities stretching back to antiquity, it was
formally unified less than 150 years ago. The Austrian politician Metter-
nich dismissed Italy as 'a geographical expression', and although it is
today a single political entity with a fairly unified form of government,
these historical, cultural, and political identities still loom large in the
overall national consciousness (Dickie 1996). The psychological chasm
dividing north from south and the recent rise of the Northern League are
the most apparent signals, but Italian diversity is marked in several lesser
ways: from the persistence of distinct language regions like Sardinia and
Friuli, to the powerful sense of localism that structures Italian life, to the
creation of special autonomous regions that endow residents with certain
political rights (Gribaudi 1996; Agnew and Brusa 1999; De Mauro 1996;
Parker 1996).

Given such extraordinary cultural, political, and economic diversity,
one could plausibly argue that all of Italy constitutes a borderland, laced
throughout with various separations and frontiers. Italy's fitful development as a unified state has sought (often unsuccessfully) to soften some
of these divisions. Likewise, Europe's recent transformations have influenced the boundaries delimiting Italy from its neighbours. As a founding
member of the European Union and an eager adopter of the Euro, Italy's
northern political boundaries with France and Austria are no longer
marked by formal customs barriers and different currencies. Italy's northeastern boundary with Yugoslavia, a source of contention since Italy's unification in 1870, has witnessed numerous changes. With Yugoslavia

splintering into several successor states, Italy now borders the much smaller country of Slovenia, while the larger successor state of Croatia lies within the border sphere as well. This has expedited and increased interactions across the boundary. It has also changed the political landscape of the Trieste hinterland and the Istrian peninsula, of interest to all three countries.

I have argued elsewhere that these international developments, coupled with Italy's legacy of regionalism, have helped create distinct borderland identities (Kaplan 2000). In this chapter I examine the history and peculiarities of two affected regions, the Südtirol/Alto Adige region bordering Austria and the Julian region on the borders of Italy, Slovenia, and Croatia (see figure 7.1). Each region comprises a geographical layering—a palimpsest as it were—which reveals its separate historical epochs, changes in political control, cultural diversity, and the continued struggles for definition that make both regions a part of Italy yet also apart from Italy. The purpose of this chapter is to describe the geographical elements that clearly define each region as a borderland and establish its unique identity.

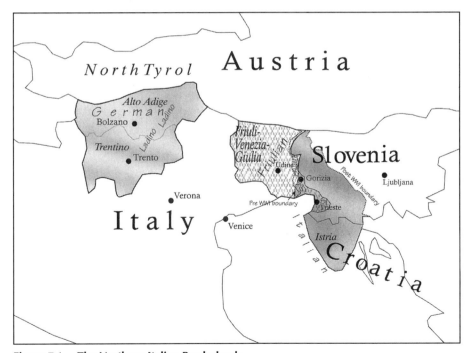

Figure 7.1.   The Northern Italian Borderlands

SOUTH TYROLEAN BORDERLAND

That the German-majority South Tyrol lies within Italy seems a profound accident of history. Up until World War I, this region, along with Trentino, belonged to Austria. Both provinces were given to Italy in 1919 and soon suffered under fascist domination. Following Italy's surrender in World War II, they were briefly under German Nazi authority and were then returned to a democratic Italy. The last fifty-five years have seen the development of a strong autonomous region, perhaps the most independent in Italy.

Austrian Rule

Prior to 1919, the population of Bolzano (in German, Bozen[1]) and the nearby valleys was composed of German speakers and a large, concentrated population of Ladin speakers just to the east-northeast of Bolzano. They were possessed of a powerful Tyrolean identity, marked by the legacy of patriots such as Andreas Hofer; a conservative, 'anti-modernist' culture; and the alpine environment (Luverà 1996). Beyond this, their incorporation into the Austrian Empire was fairly straightforward. In fact, as Luverà (1996: 55) points out, the term *Südtirol* was used to describe the culturally distinct area that is now called Trentino, a region comprising the city of Trento and several nearby valleys. The Italian population was found almost exclusively here and was a clear ethnic and linguistic minority overall.

Despite their linguistic differences, the identities and legacies of Trentino and the South Tyrol were interlinked (Andreotti 1995). They share a common history from the Roman period onward, they were joined together in a common bishopric, and they were both a part of the thirteenth- to fourteenth-century Tyrolean Confederation. This sense of shared identity is clear from statements by the above-mentioned Hofer— who described the Trentini as 'beloved Italian Tyroleans'—and by the association of Trentino and the South Tyrol to this day (Grigolli 1997).

The landscape of both provinces reflects very clearly the Germanic Tyrolean heritage and identity. It also denotes a history of independence that set this area off from other German-speaking regions. Castles are common features of a borderland, as they are constructed primarily for defence and to project authority, and the large number of such castles in the South Tyrol and in Trentino predates Italian rule. In many cases, the castles predate a unified Austrian Empire. Such castles are located on high ground for defence, and many overlook some of the principal river valleys of the region. For example, the castle of Trostburg, at the confluence of the Gardena and Isarco Rivers, was the home of one of the Tyrolean counts, and hearkens back to the period of Tyrolean independence prior to 1363 (Mondaini 1996). The architecture of the homes and the design of the cities is also a clear indication of the Tyrolean legacy. To go to a village is to witness a profusion of Tyrolean architecture (see figure 7.2), creating an image far different from that of the classic Italian village. Of the many distinctions, one that is immediately striking is the lack of apartment buildings, so common to all but the tiniest Italian settlement. The Tyrolean style is perpetuated to this day in new construction.

Under Italian Fascism

The incorporation of this region into Italy after World War I fulfilled the desire of some Italian nationalists to acquire territory up to the Brenner Pass. The Germans and Ladins who lived in the region around Bolzano became the 'new' Südtiroleans and a distinct minority group. As such they were beset by two boundaries: the cultural boundary dividing them from Italian Trentino and the Italian nation, and the political boundary dividing them from the much-diminished country of Austria and the North

Figure 7.2.   Village with Tyrolean Architecture
Photo by author.

Tyrol. Without Italian government intervention, there is a good chance that the entire South Tyrol would have remained culturally German, but Mussolini's designs included efforts to aggressively Italianise the new province by mandating that all offices, institutions, and individuals operate exclusively in the Italian language (see Egger 1978: 18 for a complete listing of fascist-era laws). The litany of fascist rulings demonstrates the power of the state to alter the language of usage. This pertained to the living and the dead, as even gravestone inscriptions were ordered to be written in Italian. These efforts never caused German speakers to shift their language of usage, but the rulings still resonate, especially in the toponymic landscape of the South Tyrol. They also serve to inflame a sense of continued grievance among the German population.

The imprint of Mussolini's 'fascist architecture' is evident throughout Italy but carries a special meaning in this border region. Old monuments were removed or razed to erase the significance of a Tyrolean past. The monument to the medieval poet Walther von der Vogelweide, constructed in 1889, was removed from the central square in 1935 to a more remote area. New monuments were put up at strategic locations to project Italian power (see figure 7.3).

A further legacy lies in demographic changes. Mussolini lured Italian nationals to this territory by granting them favourable opportunities for employment in services and by establishing new industries that could only operate in Italian. According to an account based on census figures, the Italian population in the South Tyrol increased from approximately 7,000 in 1910, to about 81,000 in 1939, to almost 105,000 by 1943 (Egger 1978: 28). Demographic changes were further influenced by the emigration of German speakers following an 'option', hammered out between Mussolini and Hitler, that forced German speakers to choose between their ethnic identity and their homeland. Those who wished to remain 'German' would have to leave the South Tyrol and settle in German territory. The majority stayed, but about 75,000 Germanophones left, most of them for good (Egger 1978).

From that point on, the South Tyrol has remained about one-third Italian-speaking (with a bit less than 30 percent according to the most recent figures). Because the Italians migrated primarily to the cities, the rural landscape was left solidly German (and Ladin in Val Gardena and Val Badia). The primary city of Bolzano was expanded to include a new industrial district in South Bolzano and new Italian neighbourhoods across the River Isarco from the old city (Cole and Wolf 1974). The result was a city that at one point was almost 80 percent Italian and that still has an overwhelming Italian majority (73 percent as of 1991; ASTAT 1998). The second city of Merano also gained an Italian majority for a while; it is now

Figure 7.3.   Arch across the Torrente Talvera in Bolzano, Built in 1928

Photo by author.

split fairly evenly between the two populations (49 percent Italian, 50 percent German as of 1991; ASTAT 1998). Among the 118 communes in the
province, there exists a roughly inverse relationship between population
size and Italian proportion. Only 30 of the 102 communes with populations under 5,000 are more than 5 percent Italian, and most just barely so
(ASTAT 1998). Within Bolzano itself, 1981 data show a German majority
within the historical centre and Italian majorities elsewhere (data courtesy
of ASTAT; no similar data acquired by the 1991 census).

Finally, fascism's legacy is imprinted throughout the province in place
names. In 1923, a commission was created to replace every geographic
place with an Italian name (Klein 1986). The commission was led by the
geographer Ettore Tolomei, who had argued in prewar books that the
German place names were 'deformations' of original place names in Latin
or Italian (Klein 1986: 98). Place names were Italianised according to several criteria and ranged from slight changes in spelling, to translations of
German words, to the creation of completely new names. The result was
some 160,000 new names—some clearly ludicrous, others that simply
annoy Germanophone sensibilities. Foremost among these changes is the
provincial name of Alto Adige—first used in the 1880s as the name of a
Trento newspaper (which is still the principal Italian newspaper in both
provinces).

Towards Greater Autonomy

In the aftermath of World War II, the South Tyrol contained an abused and embittered German-speaking population anxious to attach its territory to Austria. While the situation was unresolved, a fair amount of nationalist violence ensued throughout the 1950s and 1960s. In the electoral realm, German speakers found their voice through the establishment of the Südtiroler Volkspartie (SVP), which won its first province-wide election in 1948 and has never had to relinquish control of the provincial government.

The newly democratic Italy worked to accommodate regional peculiarities, designating the territory Trentino–Alto Adige as an 'autonomous regione' in 1947 (Eyck 1990). Many of the fascist regulations were reversed, and the use of German (and to a lesser extent Ladin) was again allowed in schools, in exchanges with the government, in official meetings, and in place names (see figure 7.4).

These measures were not successful in assuaging the bitterness of many South Tyroleans. Official promises of 'safeguarding fundamental ethnic rights', 'respecting [German] customs and [German] schools', and not imposing Italian culture on the South Tyrolean population (from a 1947 speech by Alcide DeGasperi, cited in Grigolli 1997: 88) were viewed with a great deal of scepticism. German speakers also believed that the laws did not erase the dominance of the Italian language. Initially, the constitutional arrangement gave each of the two provinces some powers but subordinated these to the larger powers of the region. As Italians dominated the overall region by a margin of three-to-one, this diluted German power. There was no requirement that Italian government employees in the South Tyrol be conversant in German, and studies clearly indicated—and still indicate—that few Italians bothered to learn the German language, even within mixed marriages (Egger 1978; Alcock 1992). There was also resentment over the limited powers of the Alto Adige province vis-à-vis the Trentino–Alto Adige region, a balance that effectively diluted the voting strength of the German population (Unterberger 1992).

The relations between South Tyrol and Italy improved significantly through a set of agreements that improved the status of the German language and the powers of the Alto Adige province. In 1969, a settlement was drafted and passed enthusiastically by the Italian parliament and narrowly by both the SVP and the Austrian parliament (which was considered a party to the dispute). This mandated more linguistic rights for German speakers, more power to German and Ladin schools, bilingualism in the civil service, and proportionality such that the German share of public employment equalled their share of the population (Eyck 1990). Later

Figure 7.4.   Trilingual Signs—German, Italian, Ladin
Photo by author.

agreements continued to improve the powers of the Alto Adige province, the last of which was implemented in 1992 (Alcock 1992; Unterberger 1992; Lapidoth 1996). While the authority vested in the Alto Adige and Trentino provinces is extraordinary in comparison to all other Italian provinces, the SVP has officially requested that these powers be expanded to the extent where the region would function as little more than a joint assembly of the two provincial legislatures (Ferrandi 1999a). Given the shared history of these two provinces, this is considered a most grave request and has ignited fears among the Trentini that they could lose their special autonomous status or be swallowed up by another region if they are separated from the Alto Adige.

The new regime in the South Tyrol is evident on the ground. Tyrolean heroes—neglected or secreted away by Italian authorities between the wars—have come into renewed prominence. The statue of Walther von der Vogelwiede has been restored to Bolzano's central square, and the birthplace of Andreas Hofer is a provincially recognised shrine. The Italian influence is muted throughout the province. This is clearly apparent in the small towns and villages where Italian is spoken rarely. It is also evident in majority-Italian Bolzano. The historical core—prime area for tourism and the focal point of the city—is clearly Germanic and contains a majority German-language presence. Italian culture is relegated to the 'new' Bolzano across the river.[2]

Much of the influence also stems from South Tyrol's reliance on tourism. According to data from *Conoscere l'Italia* (ISTAT 1997), the South Tyrol is among the top destinations in Italy and, in relation to its population, has entertained more tourists than any other Italian region—almost seven times as many tourists and nearly eleven times as many foreign tourists as would be expected given the size of its population. What (literally) drives this tourist boom is Germans. Eighty-one percent of all foreign tourists to the province are German, and another 9 percent are either Austrian or Swiss. These far outstrip the number of domestic Italian tourists, who prefer Trentino. German tourists are not coming for an Italian experience per se—although many of the hotels do offer guided tours of Venice, Verona, and Milan—but are looking to enjoy the beauty of the 'sunny side of the Alps' in comfortable surroundings. For this reason, South Tyrol's tourist economy, although bilingual, seems more oriented to its German market. And the landscape reflects this linguistic orientation in tourist brochures, hotels, restaurants, menus, signage, points of interest, and guided trips. German Pullman buses lumber over sinuous mountain roads, followed by BMWs, Mercedes, and other automobiles from Germany. Beer *stubes* and *gasthofs* are common features throughout.

Place names have been altered to reflect the new balance of power in the South Tyrol. The compromise developed after World War II was to add original German and sometimes Ladin toponyms to the Italian place names imposed by the fascists. Beginning with the conspicuous signs announcing entry into Südtirol/Alto Adige, every place is marked by at least two or, in the Ladin valleys, three names. One of the biggest political issues of 1999 was whether such multiple names should continue or whether some places (smaller villages, streets, etc.) should have only German names. Occasionally individuals take matters into their own hands by crossing out the Italian name, although that does not occur as commonly as might be expected given the heated nature of the debate. The provincial government has proposed that the names of 'less significant' places—localities with fewer than one hundred residents as well as some other landmarks—should be in one language only (Ferrandi 1999b). This proposal has generated an enormous degree of controversy (Cagnan 1999). Likewise, unofficial names, although not subject to any laws, are also largely bilingual, reflecting perhaps the Italian presence as well as the number of Italian tourists.

THE JULIAN BORDERLAND

Like the South Tyrol, the Julian region once belonged to the Austrian Empire but was earlier part of imperial Venice. Venetian influences diffused throughout the towns and cities on the Adriatic coast, including the Istrian peninsula and Dalmatia. After World War I, Italy was granted a large portion of new territory, including all of Istria, Fiume (as of 1924), and half of what is now Slovenia. Following Italy's defeat in World War II, these lands were taken over by the Nazis, then placed under Tito's control, and were finally re-separated in 1954. Istria, Fiume, and much of the Triestine Carso were given to Yugoslavia, while Italy retained a thin corridor that stretched to include Trieste itself (but not much more), as well as a newly 'borderised' Gorizia. The lands granted to Yugoslavia shifted political authority again after 1991, when Slovenia and Croatia declared themselves independent countries. Political boundaries have thus been superimposed and then reimposed on lands united by history, culture, and economic interaction.

From Venetian Littoral to Austrian Port

During the twelfth through the fourteenth centuries Venice emerged as a major mercantile and naval power. Venice sought territory as a means to secure shipping lanes and monopolise resources and markets. Much of this expansion was directed around the Adriatic Sea, first to the northeast (including Udine and Trieste) and then southeast along the Istrian and Dalmatian coast. Trieste, which had been established in Roman times, was clearly affected and wavered between some degree of autonomy and dependence on Venice (Arneri 1998). Still, Trieste was largely successful in warding off Venetian domination when compared to nearby cities.

Venetian control can be witnessed today in the distinct architecture of the towns and cities in much of Friuli, coastal Istria, and Dalmatia: the layout of the streets, the *loggia* (a typical Venetian gathering place), the prominent signature of the Venetian lion on the main buildings, and various place names (see figure 7.5). Trieste's relative independence from Venice is reflected in the lack of these architectural elements. Venetian domination is also manifested in the geographic split between the Italian

Figure 7.5.   Venetian Architecture in Piazza Tito
Photo by author.

coast and the Slavic interior and in the widespread diffusion of the Venetian dialect along the Adriatic littoral. Within Trieste, however, the pre-
dominant language through the eighteenth century was a dialect of
Friulian (Arneri 1998).

By 1382, Trieste had become part of the Austrian Empire. The first centuries of Austrian rule took place amidst significant Austro-Venetian conflict, but by the early eighteenth century Austria had clearly eclipsed
Venice as the dominant naval power in the region (Arneri 1998). It is this
growth that led to the desire to rebuild Trieste as a great free port. Despite
a slow start, Trieste became a major port, a role it continued to enjoy until
its annexation to Italy. The easing of customs duties attracted merchants
from around the Mediterranean, turning the city into a true cultural
mélange.

Trieste grew along with its burgeoning maritime significance, creating
a design legacy that still dominates the city. Next to the old medieval city
was built the Borgo Teresiano, named after the Empress Maria Theresa. A
large area of the city was platted in regular lots, wide streets (unusual in
Italian cities) were laid out, and a grand canal was built to allow large ships
to dock right next to newly constructed warehouses (De Vecchi et al.
1996). These landscape elements and architectural styles mark Trieste as
distinctly Austrian in its appearance and in the lifestyle of the city itself

(e.g., traffic). The diverse population that Trieste attracted as a seaport also led to a very eclectic set of churches and other buildings. An enormous Serbian Orthodox Church, a Greek Orthodox Church, a Muslim cemetery, and one of the largest synagogues in Italy attest to Trieste's port status as well as the tolerance of the Austrian authorities (see figure 7.6).

During the nineteenth century, the Italian Triestine population was allowed considerable autonomy within the Austrian Empire. The city had its own government, economic position, and control over its own schools (Stranj 1992). Trieste was also becoming more culturally diverse. Throughout the nineteenth and early twentieth centuries, large numbers of Slovenes moved to the city. Between 1880 and 1910 the Slovene proportion increased from 5 to 16 percent in Trieste's centre and from 29 to 52 percent in the suburbs, and it predominated in rural areas (Greenfield 1967). While Slavic numbers and cultural influence grew, the Austrian Empire gave disproportionate authority to those they considered 'historical nationalities', which meant the Italians. This made it more difficult for the Slovene population to gain proportional representation and schooling in their own language (Stranj 1992).

The geographical dichotomy between Italian city/Italian coast and Slovenian hinterland is evident in the landscape today. Unlike Bolzano, which became Italian through the efforts of the fascist government after World War I, Trieste has an Italian heritage of long standing. During Austrian rule, the new city created by the Austrian Empress Maria Theresa was called *Borgo Teresiano* and an adjacent area was named *Borgo Giuseppino* after Emperor Joseph II—Italian tributes to Austrian rulers. Italian merchants and other business figures constructed several major buildings in this period, confirming Trieste's position as a very Italian city under Austrian auspices.

Likewise, the Slovenian legacy dominates the Carso area that surrounds Trieste. In this hilly, limestone area inland from the sea, the architecture, language, and culture were almost exclusively Slovene and are primarily so to this day. Old villages in what is now the Italian side of the Carso carry a distinct look and feel that unite them to villages on the Slovenian side. Both sides of the border are populated with *gostilna* rather than trattorias; the villagers continue to speak Slovenian; many of the statues, gravestones, and memorials are inscripted only in Slovenian; the main newspaper is the *Primorski Dnevnik;* and the area continues its ties to the Slovene motherland.

There is no question that Italian reunification had an effect on the mentality and identity of Trieste's inhabitants. To begin with, Austria's Italian holdings diminished substantially as Venetia (which then included the cities of Venice, Verona, Mantua, and Udine) was transferred from Aus-

Figure 7.6.　Serbian Orthodox Church of San Spiridione in Trieste
Photo by author.

trian to Italian rule in 1866. The Triestine area and Trentino were left as small remnants of Austria's mid-nineteenth-century domination of northern Italy. The creation of a politically independent Italy, along with a renewed sense of cultural vulnerability—arising from the Slavic infusion—promoted a stronger sense of Italianness in contrast to the more cosmopolitan attitude that had previously prevailed. The increased presence of Slovenes (Stranj 1992) and feelings that the Austrian government might be tilting in their direction (Greenfield 1967; Stella 1987) may have further intensified Italian desire to become a part of the Kingdom of Italy.

Boundaries in Flux

Irredentist sentiments in Trieste were fairly ambivalent in the period leading up to World War I (Greenfield 1967; Stella 1987). The late nineteenth century was marked by Trieste's municipal government's efforts to expand its power, while imperial authorities 'oscillated confusedly between a vain desire for centralization and various federalist plans' (Stella 1987: 162). The Italian population was divided between a few thousand irredentists and those who sought local autonomy within the plurinational Austrian state (Gross 1978; Stella 1987). Irredentist sentiments waxed and waned between 1890 and 1914 as Trieste grew in economic and demographic importance. It is impossible to know whether the sparks of irredentist sentiment may have someday flamed into a full-fledged mass movement, since Trieste, Istria, and much of the Slovenian culture region were granted to Italy after World War I for reasons having more to do with military victory and political alliances, than with the attitudes of the region's inhabitants. But for Italian nationalists, the acquisition of territory up to the city of Fiume marked the culmination of Italian spatial ideology and the completion of Italy's own manifest destiny.

When this region was turned over to Italy, the initial promise was that the fairly tolerant policies that had marked the multinationalist Austrian regime would be continued and even enhanced. Certainly, the new region of 'Venezia Giulia' was quite diverse: It included 470,000 Slavs (Croats and Slovenes) in addition to 350,000 Italians (Petacco 1999). But when Mussolini took power, Italian became the only accepted nationality, and everything was done to enforce this nationalist ideology. The use of Slovene and Croat disappeared from the schools, names were ordered changed, newspapers were outlawed, Slavic songs could not be sung, and church officials were replaced with more compliant prelates (Stranj 1992; Arneri 1998; Petacco 1999; Bufon n.d.). Such was the official disrepute of the Slavic languages that stationery was sold with the inscription 'Italian spoken here' (Petacco 1999).

Fascism's imprint was evident throughout the newly acquired territory but was especially pronounced in Trieste. Triestines had long agitated for their own university. In 1938, the Università di Trieste was constructed as a monument to Italian power. It was placed on a hill overlooking both the city and the coast, with its back to the Slovene-occupied hills (see figure 7.7). Beyond its physical attributes, the university, as the flagship of Triestine education, promoted a view of Trieste as an Italian city, and in the process shunned any attention paid to the histories, languages, and cultures of the Slavic people surrounding it (Kappus 1995). Trieste's cosmopolitan past was eradicated as portions of the old city were demolished, the Great Synagogue (built in 1797) was destroyed, and the several monuments to an exclusively Italian era were established—including the renaming of the Piazza Grande to the Piazza dell'Unità d'Italia. The position of Trieste was also altered from that of the most important port and third city of the Austrian Empire to something of a peripheral backwater within Italy (Petacco 1999).

After World War II, the boundary shifted once again. For a period of time, the status of Trieste and much of the Italo-Yugoslav boundary was in flux. Tito was the first to defeat the German Nazi army, which had taken over the region in the last two years of the war, and he initially claimed Trieste for himself. There followed several proposals and counterproposals regarding the status of Trieste and many towns on the Istrian peninsula. For example, Pola, a city on the southern tip of Istria made up primarily of Italian fishermen, was eventually given to Yugoslav authorities (Petacco 1999). Trieste was eventually placed under Italian adminis-

Figure 7.7.   University of Trieste
Photo by author.

tration, although not made a formal part of Italy until 1954 (Klemencic and Bufon 1991; Kappus 1995). In the process, Trieste lost almost all of its Istrian hinterland to Yugoslavia. What remained was merged with Friulian territory, with which it had very little in common, creating the new province of Friuli–Venezia Giulia.

Cities without Hinterlands

The political boundary drawn between Italy and Yugoslavia separated a region that had been linked together culturally and economically. Left on the Italian side of the border were a large population of Slovenes. According to Stranj (1992), 70 percent of the Italian Carso surrounding Trieste was owned by Slovenes prior to 1945, and the area continues to have a major Slovene presence. Official Italian sources from 1961 and 1971 indicated a Slovene population within the province of Trieste (which includes the city of Trieste and the Carso) at about twenty-five thousand, still a majority outside the city itself. Considerable Slovene populations lived and continue to live along the Italian side all the way north to Austria. Estimates of these proportions differ, since the Italian census did not tabulate ethnicity in these districts. An Italian estimate from 1971 census data suggested a population of over twenty-seven thousand, with majorities in fourteen communes (the smallest political jurisdiction in Italy, similar to a township). Differing estimates tabulated by the Slovene Research Institute, which argues that many Slovenes may have been reluctant to divulge their identity, indicate that almost fifty thousand Slovenes live within the province of Trieste and another thirty-six thousand Slovenes inhabit the border regions farther north (Stranj 1992). Whatever the precise figures, there is little question that the numbers have been altered by Slovene emigration and Italian immigration from Istria.

Despite some substantial losses, there remains a significant Italian population in Istria (Radin 1995). Fortunately the Yugoslav government did count nationality and mother tongue in its census. The number of Italian nationals in Istria stood at almost eighty thousand in 1948. There followed a large drop, as Italians (and some pro-Western Slavs) fled Tito's regime (Stranj 1992; Petacco 1999; Bufon 1999); in 1953 only about thirty-six thousand Italians remained. By 1981, only fifteen thousand Italian 'nationals' remained in Istria, but by 1991 that number had risen to over twenty-four thousand. This latter fluctuation in particular raises the same concerns regarding the willingness of individuals to identify themselves as Italian nationals (Bufon 1999). What is more, the number of 'mother tongue' Italian speakers in 1991 was close to thirty thousand (Radin 1995). The port city of Capodistria (Koper), some thirty kilometres from Trieste, was three-quarters Italian in 1910. The proportion declined steadily, regis-tering less than 2 percent Italian in 1991 (Bufon 1999). In addition, the Italian population here is old; 48 percent of Istrian Italians are over age fifty, compared with 30 percent of the Istrian population as a whole (Radin 1995).

The boundary also disrupted economic relations. Trieste was clearly a central place that served the entire Carso and much of Istria during the pre–World War I Austrian period and the Italian interwar period. Sloven-ian Carso villages were split apart by the new boundary. Culturally Italian cities like Capodistria—very much linked to Trieste and the entire upper Adriatic region—were now relocated in an altered cultural, political, and economic landscape. In the north, the city of Gorizia had served as the major marketplace for the entire Isarco Valley, but the Italo-Yugoslav boundary was placed right outside the city itself. In areas in nearby Gori-zia, some villages were cut in two, and transportation links on the Yugoslav side of the boundary were severed (Bufon 1996).

Moreover, the Yugoslav side of the boundary was left without a major urban centre (Bufon 1996). The development of Nova Gorica (or New Gorizia) was the most visible response to this change. It was a city 'born by decree' in 1947, after the de facto boundary had been fixed but before new treaties made the boundary more permeable (Jurca and Torkar 1994: 43). Nova Gorica allowed socialist urban planners and architects to build a new city from the ground up, adhering to modern plans of design (the principal planner had been a student of Le Corbusier's) and providing a positive symbolic counterpoint to the messy, irrational city of Gorizia. Today it is commonplace to cross the border daily and 'the boundary does not seem to exist' from the air (Jurca and Torkar 1994: 42). Yet the city of Nova Gorica continues to mark its place as a legacy of a different ideologi-cal system. It is also a thriving city, and the largest centre in western Slov-enia.

The new boundary disrupted social and economic relations throughout the region. But the strength of these local ties also forced the Italian and Yugoslav governments to forge a series of agreements across an ideologi-cal divide, in sharp contrast to other places where ideological separation created nearly impermeable boundaries. Boundary crossings, especially for local residents, were liberalised as early as 1949, and further still in 1967. Some of these early agreements were necessary to enable farmers to work all of their land; later agreements were intended to expedite local commerce and allow a return to normal economic relations (Klemencic and Bufon 1991; Bufon 1996). Cross-border interaction and trade flour-ished. Once border crossings were liberalised, local traffic in Gorizia increased almost ninefold (Bufon 1996). By 1985, there were over 31 million crossing in the Trieste area, over 8 million in the Gorizia area, and a total of 725 billion lire (about US$400 million) worth of trade across these boundaries (Klemencic and Bufon 1991). While still a member of the Yugoslav Federation, Slovenia, as the most economically dynamic and Western-oriented republic, was always pushing for greater ties (Mlinar 1996). These aims were intensified after Slovenia's independence in 1991. As a result, borders have been further loosened and local social and economic exchanges have been increased (Minghi 1994).

The strength of the cross-border economy is clearly visible. On Saturdays, lines of cars and buses from Slovenia and Croatia cross into Gorizia and Trieste, their drivers looking for goods to buy and bring back home. Regular stores and flea markets in these Italian cities (and in majority-Slovene villages) cater to these 'tourist-shoppers'; the most prominent is the Trieste Shopping Fair (Minghi 1994). For the Italians, the loose borders have opened up tremendous recreational opportunities. The beaches of Istria—cheaper, cleaner, and sandier than in Italy—beckon weekend vacationers, most of whom use lire instead of the local tolars and kuna. A further attraction is gambling. There are only a few casinos in Italy (the closest is on the Venetian Lido), whereas in Slovenia gambling is relatively unfettered. To take advantage of the Italian market, casinos are located along the boundary, often right next to the checkpoint (see figure 7.8) and hard by a couple of gasoline stations and duty-free shops.

Certainly the creation of an independent Slovenia has had dramatic psychological effects on the borderland. Of all the former Yugoslav federations, Slovenia is by far the most prosperous; in fact, it has the highest gross domestic product per capita of all post-communist societies. Following are a few examples of this new status and its Western orientation. First and foremost is that Slovenia has bid to become a part of the European Union and is considered to be a viable candidate in the third wave, perhaps in 2005 (Manzin 1999). Successful admission would eliminate cross-border checks and could further fuse Gorizia–Nova Gorica into a single urban system. A second example is the recent attempt to host the 2006 Winter Olympics. The name for the bid was '*senza confini*' (without borders) and was truly a borderland effort from the Friuli–Venezia Giulia region of Italy, the Carinthia region of Austria, and Slovenia (*Il Piccolo* 1999). In fact, the regional Friuli–Venezia Giulia government worked against the Italian state, which was rooting for Turin to win (which it eventually did). This bid is an example of a whole series of inter-regional collaborations, many of which are documented in the pages of Trieste's main newspaper, *Il Piccolo* (see Radossi 1999). Third, the emergence of an independent Slovenia has energised the Slovene population in Italy and has perhaps comforted the remaining Italian population in Slovenian Istria.

Figure 7.8.   Casino on the Italo-Slovene Boundary
Photo by author.

There does not appear to be significant irredentist sentiment among the minority populations on either side. Slovenes in Italy feel a considerable degree of pride in their heritage, wish to retain their language, and are currently pressing for greater cultural protection. They aspire towards the political benefits enjoyed by the German-speaking population of the South Tyrol and a greater formalisation of their status. Italians in Slovenia, particularly those who are younger, increasingly cast their lot with the new state. A survey conducted in 1993 (Bergnach and Radin 1993) showed that most Istrian Italians had a strong sense of ethnic identity and hoped to continue to maintain this identity. But most expected good relations with the majority and, especially among those living in Slovenia, had an attachment to the state.

CONCLUSION

The South Tyrol and the Julian region are true borderlands in several respects. Both are distinct from the rest of Italy in their political arrangements, their economic interactions, and especially their culture. Much of this stems from their historical legacy. These regions have belonged to Italy only since 1919. The boundaries have since undergone tremendous physical and psychological impacts. The imprint of fascism was especially powerful, as it aggressively imposed Italian culture and authority on each region. In the Julian region, World War II resulted in further alterations of the boundary, whereas in the South Tyrol, international acceptance of the boundary has been in place only since the 1960s. Attempted control by Italian authorities and localised resistance stir memories and resentments that are reflected in architecture, statuary, and signage. These geographical elements manifest and create layers of meaning that underscore the position of each region as a borderland and are key in distinguishing these borderland regions from the rest of Italy.

Both regions exist at the margins of Italian consciousness. Trieste's main newspaper recently reported that many Italians knew almost nothing about the city. The South Tyrol is even more removed than Friuli–Venezia Giulia from national politics, as it has been governed for the last fifty years by a Germanophone-dominated regionalist party. Tellingly, it is not included in the Northern League's plans for an independent Padania (Agnew 1999). And it is the only region in Italy that lures far more foreign than domestic tourists.

Both regions are also marked by messy boundaries, with large populations of minority groups. In the case of the South Tyrol, this cultural mixture extends one way, as there are no Italians within Austria. In fact, the line dividing the provinces of Alto Adige from Trentino represents more of a cultural boundary than does the international boundary between Italy and Austria, where populations on both sides are culturally similar. In the Julian region, the political boundary more closely parallels the cultural boundary but is marked by cultural minorities on both sides: Slovenes in Italy and Italians in the Istrian portion of Slovenia and Croatia.

Italy has recognised the cultural and political peculiarities of each region by designating them among five 'special' autonomous regions (the others are Valle d'Aosta, Sicily, and Sardinia). The South Tyrol has been further recognised by the extraordinary devolution of powers from the combined region to the two constituent provinces of Trentino and Alto Adige. This has allowed the German-majority province of Alto Adige to enjoy extraordinary authority. It has also allowed it to retain a large proportion of tax receipts. Friuli–Venezia Giulia was designated later as a special region (in 1963) and enjoys fewer prerogatives.

The differences between these border regions are also quite apparent. Although both regions were originally a part of the Austrian Empire, they have fronted very different countries since becoming part of Italy. The

South Tyrol abuts Austria, a Western, capitalist country that has belonged to the European Union since 1995. As a result, the two countries share a common base currency—the Euro—and have abolished checkpoints. Friuli–Venezia Giulia mostly borders Yugoslavia, with a separate ideological system and a marked difference in living conditions. The gap has narrowed considerably with Slovenia's independence. However, Slovenia remains outside the European Union, and Croatia—close by the boundary and with a significant number of Italian speakers—is even farther behind.

Internally, the two regions diverge culturally and politically. The province of Alto Adige contains a clear majority of German speakers, a group found throughout the province. The Italian population here is limited to the big cities of Bolzano and Merano and a few other cities and towns. German speakers overwhelm the villages, and these numbers are augmented by the huge vacation population made up primarily of tourists from the German Republic. Even within Bolzano, there is a clear population divide between the German-speaking historical core and the Italian New Bolzano.

A very different dynamic exists in Friuli–Venezia Giulia. The Slovene population is a clear minority throughout the region and is concentrated along the boundary. There are a few majority Slovene villages in the Triestine Carso. There is also a Slovene presence in the cities of Gorizia and Trieste, evidenced by some cultural institutions and academic centers. But these two cities feel culturally Italian, distinct from the German Tyrolean feel of Bolzano and Merano. On the Istrian peninsula, the Italian legacy continues to be felt and is evident in the architecture, street and town signs, the Italian associations, the few Italian schools, and even the influx of Italian tourists. But the population of Italian nationals has declined considerably, and the language heard on the streets is more likely to be Slovene or Croat.

Cultural distinctions have steered political differences between the two Italian regions. In the South Tyrol, the Germanophone party controls the province, and the German speakers behave in many ways like a majority. Multiple institutions support German dominance: newspapers and other mass media, banks, shops, cultural associations, and the impact of tourism itself. In this way, the Alto Adige shares some similarities to Quebec, where a linguistic minority enjoys majority status within its own province. Unlike in Quebec, however, there is little separatist sentiment here. The SVP disavows any such sentiment—in marked distinction to the avowedly separatist Parti Quebecois—and irredentist graffiti is quite rare throughout the province. (There were more signs protesting the U.S. military presence in the region.) Perhaps this has to do with the increased affluence of the region. When considered in terms of production and consumption per capita, Trentino–Alto Adige is one of the wealthiest regions in Italy (ISTAT 1997). One old-line separatist has lamented that money 'has changed the mentality' of residents (Luverà 1996: 53)

It could be argued that a distinct Südtirolean identity is emerging. Certainly the current leader of the SVP and president of the province, Luis Durnwalder, has stated, 'We hope that in the Alto Adige is born a bilingual society in which each person possesses the language of the other' (L'Intervista 1999). And the mountain climber Reinhold Messner, perhaps the best-known celebrity in the province, has claimed 'there no longer exists a Tyrolean identity, but rather a South Tyrolean identity' (Luverà 1996: 54).

The Slovenes in the Friuli–Venezia Giulia have far less power; they are treated and behave very much like a minority. In fact, Trieste (which also includes many of the Carso villages) has wavered between a strongly Italian nationalistic stance and one more accommodating to the Slovene population. The physical manifestation of this can be seen in the signs marking the villages of the Triestine Carso. At present, they are bilingually Italian and Slovene, but that depends on the governments of Trieste and neighbouring communes, which are controlled by Italian majorities. The previous administration imposed Italian-only signs. This goes to show how little power resides in the hands of the Slovenian minority. Similarly, the minority Istrian Italian population has been subject more to the vagaries of the Yugoslav, Slovene, and Croat governments and has little internal power. Much of the activity of the Italian community is in fact subsidised by the Italian government. Minority populations on both sides, however, appear to be relatively satisfied with the location of the boundary, although there is a concerted effort among both parties to increase their rights and privileges.

Over eighty years have now passed since the Austrian Empire ceded two southern territories to the Kingdom of Italy. Since that time, the South Tyrol and the Julian regions have experienced fascism, Nazism, a world war, genocide, boundary shifts, the Cold War, the breakup of Yugoslavia, the melting of the Iron Curtain, and the growth of the European Union. While these regions float on the frontiers of Italian consciousness, they have sat firmly on the front lines of the most significant European events. Now they are again in focus, this time as participants in a mass reshaping of spatial identities. Although the political boundaries are not likely to change any time soon, the consciousness and identities of people living next to them is changing fast. A borderland identity—still in its infancy—may come to complement an ensuing range of identities, extending from the town, to the region, to the nation, and to Europe itself.

NOTES

Thanks must be given to a number of people who have significantly aided in the preparation of this chapter. I am especially indebted to the Academy of Finland and to Kent State University, which gave me money and time to conduct this fieldwork. In Italy, I received an enormous amount of professional assistance and friendship from Professors Giuliana Andreotti, Igor Jelen, Paola Pagnini, Milan Bufon, and Anton Gosar. I also wish to thank Veronica Jurgena for her invaluable help.

1. To avoid semantic awkwardness, one linguistic form will be used for place names. In this instance, the Italian form is used.

2. This information was gathered for the 1981 census and from a special tabulation conducted in 1987. As of 1987, the central part of Bolzano—its historical core—contained approximately 51 percent German speakers. The three other broadly defined districts had Italian majorities: Oltrisarco (74 percent), Europa–Don Bosco (88 percent), and Gries–S. Quirino (67 percent). I appreciate the help of Gregorio Gobbi of ASTAT in procuring this information.

REFERENCES

Agnew, J., and C. Brusa. 1999. New rules for national identity? The Northern League and political identity in contemporary northern Italy. *National Identities* 1, no. 2: 117–33.

Alcock, A. 1992. The protection of regional cultural minorities and the process of European integration: The example of South Tyrol. *International Relations* 11: 17–36.

Andreotti, G. 1995. *Euroregione Tirolo: Un Nouvo Modo di Pensare l'Europa.* Trento, Italy: Edizione Colibrì.

Ara, A. 1994. The 'cultural soul' and the 'merchant soul': Trieste between Italian and Austrian identity. In R. Robertson and E. Timms, eds. *The Habsburg Legacy: National Identity in Historical Perspective,* 58–66. Edinburgh: Edinburgh University Press.

Arneri, G. 1998. *Trieste: Breve Storia della Città.* Trieste: Edizioni Lint.

ASTAT. 1998. *Annuario Statistico della Provincia di Bolzano.* Bolzano: Istituto Provinciale di Statistica.

Bergnach, L., and F. Radin. 1993. Le attese della minoranza italiana in Istria. *Istituto di Sociologia Internazionale* 3, no. 2: 8–12.

Bufon, M. n.d. The Slovenian minority in Italy and the independence of Slovenia. Unpublished manuscript.

———. 1996. Social integration in the Italo-Slovene Gorizia transborder region. *Tijdschrift voor Economische en Sociale Geografie* 87, no. 3: 247–58.

———. 1999. Slovene Istria and its neighborhood: Problems of shaping social and cultural spaces. *Mediterranean Ethnological Summer School* 3: 159–75.

Cagnan, P. 1999. I toponomi dividono gli esperti. *Alto Adige,* 6 July: 3.

Cole, J., and E. Wolf. 1974. *The Hidden Frontier: Ecology and Ethnicity in an Alpine Valley.* New York: Academic Press.

De Mauro, T. 1996. Linguistic variety and linguistic minorities. In D. Forgacs and R. Lumley, eds. *Italian Cultural Studies: An Introduction,* 88–101. Oxford: Oxford University Press.

De Vecchi, F., et al. 1996. *Trieste: A Guide to the City.* Trieste, Italy: Bruno Fachin Editore.

Dickie, J. 1996. Imagined Italies. In D. Forgacs and R. Lumley, eds. *Italian Cultural Studies: An Introduction,* 19–33. Oxford: Oxford University Press.

Egger, K. 1978. *Bilinguismo in Alto Adige: Problemi e Prospettive.* Bolzano, Italy: Casa Editrice Athesia.

Eyck, F. G. 1990. South Tyrol and multiethnic relations. In J. V. Montville, ed. *Conflict and Peacemaking in Multiethnic Societies,* 219–38. Lexington, MA: Lexington Books.

Ferrandi, G. 1999a. La SVP insiste: Poteri alle due Province. *Alto Adige,* 6 July: 9.

———. 1999b. Più di cento abitanti, nome bilingue. *Alto Adige,* 21 September: 13.

Greenfield, K. 1967. The Italian nationality problem of the Austrian Empire. *Austrian History Yearbook* 3: 491–526.

Gribaudi, G. 1996. Images of the South. In D. Forgacs and R. Lumley, eds. *Italian Cultural Studies: An Introduction,* 72–101. Oxford: Oxford University Press.

Grigolli, G. 1997. *Viaggio nell'Autonomia.* Trento: Casa Editrice Publilux.

Gross, F. 1978. *Ethnics in a Borderland: An Inquiry into the Nature of Ethnicity and Reduction of Ethnic Tensions in a One-Time Genocide Area.* Westport, CT: Greenwood Press.

Hine, D. 1993. *Governing Italy: The Politics of Bargained Pluralism.* Oxford: Oxford University Press.

Il Piccolo. 1999. Tre depuratori sul Carso solveno finanziati dall'UE. 15 June: 23.

ISTAT. 1997. Conoscere l'Italia. Rome, Italy: Istituto Nazionale di Statistica.

Jurca, N., and V. Torkar. 1994. Nova Gorica ha meno di cinquant'anni. In A. Angelillo, A. Angelillo, and C. Menato, eds. *Città di Confine: Conversazione sul Futuro di Gorizia e Nova Gorica,* 41–57. Portogruaro, Italy: Nuova Dimensione Ediciclo.

Kaplan, D. 2000. Conflict and compromise among borderland identities in Northern Italy. *Tijdschrift voor Economische en Sociale Geografie* 91, no. 1: 44–60.

Kappus, E.-N. 1995. Unaltered history: The role and use of history in ethnic identity management among Slovenes and Italians in Trieste, Italy. *Anthropological Journal on European Culture* 4: 25–42.

Klein, G. 1986. *La Politica Linguistica del Fascismo.* Bologna: Il Mulino.

Klemencic, V., and M. Bufon. 1991. Geographic problems of frontier regions: The case of the Italo-Yugoslav border landscape. In D. Rumley and J. Minghi, eds. *The Geography of Border Landscapes,* 86–103. London: Routledge.

Lapidoth, R. 1996. *Autonomy: Flexible Solutions to Ethnic Conflicts.* Washington, DC: United States Institute of Peace Press.

Lepschy, A. L., et al. 1996. Linguistic variety in Italy. In C. Levy, ed. *Italian Regionalism: History, Identity and Politics,* 69–80. Oxford: Berg.

L'Intervista. 1999. Società bilingue ecco l'obiettivo. *Alto Adige,* 8 July.

Luverà, B. 1996. *Oltre il Confine.* Bologna: Il Mulino.

Manzin, M. 1999. Più lontano l'ingresso della Slovenia nell'Europa unita. *Il Piccolo,* 8 October.

Minghi, J. 1994. The impact of Slovenian independence on the Italo-Slovene borderland: An assessment of the first three years. In *Political Boundaries and Coexistence: Proceedings of the IGU Symposium.* Basel, Switzerland: Peter Lang.

Mlinar, Z. 1996. New states and open borders: Slovenia between the Balkans and the European Union. In L. O'Dowd and T. Wilson, eds. *Borders, Nations and States: Frontiers of Sovereignty in the New Europe,* 135–53. Aldershot: Avebury.

Mondaini, D. 1996. *Gente di Val Gardena.* Florence: Istituto di Studi per l'Alto Adige.

Parker, S. 1996. Political identities. In D. Forgacs and R. Lumley, eds. *Italian Cultural Studies: An Introduction*, 107–28. Oxford: Oxford University Press.

Petacco, A. 1999. *L'Esodo: La Tragedia Negata degli Italiani d'Istria, Dalmazia e Venezia Giulia*. Milan: Mondadori.

Putnam, R. 1993. *Making Democracy Work: Civic Traditions in Modern Italy*. Princeton, NJ: Princeton University Press.

Radin, F. 1995. Il gruppo etnico Italiano e la nuova democrazia: Aspetti giuridico-costiituzionali. In L. Bergnach, ed. *L'Istria Come Risorsa per Nuova Convivenze*, 77–91. Gorizia, Italy: Grafica Goriziana.

Radossi, A. 1999. Interreg Notizie: La cooperazione transfrontiera tra Friuli-Venezia Giulia, Austria e Slovenia. *Il Piccolo*, 15 October: 14.

Stella, A. 1987. *Trento, Bressanone, Trieste: Sette Secoli di Autonomia ai Confini d'Italia*. Turin: Utet Libreria.

———. 1997. *Storia dell'Autonomia Trentina*. Trento: Edizioni U.C.T.

Stranj, P. 1992. *The Submerged Community*. Trieste: Editoriale Stampa Triestina.

Unterberger, A. 1992. Case of South Tyrol. *Austria Today* 3: 1–5.

Vittur, F. 1994. *Una Vita, Una Scuola: Cenni di Storia della Scuola Ladina*. Bolzano: Istitut Pedagogich Ladin.

Chapter Eight

Common Spirit in the Upper Rhine Valley?

Susanne Eder and Martin Sandtner

The Regio TriRhena is situated on the southern end of the Upper Rhine Rift Valley. It is a cross-border region where the living conditions of the inhabitants are changing, although less abruptly and drastically than in other European border zones. The progressive integration of European Union member states on the macro scale and efforts to improve the inter-regional co-operation on the micro scale have had far-reaching effects. Here, cross-border projects have been initiated and developed on individual, business, and national levels during the past fifty years. The region, originally known by the name 'Regio Basiliensis' (named for Basel), has a total of 2.2 million inhabitants and stretches over parts of three countries: Germany's Southern Baden, with the city of Freiburg; France's Upper Alsace, with Mulhouse; and Northwest Switzerland, with Basel (see figure 8.1). Geographically, the area constitutes a unity: Low mountain ranges mark the boundaries of the fluvial plain of the Upper Rhine to the south, east, and west. Internal and external EU borders cross through the trina-tional region. Traditionally characterised by comparatively 'open' borders, the region experienced periods of severe breakdowns in commu-nication during and after the two world wars. In the early 1960s, however, remembering their common roots and destiny, the inhabitants began to re-establish cross-border co-operation, making everyday life easier. At first the co-operation was a result of private initiative, with regional govern-ment becoming involved at a later stage. Due to the many years of experi-ence the TriRhena has gained in cross-border co-operation, it may be seen as a model region. It is also a suitable research subject for the develop-ment and status of a regional identity across borders.

This chapter deals with aspects of transborder regional identity in the Regio TriRhena, discussing its historical and cultural development and

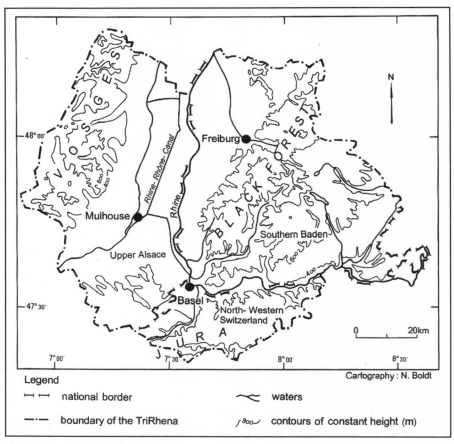

Figure 8.1.   Regio TriRhena

the efforts made to promote co-operation across the borders after World War II. The results of a recent empirical investigation (a telephone survey of 851 interviewees in the three parts of the Regio) are presented, examining the central question of a common transborder identity in the region and the sociocultural factors (language, culture, symbols, demographics) that influence it. The level of regional affinity is compared to the territorial identification with other spatial levels. The chapter concludes with a summary of the observations, placing them in a wider context.

HISTORICAL ASPECTS

Since the period of early Celtic settlement, the different parts of the Regio TriRhena seem to have experienced phases of similar historical development. The similarities promoted regional affinity; however, the region also lived through periods that discouraged regional identification, particularly as it was located in the intersection of different spheres of influence of several competing European powers. Military conflicts were frequent, and there were periods of development without any cultural exchange between the parts of the region. At times the Rhine River was seen as symbolically uniting the region, at times it was a dividing element between inimical forces. Today it functions as a symbol and namesake of the region, although over large distances it is a barrier for the inhabitants (for example, there are only four bridges in the densely populated area between Basel and Breisach near Freiburg). Nevertheless, the majority of the inhabitants see the river as a symbol unifying the regions bordering it. Table 8.1 shows the percentage of interviewees who see the Rhine, the region's history, and its culture as separating, as unifying, or as both. This is an important prerequisite for the establishment of regional identity: According to Paasi (1991: 239–40), a region is seen as a dynamic sociocultural unity that is constituted territorially *and* symbolically as signs and objects represent common values and are associated with social and psychological phenomena typical of the region and its inhabitants. However, a regional identity that only relies on symbols is unintentional and noncommittal and therefore easy to manipulate (Mai 1989: 13; Schuhbauer 1996: 31). The following sections about the area's history demonstrate the closeness of the separating and connecting elements.

Table 8.1. Perception of Various Symbols in the Regio TriRhena

		Symbol		
		Rhine	*History*	*Culture*
Northwest Switzerland	separation	20.4%	34.8%	12.4%
	connection	53.1	21.0	47.6
	both	18.0	17.1	15.7
Southern Baden	separation	27.2	39.7	10.2
	connection	46.1	24.6	66.8
	both	21.6	21.1	14.7
Upper Alsace	separation	32.6	26.4	19.8
	connection	47.7	34.1	49.0
	both	12.8	19.8	15.6
Total	separation	27.1	34.4	13.7
	connection	48.3	26.6	56.5
	both	18.0	19.7	15.2

Source: Author's investigations 1999.

Shared and Divided Settlement Area

Celtic settlement of the area in the third and second centuries B.C. stretched over both sides of the Rhine. With the founding of the Roman colony Augusta Raurica on the Rhine's southern bank near Basel in 43 B.C., the settlement area was divided. The Rhine became a fortified borderline between the Roman Empire to the south and the Celtic-Germanic territory to the north. The Romans soon expanded their territory into Southern Alsace and Southern Baden, integrating the entire region into the larger territory of *Germania Superior* (Wallner 1985: 13–14). The invasion by Alemannic tribes from the northeast in the third century A.D. divided the area once again, with the Rhine as the northern borderline of the Roman Empire. In the course of the fifth century, the Romans were finally driven out and the entire region became Alemannic. Up to the early Middle Ages, the area remained unified. To this day the frequent Alemannic place names found in all three parts of the Upper Rhine region provide evidence of this crucial period in the area's cultural development.

Disordered Territorial Situation in the Middle Ages

With the decision to divide his empire into smaller entities, or *Gaue*, Charlemagne, around 800 A.D., began a period of increasing territorial fragmentation. Several local and supra-regional dynasties competed for hegemony in the region. The House of Habsburg, with its origins in Southern Alsace, expanded its territory into today's Southern Baden and the Canton Aargau. At the same time, the city and the diocese of Basel strove for regional hegemony and extended their influence towards the south and southeast. The Swiss Confederation, too, tried to assert its influence on the region. In the fifteenth century, the city of Mulhouse sought protection from the House of Habsburg and joined the Swiss Confederation as a 'loosely attached' community (*Zugewandter Ort*) in 1515.

Armed conflicts and alliances reflected the power struggle in the region during the Middle Ages. By the late Middle Ages, the territorial fragmentation had led to a chaotic economic situation, different coinage systems impeding trade relations in the region. In 1387, twenty-eight regional sovereign leaders signed a coinage treaty. At least economically, the area was once again unified, and with the help of a common currency the Upper Rhine experienced an economic upswing.

Definition of Current Borders in Modern Times

The territorial borders shifted again after the Thirty Years' War, when Alsace (then part of the Habsburg Empire) fell to the French Kingdom, and the Swiss Confederation left the Holy Roman Empire of the German

Nation. The boundaries changed once more during the French Revolution and the Napoleonic Wars. It was only with the rise of modern nation-states following the Vienna Congress in 1814–1815 that the political map of this part of Europe was finally settled. The Rhine became the borderline between the Grand Duchy of Baden, the Swiss Confederation, and the Kingdom of France. Customs regulations made trading across the borders increasingly difficult. When Baden joined the German customs union in 1835, Swiss companies from Basel were able to obtain access to the large German market by founding branches in Southern Baden (Moehring 1992: 65). Industrialisation in Southern Baden and in Southern Alsace was to a considerable degree brought about by Swiss capital.

Alsace: Between German and French Influence

Alsace occupies a special position in the region. Starting in the seventeenth century, the area between the Vosges Mountains and the Rhine was part of the French Kingdom. The expansive freedom it initially enjoyed was replaced with stronger bonds to France after the French Revolution and the subsequent rise of centralism. In the following centuries, Alsace suffered because of its border position between two conflicting nations. During this period, its nationality changed four times. After the German-French War in 1870–1871 it became German for about fifty years, and after the First World War it was French. During the Second World War, Alsace was under German occupation for four years before finally rejoining France in 1945. Each changeover of power was accompanied by forceful attempts to 're-educate' the Alsatians at a cultural level, leading to increasing identity crises as inhabitants tried to define and redefine their identity from partly conflicting elements out of their German and French past and present.

The Role of History Today

Mirroring the ambivalent role of history in the region, perception of the past is rather varied (see table 8.1). Whereas in Northwest Switzerland and Southern Baden it is regarded as primarily separating, the majority of Upper Alsatians emphasise the common aspects of the region's history. This comes as a surprise insofar as the Alsatians have suffered most from the repeated changeovers of power in recent history.

ASPECTS OF CULTURE AND LANGUAGE

Culture

Culture or sociocultural peculiarities function as a background for social relations and are a precondition for territorial community spirit (Trouillet

1997: 8; Werlen 1993: 2–3; Hard 1987: 133–34). Cross-border contacts in the TriRhena were numerous in the past. German-speaking Switzerland, Alsace, and Southern Baden have the same cultural and linguistic Alemannic roots. This is reflected in the attitude of the inhabitants towards culture: The majority see *culture* as a unifying element in the Regio. Asked about the functions of the borders, only 19.6 percent of the interviewees said that the national boundaries within TriRhena were also cultural barriers. As a large number of the inhabitants obviously share a common concept of the cultural area's range, an important aspect for the formation of a shared regional identity is fulfilled. There are, however, some differences between the three adjoining areas. Only 13.3 percent of the inhabitants in Northwest Switzerland see their cultural area enclosed by the national border, whereas 18.1 percent of Southern Badeners and 26.7 percent of Alsatians feel that the borders of their cultural territories and their nationality correspond. Obviously the French concept of the *'Grande Nation'* as a clearly defined cultural unity exists at least for part of the Alsatian population. Accordingly, the percentage of those Alsatians who regard culture and tradition as separating elements in the trinational region is higher than in the two other groups.

Language

The spatial range of the Alemannic sphere of influence is still unclear today. Historical boundaries are set using the territorial borders of the diocese of Basel; linguistic boundaries are marked along the perimeter of the Low Alemannic dialect. Many inhabitants of the region, however, are not aware of these common grounds; they are not even aware of the common linguistic roots of their three similar dialects. Our investigation showed that 45.1 percent of the region's inhabitants consider 'language' a separating element in the trinational region. Only 33.2 percent of them regard it as a unifying element.

The Alsatian variant of the Alemannic dialect, *Elsässerdytsch,* lost its cultural importance during the successive periods of German and French rule. Since the last changeover of power, French has been made the official language, displacing *Elsässerdytsch* in everyday life. Although 93.4 percent of the population in Northwest Switzerland speaks the regional dialect, only about half of the interviewees in Alsace do. There exists a correlation between Alsatian dialect speakers and age: The younger the generation, the less dialect is spoken. Whereas it is spoken by 69.4 percent of the prewar generation, this is the case for only 57.7 percent of the postwar generation and for only 46.0 percent of people born after 1960.

For many Alsatians, the German dialect and culture of their past is an unpleasant reminder of the horrors experienced during the world wars, yet an increasing number of the population now see bilingualism as essential for living in a unified Europe (Trouillet 1997: 181). In this context it is interesting to note that, according to our investigation, many Alsatians (38 percent) regard language as a unifying element for the Regio Tri-Rhena. This apparent inconsistency is symptomatic of the inner cultural conflict many Alsatians have inherited from their German and French past.

Bilingualism (German-French) is very common in the Regio as a whole. About half of the region's inhabitants (49.5 percent) speak the language of their neighbours, and an additional 20.3 percent can understand it. This means that 69.8 percent possess an important requirement for regional identification: the ability to communicate with the region's inhabitants (Trouillet 1997: 16–17; Essig 1994: 48). It is worth noting that in Upper Alsace and Northwest Switzerland about two-thirds of the population can speak their neighbours' language, a result of both the Swiss school system (French as first foreign language) and the history of Alsace. In Southern Baden only 34.2 percent claim to have good command of French, but here, too, a majority of 55.7 percent are able to understand it.

The ability to speak the language of one's neighbours has significant effects on cross-border activities and personal contacts. There is a clear interrelation between bilingualism and cross-border activities: Bilingual persons are involved in a greater number of cross-border activities than people who cannot understand their neighbours' language. As is to be expected, this is true especially for the Alsatians. The same applies to cross-border contacts in the Regio: Bilingual speakers have more contacts in the region than the average inhabitant. Particularly the Alsatians fit into this category. There is, however, no significant correlation between bilingualism and cross-border regional affinity in the Regio. Only bilingual Alsatians are clearly underrepresented in the group 'no regional affinity'.

INTERCONNECTIONS IN THE EVERYDAY LIFE OF THE BORDER REGION'S CITIZENS

Cross-Border Activities Induced by Economic Gradients

Not only political and administrative systems but also national economies converge in border zones. Boundaries can thus be seen as lines of economic discontinuity. Differences between the national economic systems result in economic gradients along the borders, stimulating cross-border activity. These interconnections in the fields of working, shopping, and living are illustrated in figure 8.2.

At the interregional level, the job market in Northwest Switzerland is the most favourable. It has the lowest unemployment rate and the highest wages. Numerous cross-border commuters have been able to profit from this situation. In 1994, 29,900 Southern Alsatians and 17,200 Southern Badeners daily crossed the borders to work in Northwest Switzerland, making up 15 percent of all employees there. The commuter movement from Southern Alsace to Southern Baden, involving 5,100 employees, is also significant. Obviously, the economic differences between Switzerland, Germany, and France trigger massive cross-border commuter movements.

The agricultural situation and prevailing agricultural policies in Switzerland lead to higher food prices than in the neighbouring EU member states of Germany and France. As a consequence, Germany and France benefit from the lively shopping tourism of the Swiss. The concentration of shopping centres and malls on foreign ground in the vicinity of Basel, as well as a comparatively high percentage of employees in the retail trade

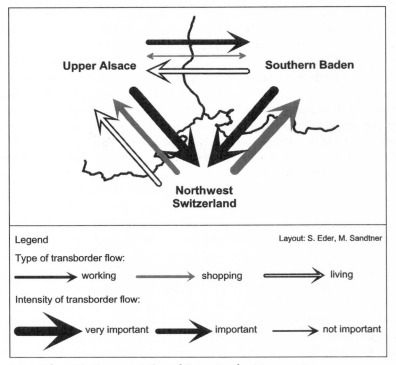

Figure 8.2. Schematic Representation of Cross-Border Movements

in Southern Alsace and Southern Baden, particularly in areas close to the Swiss border, are evidence of the cross-border shopping flux. For Northwest Switzerland, shopping tourism results in a loss of purchasing power on the order of 126.4 million Swiss francs (CHF) for the food sector in 1991. The losses are, however, partially compensated for by a positive balance of 70.4 million CHF in the non-food sector (Füeg 1991: 46). At the individual level, rather frequent cross-border shopping activities by the inhabitants of all parts of the Regio can be observed (see table 8.2): Approximately one-third of them take the opportunity of shopping beyond the border at least once a month. Some 27.7 percent of the Southern Badeners, 33.1 percent of the Upper Alsatians, and 34.6 percent of the Northwest Swiss said they would never go shopping beyond the borders.

Real estate prices are significantly lower in rural Southern Alsace than in Southern Baden or Northwest Switzerland. Since 1993, with the realisation of the freedom of movement between EU member states, Germans have been able to benefit from the differences in real estate prices, taking up residence in the cheaper Alsace. Since 1998, the Swiss also can obtain a residential permit for France. In Alsatian communities close to the centres of Freiburg and Basel, the percentage of German and Swiss residents has reached 5 percent or more. At present, these rural communities are experiencing processes of counterurbanisation, induced specifically by urban newcomers from beyond the borders.

It can be said that the population of TriRhena benefits from the economic differences among the three nations in the region. The national boundaries subdividing the region influence cross-border movements in different ways: Whereas the boundaries within the EU no longer impose any restraints, the Swiss border is still a confining factor in many respects. To date, agreement has only been reached on a partial freedom of movement. The bilateral treaties between Switzerland and the EU, at present

Table 8.2. Cross-Border Activities in the Regio TriRhena

		Activity		
		Shopping	*Recreation/gastronomy*	*Culture*
Northwest Switzerland	at least once a month	31.6%	25.9%	10.9%
	never	34.6	28.1	57.4
Southern Baden	at least once a month	38.7	23.3	12.7
	never	27.7	37.9	49.3
Upper Alsace	at least once a month	37.0	29.6	21.6
	never	33.1	28.3	42.7

Source: Author's investigations 1999.

being ratified and probably in force by 2001, are expected to bring greater freedom to the region, intensifying cross-border interconnections.

Other Cross-Border Activities and Personal Contacts

People visit the foreign parts of the Regio not only to benefit from the economic gradients along the borders but also to take advantage of the recreational potential and gastronomy. They are not so much interested in the cultural events there. However, a relatively high percentage of Upper Alsatians enjoy cultural events beyond the border at least once a month. More than half of cross-border activities are directed at both neighbouring countries. The Northwest Swiss prefer Southern Baden to Alsace, and the Southern Badeners favour Northwest Switzerland. These preferences may be explained by language barriers that exist despite the above-mentioned proficiency in the neighbours' tongue. Upper Alsatians visit Northwest Switzerland more often than Southern Baden, which may be due to the regional dominance of the centre of Basel and the high percentage of Alsatian cross-border commuters.

Friendships or acquaintances beyond the border are cultivated by half of the region's inhabitants, differences among the three parts not being significant. At least 20 percent have relatives beyond the border, half of whom are visited regularly.

CROSS-BORDER CO-OPERATION IN THE POSTWAR ERA AND INTERCONNECTIONS IN THE REGIONAL ECONOMY

The Second World War put a stop to cross-border relations in the region. France and Germany were war-time enemies; Alsace was under German siege; and Switzerland, although neutral, had to protect its frontiers against an impending German invasion. Cross-border contacts were impossible during the war and the first few years thereafter. Since the 1960s, however, a close neighbourly co-operation on the political-institutional level has developed that today is regarded as exemplary in Europe (Speiser 1993: 35). The traditionally strong regional interconnections of enterprise structures have intensified once again.

The Regional Association Regio Basiliensis as an Impulse for Cross-Border Co-operation

Reflecting the local importance given to a common background, the Regio Basiliensis was founded mainly on the initiative of private Swiss businesspeople in 1963. The association aimed to 'contribute to the conceptu-alization and promotion of the economic, political and cultural development of the region' (Speiser 1993: 31). The perimeter of the region concerned corresponded approximately to the area of today's Regio TriRhena (see figure 8.1). Similar associations were founded in the other parts of the region: Regio du Haut-Rhin in 1965 and Freiburger Regio-Gesellschaft in 1985. The private initiative aroused much interest in Europe. As early as 1965, an international 'Regio' planning congress was held, at which the guidelines for a 'Europe of Regions' were formulated, following the example of today's TriRhena. Since 1971, experts and repre-sentatives of the three regional administrations have met regularly at con-ferences (Speiser 1993: 30–36).

Political Institutions

In 1975, informal co-operation at the political level was given a formal conference structure, known today as the *Deutsch-französisch-schweizerische Oberrheinkonferenz*. Biennial conferences with representatives from all three border nations have been held regularly since 1988. An important step was taken towards cross-border co-operation with the signing of the Karlsruhe Treaty by Germany, France, Switzerland, and Luxembourg in 1996. The treaty made it possible for communities and regional adminis-trative bodies to form cross-border societies with the particular aim of solv-ing problems at a local level.

Most Recent Instrument of Co-operation: The Council of the Regio TriRhena

Over the years, the number of cross-border institutions and societies has grown, their individual territorial range differing greatly. One such organ-isation is the Council of the Regio TriRhena, founded in 1995 on the ini-tiative of the three previously mentioned Regio societies. The council functions as a network of cities, communities, regional administrative bod-ies, business associations, and universities, concentrating and co-ordinat-ing efforts in regional and cross-border co-operation and representing common interests. In addition, the council has set the goal of bringing the Regio concept to the everyday citizen, stimulating a community feel-ing across borders. The name *Regio TriRhena* consciously signifies the uni-fying element of the Rhine in the region. Obviously the marketing strategies for the region have already been successful: Whereas a similar study in 1987 revealed still significant differences for the spatial Regio con-cept in the three parts of the region (Fichtner 1988: 99), there are no more differences today. Asked to make spontaneous associations with the term *Regio*, more than half of the interviewees' answers can be considered 'appropriate' reflections of the Regio TriRhena (55.1 percent), including ideas like 'common cultural area' and 'living together across the borders' or statements referring to the institutionalised Regio. A shared territorial concept and concurring space-related attitudes promote the formation of a common regional spirit (Weichhart 1990: 20, 92; Blotevogel, Heinritz, and Popp 1989: 73).

Of the persons interviewed, 27.7 percent associate the term *Regio* with the immediate surroundings of Basel or with only a limited area of one of the three countries bordering the Upper Rhine. Such associations are significantly most frequent in Southern Baden (χ^2 = 12.53, p = 0.002). The most plausible explanation is that the term *Regio* is ambiguous, not only denoting the cross-border region but also referring, for example, to the public transport system of Freiburg and an economic area in the German part of the region. This example confirms the assumption that the concept 'region' can easily be manipulated by marketing strategies (Schuhbauer 1996: 31) as it is not clearly defined and, in this case, TriRhena is not an authentic, administrative area.

Promotion of Cross-Border Projects

The Regio TriRhena, like other cross-border institutions, deals with problems affecting more than one of the region's neighbouring countries. Examples of successful projects are the establishment of information centres for cross-border problems, conceptualisation of a landscape design for the entire Upper Rhine area (Regionalverband Südlicher Oberrhein 1998), and the realisation of the first regional cross-border railway line running from Mulhouse via Basel City to smaller towns farther up the Rhine. Many of the cross-border projects would not have been initiated without the financial support of the European Union INTERREG programmes (Lezzi 1994: 77–78). Despite positive developments on the European home market, border zones have not benefited structurally to the same extent, with the consequence that cross-border projects tend to focus on improving structural aspects of the border zone. Projects along the external and internal EU borders have been financially supported by the EU since 1990. In particular, during the second phase of the program (INTERREG II, 1994–1999) the Upper Rhine region benefited from seventy-three cross-border projects and funds of about 50 million Euros.

Evaluation of Co-operation in the TriRhena

Although the intensity of cross-border co-operation is exemplary, the flow of mutual information and the co-ordination of projects is still unsatisfactory. There is neither a democratically legitimised representative body of the border region's population, nor can the TriRhena dispose of its own budget. The projects are currently financed by communal, regional, national, or supranational administrative bodies. Experience has shown that until the cross-border agencies are given statutory sovereign rights and responsibilities, they will not be able to do much more than co-ordinate projects. In particular, nationally differing levels of administrative decision-making powers make the realisation of projects extremely difficult and time-consuming. When it comes to the promotion of business, decisions are often influenced more by each area's gain than by the region's common interests.

Interrelations at the Entrepreneurial Level

Opening branches and investing in business on the other side of the border has a long tradition in the region, in particular for Swiss enterprises (see chapter 2). In the postwar period, interrelations between businesses were intensified. Forty percent of the industry in Alsace is controlled by non-French companies, mainly Swiss and German. Alsace today is by far the most international French region, at the same time boasting the second highest gross national product per capita (Kleinschmager 1999: 6). Thanks to its active contact with the international business scene, the province has escaped the fate of other old industrial regions. However, some consider its dependence on foreign business problematic.

THE REGIO TRIRHENA AS A LEVEL
OF SPATIAL IDENTIFICATION

The examples of the Regio's history, culture, everyday life, and recent institutional efforts to promote the idea of a shared territorial concept lead to the question of whether there exists a 'common spirit' among the people. Many of the theoretically demanded preconditions for the formation of a regional identity are present in the Regio TriRhena: a majority of the inhabitants are able to communicate with their neighbours because of widespread bilingualism. Common linguistic, historical, and cultural roots, also, are important conditions for a territorial community spirit. But events of the twentieth century have also caused antipathies that are only slowly disappearing. The frequency and intensity of the partly economically motivated contacts across the borders produce a certain proximity among the region's inhabitants. According to Allport's contact hypothesis, however, these do not necessarily lead to improved relationships among the people: The circumstances of that contact are crucial; a competitive situation has the tendency to aggravate mutual prejudices (Allport 1958).

Obviously, a transborder regional identity is not homogeneously spread throughout the Regio. More than half of the Northwest Swiss do not show any attachment to the TriRhena, and the same is true for 39 percent of Southern Badeners and 42 percent of Alsatians. On the other hand, transborder regional affinity is comparatively strong or very strong in Northwest Switzerland (28.2 percent). The same goes for Southern Baden (30.2 percent) but not for the French (only 19.7 percent). The Northwest Swiss obviously are divided into a large group that shows no interest in cross-border communication and a smaller group that attaches much importance to the relationship with foreign neighbours. Among the latter are the 'Regio-activists', who provide an important impetus for the TriRhena.

Spatial Scales of Identification

To examine the significance of different spatial scales of identification, the interviewees were asked to indicate which territorial level—Europe, Regio TriRhena, state, national part of the region, or other—was most important to them. Figure 8.3 shows the significance of the various scales of identification for the region's inhabitants, differentiated according to the three national parts.

Whereas the national level plays the most important role in Switzerland, it takes only third place in Southern Baden. This phenomenon can be explained by the traumatic aftermath of recent history, which impedes an identification with the German nation. For the Southern Badeners, the identification with Europe has already become most important; German pro-European politics in the past decades obviously have been successful. The same is true for France. Here the European level is second to national identification and, compared to the Germans and the Swiss, French identification with Europe is the most pronounced. Surprising is the number of Northwest Swiss who identify themselves with Europe, considering the fact that Switzerland voted against joining the European Economic Area (EEA) in a referendum in 1992. The pro-European attitude is certainly to be seen as an exceptional feature of the border region.

The significance of the level 'national part in the region' varies. Whereas its prime importance for Southern Badeners and Alsatians suggests that it functions as a substitute for, or antithesis to, the national level here, it is relatively insignificant to the Northwest Swiss. That may be so because the territorial concept 'Northwest Switzerland' is not historically evolved but was only recently *artificially* proposed to create a single, uni-

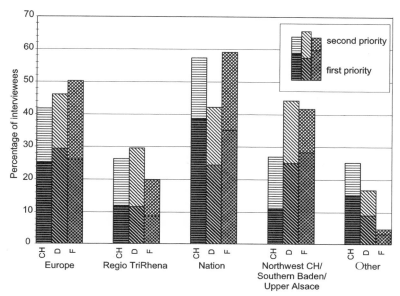

Figure 8.3. Identification with Different Spatial Levels

Source: Author's investigations 1999.

fied economic area with Basel as its centre. For the Swiss the cantonal level (listed under 'other') has priority.

The Regio TriRhena appears to be of the least significance for its inhabitants. Nevertheless, at least 11 percent of the Southern Badeners and Northwest Swiss attach priority to the term Regio-inhabitant, and it is the second most important level for an even larger number. In Upper Alsace, the Regio obviously has not yet become deeply rooted in the inhabitants' consciousness.

Sociodemographic Factors

The influence of the variables *age, sex,* and *size of place of residence* on regional identity could not be proven scientifically. The comparison of the different spatial scales of identification with educational level reveals some clear tendencies. Whereas the levels 'nation' and 'national part of the region' are the most important levels of identification for the less educated, the importance of the European level and the TriRhena increases with educational status. Interview partners with the highest level of education attach less importance to the Regio, preferring other terms, like *cosmopolitan.* As regional identity originates from identification with a territorially defined social system (Füchtner 1996: 72; Mai 1989: 12–14), it is not surprising that a regional identity is clearly more apparent for the region's natives than for newcomers. Only 38.9 percent of the natives show no regional attachment, in contrast to 48.6 percent of the newcomers.

Interestingly, only a minor correlation can be seen between cross-border activities and contacts on the one hand and regional affinity on the other. This phenomenon confirms the fact that many contacts, which may partly be economically motivated (e.g., shopping), do not necessarily lead to an intensified affinity with the cross-border area, which can be taken as verification of Allport's (1958) contact hypothesis.

CONCLUSION

This chapter shows that there is something like a transborder identity in the Regio TriRhena, at least for large parts of the border zone population. To the present day the facets of the region's varied history are mirrored in the attitudes of its inhabitants. Despite the phases of separate development, many of those interviewed consider the common grounds to be language and culture, which not only unite the region but also serve as a basis for fencing it off against the respective nation-states. This attitude influences their actions as well: Cross-border contacts and activities are part of everyday life. Yet the experience of war in recent history, which had a severe impact on the area of the Upper Rhine, is still alive. People still talk about an 'invisible wall' separating the German Southern Baden from its neighbours.

Both the intensification of co-operation on a regional and local level across the national borders and the marketing of the *Regio* concept have had a tangible effect on awareness patterns among the border zone population. The majority of the inhabitants have a clear association with the term *Regio;* the integrating character of the well-chosen symbolic namesake *Rhine* has certainly contributed to that consciousness. Yet cross-border projects of co-operation have not all been very successful until now, as the bickering over who is responsible for what in the trinational area has proved to be a hindrance to these efforts. If projects continue to not meet their goals, there is a danger that the population will grow tired of the co-ordination problems. Some of the interviewees' negative attitudes about the topic may be explained by the 'inuring effect'.

The study has revealed that at the spatial level, the border region Tri-Rhena plays only a subordinate role for territorial identity, identification with the state or with Europe being stronger. This may be explained by the fact that at the 'regional' level, TriRhena has to compete with the national parts of the region for feelings of affinity. This is especially evident in the case of Southern Baden and Alsace. Even in a region that can be seen as a single cultural area with a lot of common ground, the influence of some 150 years of nation-state dominance has left its mark.

This region, with its long-term experience in cross-border interrelations, may serve as an example for other border zones in Europe. Experience in TriRhena has shown that cross-border co-operation should take place at a low level, facilitating the realisation of projects by reducing the number of involved decision-making powers. Agreements like the Karlsruhe Treaty of 1996 guarantee the unrestricted and nation-state independent co-operation of cities and communities across borders. The promotion of projects by the EU (like the INTERREG programs) is an effective way of motivating regional decision makers to show more commitment.

The removal of the impeding effects of borders leads to an improvement of living conditions in the border zone and, as is the case in TriRhena, may transform individual, peripheral, rather isolated areas into an economically strong cross-border region with manifold international interrelations. To create transborder identity or a common regional spirit, the elimination of economic obstacles does not suffice. Use has to be made of marketing strategies, focusing for example on cultural common ground, the careful introduction of suitable symbols, and the promotion of active cultural exchange. In principle, this policy is being pursued in TriRhena. The experiences described here—if adjusted to local particularities—could be of benefit to unification processes in other border zones.

REFERENCES

Allport, G. 1958. *The Nature of Prejudice*. Garden City, NY: Anchor Books.

Blotevogel, H. H., G. Heinritz, and H. Popp. 1989. 'Regionalbewußtsein': Zum Stand der Diskussion um einen Stein des Anstoßes. *Geographische Zeitschrift* 77, no. 2: 65–88.

Essig, M. 1994. *Das Elsaß auf der Suche nach seiner Identität*. Munich: Eberhard.

Fichtner, U. 1988. *Grenzüberschreitende Verflechtungen und regionales Bewusstsein in der Regio*. Basel and Frankfurt am Main: Helbing und Lichtenhahn.

Füchtner, H. 1996. *Das Vaterlandssyndrom: Zur Sozialpsychologie von Nationalismus, Rechtsradikalismus und Fremdenhass*. Heidelberg: Asanger.

Füeg, R. 1991. *Zur Situation des Fachhandels in der Nordwestschweiz angesichts der europäischen Integration* (Studie im Auftrag des Gewerbeverband Basel-Stadt und des Kantonaler Gewerbeverband Basselland). Liestal, Switzerland: Haus des Gewerbes.

Hard, G. 1987. 'Bewußtseinsräume': Interpretationen zu geographischen Versuchen, regionales Bewusstsein zu erforschen. *Geographische Zeitschrift* 75: 127–48.

Kleinschmager, R. 1999. Das Elsass zwischen Entwicklung und Abhängigkeit. *Regio Basiliensis* 40, no. 1: 6–8.

Lezzi, M. 1994. *Raumordnungspolitik in europäischen Grenzregionen zwischen Konkurrenz und Zusammenarbeit: Untersuchungen an der EG-Aussengrenze Deutschland-Schweiz.* Zurich: Universität Zürich-Irchel, Geographisches Institut.

Mai, U. 1989. Gedanken über räumliche Identität. *Zeitschrift für Wirtschaftsgeographie* 33, nos. 1/2: 12–19.

Moehring, M. 1992. Lörrach und die Schweiz. *Stadtbuch Lörrach* 23: 51–78.

Paasi, A. 1991. Deconstructing regions: Notes on the scales of spacial life. *Environment and Planning A* 23: 239–56.

Regionalverband Südlicher Oberrhein, ed. 1998. *Regionales grenzüberschreitendes Freiraumkonzept Oberrhein.* Freiburg: Selbstverlag.

Schuhbauer, J. 1996. *Wirtschaftsbezogene Regionale Identität.* Mannheim: Selbstverlag des Geographischen Instituts.

Speiser, B. 1993. *Europa am Oberrhein: Der grenzüberschreitende Regionalismus am Beispiel der oberrheinischen Kooperation.* Basel and Frankfurt am Main: Helbing und Lichtenhahn.

Trouillet, B. 1997. *Das Elsass—Grenzland in Europa: Sprachen und Identitäten im Wandel.* Köln: Böhlau.

Wallner, E. M. 1985. *Dreieckland-Fibel.* Konstanz, Germany: Rosgarten.

Weichhart, P. 1990. *Raumbezogene Identität.* Stuttgart: Steiner.

Werlen, B. 1993. *Society, Action and Space: An Alternative Human Geography.* London: Routledge.

Chapter Nine

Urban Borderlands and the Politics of Place in Northern Ireland

Anna-Kaisa Kuusisto-Arponen

Since the outbreak of the current violent conflict (1969) in Northern Ireland, a large number of academic studies have been conducted on the reasons behind the violence and its effects. Geographers have been quite active in this field, but the studies have rarely focused on the basic concepts of geography, such as place and space, and their relation to the ethnic conflict in Northern Ireland. However, since the late 1980s research topics in the overall field of political geography have often focused on identities, borders and borderlands, and meaning of places and spaces. This trend can, to some extent, be found in Northern Irish studies (Boal and Livingstone 1983; Lee 1985; Douglas and Shirlow 1998; Graham 1998; Anderson and Shuttleworth 1998; O'Dowd 1998).

The seeds of the Northern Irish conflict were sown in the acts of resistance by the native Irish against becoming an English colony in the sixteenth century (Doumitt 1985). There have been many changes in the dynamics and the intensity of the conflict, but some of the basic problems have persisted since the beginning. Irish Catholics formed the majority of the population in the present-day area of Northern Ireland, but after English colonisation the demographic situation changed radically. Protestants began to dominate, not only in terms of population but also in political and economic life. The same territory was occupied by two mutually suspicious communities, one believing that its land had been usurped and the other fearing that its tenure was under constant threat. Territorial divisions began as early as the seventeenth century and have persisted until this day (Darby 1997). After the Republic of Ireland gained independence in 1921, Northern Ireland remained a part of the United Kingdom. The border that was laid down at the time became the main 'mental' divider between the two communities in Northern Ireland. However, the conflict-prone borderlands have not only emerged at the state border between Northern Ireland and the Republic of Ireland, but rather are continuously re-made and re-lived at the local level through divisions of urban space and conflict strictly related to the question of the legitimacy of the partition.

The main focus of this chapter is to illustrate the processes and experiences that characterise the various boundary-making practices in the Northern Irish borderlands. Here, the concept of 'borderland' refers not only to the actual border between the Republic of Ireland and Northern Ireland (see figure 9.1) but also to the boundaries and divisions that exist in the everyday urban (and rural) environments. By looking at the city of Derry/Londonderry,[1] this chapter seeks to show that two different traditions of collective identification exist in Northern Ireland, and that the construction of boundaries on various geographical scales plays a crucial role in the conflict as well as in any attempts to resolve it.

LOCAL TERRITORIALITY AND THE URBAN
CONTEXT IN NORTHERN IRELAND

Certain places and spaces are important to most human communities. People are physically and mentally attached to specific territories (Sack 1983, 1986). Places are also sites of people's everyday life practices: shopping, working, dwelling, and leisure time. These sites achieve their meanings through social interaction that turns everyday spaces into meaningful places.

The particular ways in which places are signified and territorially bound come to define the character of the local 'politics of place'. Generally, this can be seen as the set of communal practices in which images and sense of place are produced and reproduced. The politics of place typically includes attempts to reconstruct the physical or mental appearance of the territory. Therefore it is closely connected to the construction of collective identities and boundaries across various geographical scales.

To understand people's strong bonds to community and place in the Northern Irish context, it is crucial to be aware of the historical background of the two communities and their collective identities. Often the two communities are narrowly 'locked' into the categories of Catholic/Irish/nationalist and Protestant/British/unionist. However, the roots of each community lie in a multi- rather than a mono-cultural basis. As in the case of the Irish cultural nation, there is a need also to recognise Viking,

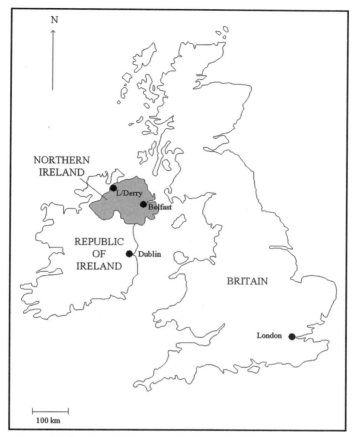

Figure 9.1.   Map of Ireland and L/Derry on Northern Irish Border

Norman, Scots, and Anglo-Irish contributions alongside those of the 'ancient' Celtic race (Kearney 1997).

The influence of English colonial rule in Ireland began in 1169. At the time, few English and Welsh colonists migrated to Ireland (Robinson 1984). The most dramatic change in Gaelic Ireland was experienced during the seventeenth-century Plantation, when colonists came from England, Wales, and Scotland. To a large extent they were Protestants. This Plantation introduced into Ireland, and in particular into Ulster, a community of 'strangers' who spoke a different language and had a different faith, as well as an alien culture and way of life (Darby 1997). Moreover, the native Catholic population was discriminated against and many were forced to move away from their ancestral lands to the fringes (Doumitt 1985).

The background of colonist Protestants was more heterogeneous than is often acknowledged. They came from different social classes, had migrated from various parts of the British Isles, and varied in their understanding of the Protestant faith, which took the form of Presbyterianism, Methodism, and the Church of Ireland. Not all Protestants were in favour of a British state or a British identity. For example, a group of middle-class Ulster Presbyterians in the eighteenth century were among the first to act in the republican project.

In general, however, Presbyterians were staunch loyalists. Even the segments of the wider Protestant community that attempted to forge a collective sense of Irishness (between 1770 and 1790) did so only for economic reasons. Their aim at the time was to assimilate with the indigenous majority (Catholics), but only as a means of gaining autonomy from England (Kearney 1997). During the eighteenth century it became obvious that a universalist version of Irish republicanism was a failure, and Ireland was to become the battlefield for two mutually exclusive and sectarian nationalisms.

The nineteenth century witnessed a growing separation between Ulster and the rest of Ireland. The effects of the Industrial Revolution in Ireland were mainly confined to the northern parts of the island, leading to closer industrial and commercial dependency of northern areas on Britain. The greater prosperity of the north, its economic structure, even its physical appearance all increased its alienation from the rest of Ireland (Darby 1997). The Home Rule campaign in the 1880s was very important for the future development of the (economically) divided island. In the Home Rule campaign some aspects of strict political division between nationalists and unionists surfaced for the first time.

The struggle for national independence came to an end with the passing of the Government of Ireland Act (1920), which created a separate Northern Irish government to rule the six counties in the North and led to the establishment of the new Irish Free State in the south in late 1921. Consequently, the actual border was laid down between the north and south of Ireland. The Anglo-Irish Treaty (1921) gave dominion status to the twenty-six counties of southern Ireland, while the six northernmost counties of Ulster remained part of the United Kingdom. One island was now divided into two separate territories. The boundary between south and north divided the Catholic Irish, but a number of Protestants found themselves living in the new Irish Free State, which was predominantly Catholic. Although Irish nationalists in the south had achieved one of their goals, an independent Ireland, this was not enough. It did not include the whole Irish nation and national territory.

DIFFERING SENSES OF PLACE BETWEEN
THE TWO COMMUNITIES

The two major communities in Northern Ireland have developed striking differences in their sense of 'place'. Generally, Irishness has been characterised through Gaelicism, Catholicism, and strong cultural nationalism. This definition totally excludes the Protestant community. Therefore, Protestants often define themselves foremost as not being Irish or Catholic and only secondarily as British. Moreover, unionist collective identity is based on being in opposition to Irish nationalism (Graham 1994; Connolly 1997). This has led to a situation in which Ireland became divided less by the actual border than by juxtaposition of an increasingly confident Irish identity alongside a confused and heavily qualified sense of Britishness (Graham 1997).

Different practices for defining one's community against the 'other' have affected the formation of a local sense of place. The sense of place is one result of the dialectical relation between community and place, whilst simultaneously defining this relationship. It is formed from the ways in which people experience representations of present and past landscapes, and it forms an important part of collective territorial identity and geographical understanding (Duffy 1997). In contrast, the 'sense of placelessness' refers to a lack of unifying narrative of place (Relph 1976). Relph (1976) describes 'placelessness' as both an environment without significant places and the underlying attitude that does not acknowledge significance in places. Although the Protestant community in Northern Ireland has communally significant places, the lack of a connecting sense of place has arguably created a situation in which the wider web of significant places does not exist. The Protestant community does not have a narrative acknowledging the significance of places in the same manner as does the Catholic community. In the Northern Irish context, the Catholic community seems to achieve a stronger sense of place, while Protestant community can be characterised by a certain sense of placelessness.

The Catholic community's sense of place fluently combines spatiality, history, and communal identity. Within the community, a strong connection between cultural traditions and history, as well as the iconography of cultural landscape, is emphasised (Kuusisto 1999). One of the most powerful 'tools' in the construction of a Catholic sense of place was the myth of Ireland's west. The West became the heart of Irish identity and was pictured as rural, wild, and primitive. In fact, this image of the West was in contradiction to the reality. The West was one of Ireland's poorest areas, and many people emigrated from there (Duffy 1997). However, the romanticised West contained the basic features of nation—national landscape, common heritage, native Irish people, Gaelic language, and Irish place—and therefore the myths surrounding it remained unchanged, although everyday life in the West of Ireland was much harder than was pictured.

In the Catholic community's understanding of place, nativeness and motherland are celebrated, while the Protestant community bases its understanding of place on a more political definition. By politically defining the boundaries of the island of Ireland (and especially its northern parts), Protestants could avoid engaging with the contested cultural definitions of the Catholic community. For some Protestants, Northern Ireland still is more a target of conquest than a socially and culturally constructed entity (Kuusisto 1999). The lack of a confident sense of place among the Protestant community emphasises this fact. The absence of strong and coherent representative landscape, steadfast myths or traditions, and cultural features has historically created problems in the construction of a collective Protestant identity.[2] Moreover, relations between place and the local Protestant communities appear 'confused' as well, indicating that the narrative from the Ulster Plantation until the present day has not created a coherent sense of place for the Protestant community. Whereas for Protestants the locality (for example, single-identity housing estate) may appear as a base for politically grounded opposition, for Catholics the locality is a site for political resistance and a nurturing site of collective cultural identity and Irishness.

L/DERRY ON THE BORDER BETWEEN TWO IRELANDS

The city of L/Derry is located on the northwest border between Northern Ireland and the Republic of Ireland. Being located on the 'frontier zone' has its own difficulties, but in addition the city is divided internally by many local, national, physical, mental, political, economic, social, cultural, and religious boundaries. It can be argued that the cityscape of L/Derry is formed from a mosaic of borderlands. This combination makes up a challenging social environment. The city centre is located not more than ten kilometres away from the border, which nowadays is open to traffic and not guarded by the security forces as it was during the high-intensity years of the conflict. Currently the state border is subject to much daily crossing as many people from the Republic of Ireland commute to work in Northern Ireland. Lower fuel prices also attract motorists from Northern Ireland to fill their tanks on the Irish side of the border. Furthermore, various institutional border-crossing projects and new cross-border bodies have been set up since the implementation of the Good Friday Agreement.

However, although crossing the national boundary has become part of the everyday, this appears to have no direct relation to the persisting territoriality on the local neighbourhood level. The state boundary is most often crossed for economic reasons, whether for cheaper petrol or as a result of EU funding for a youth program that may require a cross-border element. Boundary crossing as a learning experience or for better mutual respect is still quite rare, even though this is the pronounced goal of much national policy making.

In the 1940s and 1950s, when the political violence between the two communities had not yet reached its peak, there were many cross-border activities among the Northern Irish borderlanders. Many old people from L/Derry tell stories about going to the same dances with people from the South and North, dating, and having what they thought to be lifelong friendships across the border. Although later on it became almost impossible to sustain the relationships because of the security operations at the state border, the times of sharing and friendships are remembered by many on both sides of the national borderline.

The current peace process has again changed L/Derry's situation on the border from disadvantageous, strictly guarded borderline to an opportunity. Although this opportunity is as yet mainly seen in economic terms, L/Derry has good prospects to become one of the flagships of cross-border activity in Ireland. The major challenge for the institutional and nongovernmental actors involved is to be able to create an environment supportive of overcoming the dividing legacies of the past.

THE URBAN LANDSCAPE OF TERRITORIALITY

It is widely recognised that the role of territoriality in the Northern Irish conflict is essential (Boal 1974; Anderson and Shuttleworth 1998; Graham 1998; O'Dowd 1998). People have collectively identified themselves through local-level territories in much the same manner as they did on the state level during the nineteenth and early twentieth centuries. A collective defence of local territory gives people security, and by collectively identifying with a specific micro-community and territory, people can better cope with the troubles that they have to face as a result of living in a society in conflict (Kuusisto 1998). Many social, economic, political, and cultural practices are divided along neighbourhood boundaries. In the absence of a consensus over the place of Northern Ireland as a whole, a strong politics of place has become characteristic of local communities and their everyday life.

Most people in Northern Ireland live the segregated reality both consciously and unconsciously. The majority of working-class Protestants and Catholics live in segregated single-identity housing estates (70 percent or more Catholic or Protestant), as do some of their middle-class counterparts. On average, 50 percent of the total population in Northern Ireland lives in areas that are 90 percent or more Catholic or Protestant (Smyth 1996). However, the option of mixed housing seems to appeal to people with an economically secure background. In these cases, mixing seems to offer no threat, but most often mixing would be perceived as a personal security threat, especially by the working-class communities. Calculations based on 1991 census data (religion by local governmental districts and wards) in the city of L/Derry indicate that there are twenty Catholic single-identity housing estates, four Protestant single-identity estates, and six mixed estates in the city. Territorial order within these segregated estates is strict, and often boundaries are nonpermeable. Sometimes territorial order is contested by people within one community, and in fact these intracommunal clashes have increased since the cease-fires, but most confrontations take place between the two communities. Territoriality has created a cityscape of borderlands, where numerous visible and invisible borders define the essence of the urban space.

Segregated housing is not the only marker of territoriality and politics of place embedded in Northern Ireland. The urban space in Northern Ireland has for a long time been an indicator of territorial order and belonging. Symbolism in urban landscapes emphasises territoriality and power over the specific place. Symbols such as painted curbstones, national flags, murals, political graffiti, banners, and posters are essential parts of 'banal nationalism' (Billig 1995) (see figures 9.2 and 9.3). 'Banal' in this context refers to symbolism and nationalistic practices taking place in everyday life, not strictly to Billig's idea of so-called forgotten and unconscious ways of 'flagging' the nation.

Billig (1995) also argues that nationalism is an endemic condition, emphasising the fact that nationalistic ideology is not pushed aside after the national context and the nation are defined but continues to exist within the nation. In the context where 'active' nationalism does not exist or nationalism has become a structural part of everyday life, these signs of banal nationalism are often unacknowledged. However, the banal signs of nationalism are essential in the reproduction of national identity and national institutional structures. In Northern Ireland, the bloody and violent forms of nationalism have not totally vanished, and the marking of one's territory with nationalistic symbols is common. The two communi-

Figure 9.2.   Bloody Sunday Memorial Mural
Photo by author.

ties manifest themselves in (banal) nationalistic terms through language, clothing, and sports. Calling the 'others' 'Jaffas' or wearing a Celtic football shirt, supporting the Rangers or taking part in Loyal Orders' marches, clearly illustrate banal nationalism in Northern Irish society.[3] Signs, habits, and loyalties (on both sides) are part of the everyday nationalistic landscape, although sometimes their essence as reproducers of nationalistic thinking among communities is not consciously proclaimed (Kuusisto 2001).

Mental segregation is an interrelated part of the construction of places in Northern Ireland. For example, the urban micro-context of L/Derry is divided by many more mental than physical boundaries. Through differ-

Figure 9.3.   Political Graffiti in Protestant Estate
Photo by author.

ent institutions, such as schools and churches, stereotypical images of and thinking about the 'other' are diffused among the members of the community. These 'inherited' loyalties are deeply rooted, and changing them is extremely difficult because most people have never been offered any other mode of thinking. The mental divisions of the city of L/Derry are deeply rooted in events of legendary proportions, such as the Siege of Derry in 1689 and Bloody Sunday in 1972, as well as in symbols of territoriality. These events of the past give special meaning to certain parts of the city, and most important, these meanings are passed down to future generations.

A good illustration of L/Derry's mental segregation and the city's banal borderlands is the 'no-go areas' held by both communities. Usually these no-go areas are occupied by the 'opposing' community, and the images that one's own community attaches to this area are negative. In other words, Catholics from a Bogside housing estate would most likely not go to the Protestant Irish Street estate, and vice versa. The Catholic community's knowledge of the areas of Waterside (a perceived Protestant area) and Fountain (the last Protestant enclave in Cityside) is almost nonexistent; those areas are defined as belonging to the Protestant part of the city and are no-go areas for Catholics. As a Catholic person might argue, 'Those are the areas where "they" [Protestants] live. There is nothing we need or want to see'. Obviously, similar perceptions about the Catholic community and their territories also flourish within the Protestant community. Stereotypes about the 'other' community and the mental boundaries divide Northern Irish society even more than segregated housing or the actual physical peace lines and walls.

The stereotypical thinking of the two communities stresses that people are living on different housing estates, voting for political parties along community lines, having trouble accepting mixed marriages, enrolling their children in segregated schools, reading different newspapers, playing different sports, and socialising among their own kind. Although this is too often an apt description of the situation, a growing 'middle ground' is gradually emerging. In this 'category' people are at least in some ways more tolerant towards the differences in society. Political support for those in the middle is channelled through parties in the centre such as the Alliance Party of Northern Ireland (APNI), the Worker's Party (WP), and the Northern Ireland Women's Coalition (NIWC). Poole (1997), however, argues that although a person may exhibit a few de-ethnicised characteristics, such as sending one's children to an integrated school or supporting cross-community political parties, people still tend to identify more strongly with one side than the other. Therefore, two major ethnic groups remain in Northern Ireland (Poole 1997), but the degree to which people support the shared collective values within the community varies.

All of the visible and invisible, conscious and unconscious ways to express one's collective identity and territorial attachment to a specific place have created a great number of mutually exclusive boundaries between the communities. Such boundaries are rarely crossed in a positive and constructive manner. Segregated everyday practices signify a territorial order that forces people to live and act in a particular way. However, territoriality should be seen as one form of culture that human communities have developed from commonly accepted values, rules, norms, morals, and knowledge available at each respective time and context. This makes territoriality a social construct that is contextual and alterable.

Local territorial politics in Northern Ireland is about power, control, and influence. It is formed within the social and spatial practices of the community, and its two primary functions are (1) creating a feeling of safety within the community and (2) (re)producing the division between 'us' and 'them', 'friend' and 'enemy', for example, between Catholic and Protestant communities. Painter (1995), when referring to states' roles as territorial agents, argues that some discourses are being naturalised in the course of time, meaning that the prevailing spatial order is viewed as 'this is the way it has always been' and thus, for example, the idea of states as the only territorial agents persisted rather fixed for centuries. 'Naturalisation' has also taken place in the discourse of local territorial politics in Northern Ireland. On some occasions it may seem that local territoriality is an eternal phenomenon and a permanent part of communities; however, these matters are social and can be challenged and changed.

TOWARDS A BREACHING OF THE BOUNDARIES

'Crossing borders', 'sharing space', 'place', and 'community' have been the catchwords in Northern Irish politics since the peace process began, but actually the gap between pursuing and achieving these political goals has become wider since the Belfast Agreement of 1998. Moreover, a promising beginning to multiparty negotiations seems to have resulted in deadlocked situations time after time because of the historical disagreements between the communities. A new Northern Irish Assembly was formed and then suspended two months later in February 2000, only to be reconvened by May. Similar swings of the pendulum have been experienced throughout the peace process. In national politics summer 2001 witnessed serious setbacks, which were further escalated by the resignation of the first minister of the Northern Irish Assembly, David Trimble, and rioting in many localities. The life cycle of the Northern Irish peace process illustrates how after each political battle and compromise the time of settlement has been very short lived because the dark shadows of the next crisis are already lurking in the background. Nonetheless, it is clear that the peace process established a new era in the history of the Northern Irish conflict. Political agreement has facilitated contacts across local community boundaries. These new channels of communication will hopefully diminish the role of violently communicated boundaries and make boundaries between the communities more permeable. However, it is important not to take too technocratic a view. Theoretically, it may seem easy to 'slide' from a strong territorial definition of a community's national or local space to a weak one and simultaneously weaken the role of violently communicated territorial identities. Although it is argued that these changes are possible, they should not be presented as the only right solution. In all cases, the coercive character of reforms should be abandoned. As seen many times during the Northern Irish conflict, coercion has generated more resistance and violence than mutual understanding and peace.

The peace process and the Belfast Agreement have challenged the commonly accepted politics of place. Strict territorial order in the communities does not fit within the framework of a pluralist and shared society, which these agreements hope to achieve. In contemporary Northern Ireland, cultural pluralism as a model of mutual respect for different cultural heritage and traditions can be seen as a goal, at least on paper (*Belfast Agreement* 1998). Whatever the measures to achieve these goals, by redressing grievances derived from segregation and communal disorder, the original causes will not disappear on their own. A solution to the Northern Irish problem must create conditions that marginalise the coercive politics of territorial control and resistance (O'Dowd 1998).

To understand the dynamics of conflict and 'peacemaking' in Northern Ireland, it is not enough to analyse the politics of place on the local scale only. International agents, such as the European Union, the United States, and even individuals such as U.S. Senator George Mitchell, have made great contributions to political mediation in Northern Ireland. In conflict resolution, the involvement of external agents sometimes generates new ideas for an end to conflict. Although external agents may have a role, it should be remembered that the most drastic and difficult work is done by the people living in the troubled area.

Since the Anglo-Irish Agreement (1985), cross-border co-operation between the British and Irish governments on Northern Ireland issues has continuously increased. In 1986, a new dimension to these relations was introduced when the two governments established the International Fund for Ireland, made possible by international donors: the USA, the EU, Canada, and New Zealand (International Fund for Ireland 1999). The fund's objectives challenged the historical divisions in Northern Irish society and tried to create economic and social conditions for better community development. The geographical target area was defined to include the whole of Northern Ireland and the six border counties in the Republic of Ireland.

The International Fund for Ireland can be seen as a first major international economic involvement in the Northern Irish conflict. For the first time, at the international level, there was official support for developments to lead to a lasting peace in Northern Ireland. Simultaneously, the support for economic, social, and community development included a new politics of place. To obtain funding, people had to begin to think differently about each other and to become more open to cross-border activities. International funding was seen as a symbol of the outside world investing in the future of Northern Ireland. This was the first wave of international funding to come to Northern Ireland. Moreover, international involvement challenged the reality of a divided Ireland. Later on, other funding bodies such as the EU structural funds made their way to the very core of the Northern Irish peace process.

The European Special Support Programme for Peace and Reconciliation in Northern Ireland and the border counties of the Republic of Ireland was founded by the EU after the paramilitary cease-fire of 1994 (*European Programme* 1999). The European Union Peace Fund gets its contributions from four EU structural funds (Berg 1995). The Peace Package was launched because the EU wanted to create an impetus for resolving the conflict. It was acknowledged that Northern Ireland had serious problems in unemployment and suffered from economic underdevelopment due to long-lasting conflict.

European Union funding has enabled a number of community projects to be created. On the one hand, these projects support economic growth and welfare within communities; on the other hand, they encourage new levels of communication and co-operation between the communities. Again, external 'forces' have played their part in the game of local politics of place in Northern Ireland. In the field of politics of place, old segregative structures are challenged by new, flexible models. However, in the present situation both structures exist concurrently. The years of conflict have created an environment of distrust, in which intimidation, rumours, and violence have become typical. Economic inequalities and discrimination have exacerbated this environment of apprehension. The 'fields of distrust' have allowed bounded spaces and territoriality to take root. Therefore, breaking the cycle of distrust and strong categorising through community-based projects, whether single-identity or cross-community focused, is supported in the policies of external funding bodies. In this way the first tentative steps towards a successfully shared Northern Ireland are being taken. The role of external funding bodies and their policies should not be underestimated. However, these policies have had to find support in a particularly difficult and tension-laden environment. The question of the effectiveness of international involvement and the ambience in which the international and local scale of place politics confront each other should also be considered.

SOFTENING THE SYMBOLISM OF THE MARCHES

Living in the borderlands, whether national or local, is not always pleasant. One's territory and communal identity are constantly being challenged. The symbolism of various activities helps to reify existing divisions, and so softening their divisiveness has become an objective of the new peace process. This is best demonstrated in light of the marches. Over 3,500 marches take place annually in Northern Ireland. Although not all of them are about the Protestant-versus-Catholic division, most are either loyalist (2,584 in 1998) or nationalist (216 in 1998) (Dunn 1999). Most of the parades pass off without any problems, but in several locations the marching provokes considerable opposition and violence. In late 1997 the Independent Parades Commission was created to negotiate with the conflicting parties, those who want to march and those who oppose marching. The Parades Commission has the power to reroute or impose restrictions on the most controversial parades. The marching issue was widely discussed not only on a political level but also on a local level during the 1990s. Progress on this very sensitive issue has been slow; however, recent announcements from the Apprentice Boys of Derry and Bogside Residents' Group (BRG) indicate that negotiations and communication have led to an improvement in the situation in L/Derry.

On 29 September 1999, the *Londonderry Sentinel* wrote an article entitled: 'Boys make the first move and change date of commemoration. Lundy's Day parade brought forward' (O'Donnell 1999). The Lundy's Day parade commemorates the shutting of the city gates during the siege of 1689. This parade has a history of provoking a wave of violence in the city of L/Derry. In earlier years the parade was always scheduled for the last Saturday before Christmas, which meant economic losses for the city's business community because many shops had to be closed due to rioting and vandalism. In 1999, the Lundy Parade was rescheduled to take place on 4 December. This news was happily received among the shopkeepers of the city. Moreover, as the article in the *Londonderry Sentinel* stresses, by this gesture the Apprentice Boys 'hoped to end the harassment of their commemoration day, and that Protestant identity in the city will have its place in a shared city, which is big enough to respect differences and tolerate each other's means of cultural expression' (O'Donnell 1999).

The response from the Catholic community to the rescheduling of the parade was supportive. Social Democratic & Liberation Party (SDLP) Councillor Mary Bradley described it as 'a very positive step forward' (*Derry Journal* October 1999). Also, the BRG announced that it had no plans to oppose the Lundy's Day parade. The spokesman of BRG, Donncha MacNiallais, said that 'the Residents' Group has acknowledged the right of the Apprentice Boys to commemorate the Siege of Derry through the parade' and MacNiallais also acknowledged 'the steps taken in recent years by the loyal order to engage in dialogue and control their own members' (*Derry Journal* November 1999). The agreement between the two communities demonstrates how the national political goals of controlling parades is achieved locally. The Lundy's Day parade on 4 December 1999 occurred without any major disturbance.

International pressure to solve the marching issue is exerted through expectations related to the Northern Irish peace process. Following the cease-fires, all the major disturbances have occurred during the marching season, and especially during and after some of the most contested marches in the province. Violent confrontations in past years are not seen as 'acceptable' by the international agents involved in the peace process. To obtain international support and help, a solution to the marching dispute has to be found.

Although the local agreement seen in L/Derry in late 1999 challenges the practices of territoriality (marching and opposing), it still allows territoriality among communities to exist. The difference is that territoriality and territorial boundaries are not violently communicated. Removing violence from the parades and other such contested ways of commemoration enables the negotiating parties to focus on other problematic issues that arise when living in the 'borderlands'. It has to be remembered that while too often the conflict has become a structural part of everyday life, people in Northern Ireland have their work to do, shops to go to, and friends to see in much the same way as the rest of us. However, because of the geographical location of Northern Ireland and the destructive effect of ethnic conflict, deprivation and high unemployment are just a few of the issues that this border region also must come to terms with.

CONCLUSION

Although territorial practices change over the course of time, the underlying processes will most likely remain in some form: the control of space, inclusion and exclusion. The key is how these processes are politicised. Historically, the discourses of control, inclusion, exclusion, and territoriality in Northern Ireland have been politicised basically to 'serve' the goals of the social movements called Irish and British nationalisms and their localised identities. The politicisation has been conflict intensive, segregative, and extremist. This model of politicisation has supposedly come to the end of its road. The peace process enables, but also forces one to rethink, the practices of politicisation and the underlying process of territoriality and politics of place.

It can still be argued, however, that segregation and sometimes even sectarianism have remained ingrained within the communities. Quite often territoriality and bounded places are still essential parts of communities on both sides. The current practices of categorising 'us' and 'others' will play important roles in contemporary Northern Ireland. Over the years, the current peaceful development hopefully will be channelled into society through less politicised categories of 'us' and 'them'. This would mean more permeable boundaries between the communities and an end to practices that aim at the creation of homogenised communities. Co-operation across the local, national, and international scales is necessary. As can be seen in the case of Northern Ireland, although the various scales already operate and are involved in peace-making efforts, many actors functioning on these scales have historically occupied a central part in the conflict.

Building a shared society is a very demanding task, especially in the context of a deeply divided society such as Northern Ireland. However, it is possible, although the steps taken on this road may be small and there may be times when going backward seems to be a better option than rushing forward. The 'culture of borderscape', that is, violence, opposition, and resistance, is deeply embedded in Northern Irish society. Local safe havens and sites of resistance have aimed to create a feeling of security for local communities. During the Troubles it has become a convenient coping strategy to strictly define which side of a 'boundary' one is located on and why. In the present situation, one's loyalty to a community, and the ability to protect his or her community if necessary by violence, is still often questioned. This, however, is the context in which the old politics of place should be challenged by many new practices. In the contemporary situation, the power of old segregative structures still sometimes keeps the communities in their exclusive and uncompromising corners, but as the parade issue in L/Derry shows, communication can enable pluralistic thinking and co-operation, overcoming community boundaries. Moreover, it should be remembered that the blurring of boundaries and integration of values does not mean the homogenisation of society—quite the contrary. It means nonviolent communication between communities, valuing pluralism in society, and aiming to understand and analyse 'otherness'. It is not about changing the 'other' to be part of 'us', but rather living with and acknowledging the place of 'others'.

NOTES

I am very grateful to Paul Arthur, Gillian Robinson, Martin Melaugh, Jouni Häkli, and David Kaplan, whose comments helped me to finalise this chapter. Writing this chapter was made possible as part of Research Project SA 42657, funded by the Academy of Finland. I also want to thank INCORE for providing me with a space to work while writing the chapter.

1. There has not been a commonly acceptable way to refer to the city of Derry/Londonderry. The first term is used by the nationalist community and the latter by the unionist community. In this article, I use the term *L/Derry* without any political implications.

2. In the Protestant community the significance of parades as the core of the culture is acknowledged by the author. However, the message of the parade is often connected to a negative sense of 'siege mentality', therefore not giving the same

confidence to the cultural traditions of the Protestant community as to the traditions of the Catholic community in Northern Ireland.

3. Celtic and Rangers are both football teams playing in the Scottish League, but Celtic is affiliated with the Catholic community and Rangers with the Protestant community. These affiliations are due to the historical composition of the players in the teams.

REFERENCES

Anderson, J., and I. Shuttleworth. 1998. Sectarian demography, territoriality and political development in Northern Ireland. *Political Geography* 17, no. 2: 187–208.

The Belfast Agreement. 1998. http://www.irish-times.com/irish-times/special/peace/agreement/agreement.html. May.

Berg, J.-P., ed. 1995. The special support programme for peace and reconciliation in Northern Ireland and the Border Counties of Ireland. European Union, Regional Policy and Cohesion, Inforegio, Peace, Fact Sheet 31.07.1995 EN.

Billig, M. 1995. *Banal Nationalism*. London: Sage.

Boal, F. W. 1974. Territoriality in Belfast. In C. Bell and H. Newby, eds. *The Sociology of Community. A Selection of Readings*, 191–212. London: Frank Cass.

Boal, F. W., and D. N. Livingstone. 1983. The international frontier in microcosmos: The Shankill-Falls divide, Belfast. In N. Kliot and S. Waterman, eds. *Pluralism and Political Geography: People, Territory and State*, 138–58. London: Croom Helm.

Connolly, S. J. 1997. Culture, identity and tradition: Changing definitions of Irishness. In B. Graham, ed. *In Search of Ireland: A Cultural Geography*, 43–63. London: Routledge.

Darby, J. 1997. *Scorpions in a Bottle: Conflicting Cultures in Northern Ireland*. London: Minority Rights Group.

Derry Journal. 1999. 1 October–2 November.

Douglas, N., and P. Shirlow. 1998. People in conflict in place: The case of Northern Ireland. *Political Geography* 17, no. 2: 125–28.

Doumitt, D. 1985. *Conflict in Northern Ireland: The History, the Problem and the Challenge*. New York: Peter Lang.

Duffy, P. J. 1997. Writing Ireland: Literature and art in the representation of Irish place. In B. Graham, ed. *In Search of Ireland: A Cultural Geography*, 64–83. London: Routledge.

Dunn, S. 1999. Parades in Northern Ireland statistics. Lecture handout, University of Ulster, Magee College. 9 November.

European Programme. 1999. http://www.community-relations.org.uk/europe/europe.html. 4 November.

Graham, B. 1994. No place of the mind: Contested Protestant representations of Ulster. *Ecumene* 1, no. 3: 257–81.

———. 1997. Ireland and Irishness: Place, culture and identity. In B. Graham, ed. *In Search of Ireland: A Cultural Geography*, 1–15. London: Routledge.

———. 1998. Contested images of place among Protestants in Northern Ireland. *Political Geography* 17, no. 2: 129–44.

The International Fund for Ireland. 1999. http://www.internationalfundforireland .com. 4 November.

Kearney, R. 1997. *Postnationalist Ireland: Politics, Culture and Philosophy.* London: Routledge.

Kuusisto, A.-K. 1998. Living the territorial divisions in Northern Ireland. Master's thesis, Department of Geography, University of Joensuu.

———. 1999. Politics of place and resistance: The case of Northern Ireland. *Nordia Geographical Publications Yearbook* 28, no. 2: 15–27.

———. 2001. Territoriality, symbolism and the challenge. *Peace Review* 13, no. 1: 59–66.

Lee, J., ed. 1985. *Ireland: Towards a Sense of Place.* Cork, Ireland: Cork University Press.

The Northern Ireland Census 1991. 1992. Belfast: HMSO, Department of Health and Social Services. (Religion by local governmental districts and wards).

O'Donnell. 1999. Boys make the first move and change date of commemoration: Lundy's Day parade brought forward. *Londonderry Sentinel,* 29 September: 3.

O'Dowd, L. 1998. Coercion, territoriality and the prospects for a negotiated settlement in Ireland. *Political Geography* 17, no. 2: 239–49.

Painter, J. 1995. *Politics, Geography & 'Political Geography'—A Critical Perspective.* London: Arnold.

Poole, M. A. 1997. In search of ethnicity in Ireland. In B. Graham, ed. *In Search of Ireland: A Cultural Geography,* 128–47. London: Routledge.

Relph, E. 1976. *Place and Placelessness.* London: Pion.

Robinson, P. 1984. *The Plantation of Ulster: British Settlement in an Irish Landscape, 1600–1670.* Dublin: Gill and Macmillan.

Sack, R. 1983. Human territoriality: A theory. *Annals of American Geographers* 73, no. 1: 55–74.

———. 1986. *Human Territoriality. Its Theory and History.* Cambridge: Cambridge University Press.

Smyth, M. 1996. Population movement: The statistics. In *A Report of a Series of Public Discussions on Aspects of Sectarian Divisions in Derry Londonderry.* Londonderry: Templegrove Action Research Limited.

Chapter Ten

Place, Boundaries, and the Construction of Finnish Territory

Anssi Paasi

Boundaries, borders, and frontiers, traditional basic categories of political geography, have come to be key words in much of contemporary research. Not only have political geographers scrutinised their meanings, but they are widely used both in their concrete and metaphoric meanings by scholars in anthropology, cultural studies, or international relations. Recent debates on boundaries have been marked by a curious dualism: Some authors argue that boundaries (and even nation-states) are disappearing from the globalising world dominated by economic and 'human' flows, whereas others, often European scholars, perpetually strive to develop new conceptual and empirical approaches for concrete border studies in the situation in which cross-border regionalisations seem to be the order of the day. The backgrounds for this new engagement appear thus to be contextual and to vary from the revival of exclusive, at times violent, ethno-regionalism and nationalism to debates on the de-territorialising effects of globalisation and Internet/cyperspace (Newman and Paasi 1998).

This chapter seeks to reflect ongoing debates on boundaries, place, and identity and to shed light on the links amongst these concepts through a concrete case study on the historical production of Finnish territory and its boundaries. Consequently, it scrutinises the production of this territory as a bounded 'place', that is, a centre of meanings, and how these meanings have altered over the course of time. It is notable that the meanings of 'place' as a medium of social identification can vary. This is of decisive importance in the present-day globalising world, in which it is now argued that instead of the established, bounded, and exclusive concept of place, a more cosmopolitan view is needed—a view that would balance the particularistic and universalistic dimensions of place (Entrikin 1999). This is challenging in present-day Europe, where social processes and identities manifesting themselves at diverging spatial scales come to be increasingly fused as a consequence of political and institutional transformations and where growing flows of refugees and immigrants seriously call into question the traditional nation(-state)-centred identities and narratives of nationally bounded cultures. Finland, as the only Western neighbour of the former Soviet Union and currently the only EU member with a boundary with Russia, provides a particularly riveting 'laboratory' for analysing the dramatic shifts that took place in Europe during the 1990s, since the dominating ideology has for a long time represented Finland as a closed, relatively homogeneous cultural entity. This view is now questioned both by the opening of its boundaries and the flows of migration.

In this chapter, the construction of Finland as a meaningful territory and the roles of the Finnish-Russian border in this process are first interpreted historically to provide a background for understanding its actual significance. Second, the meanings of this border in the present transforming European and global geopolitical space are examined and the roles of identity at various spatial scales are reflected. The chapter draws on literature, statistical information, the analysis of recent media discourses, and interview materials.

THE SHAPING OF FINLAND INTO A TERRITORIAL ENTITY

The question of the link between (national) identity and boundaries is complicated because most European states have several boundaries that may have even contradistinctive histories and diverging meanings in national identity narratives. Boundaries are not merely passive, natural dividers between territories. Some may have been open and permeable, others closed, exclusive, and even instruments that have been used in the creation of the images of the 'other' or enemies and divisions between those who belong and those who do not (Conversi 1995; Cohen 1985).

International relations scholars have shown the meanings of boundaries in the rhetoric and narratives of national identity (Campbell 1992; Shapiro and Alker 1996). Boundaries are historically and spatially contingent. In Finland particularly the Finnish-Russian boundary has been of decisive importance in the construction of the images of Finnish people as a place-bound community ('us') that differs from the Soviet Union/Russia, defined as the 'other' and, on a broader spatial scale of identification, it has been interpreted as being the dividing line between 'West' and 'East', with 'West' as the cultural or ideological 'home' of the Finns. This border was closed for decades after the Second World War, being a model example of the Cold War geopolitical order; Finland was the only capitalist neighbour of the communist superpower Soviet Union. The collapse of the Soviet Union and Finland's entry into the European Union have radically modified the territorial meanings of this border. These transformations have thus had their origins on different spatial scales. Finland's two other boundaries, with Sweden and Norway, have been for decades relatively open to citizens coming from these countries. Contrary to the Finnish-Russian border, these borders have been illustrative of the fact that boundaries around places are not always exclusive entities (Massey 1995). The boundary between Finland and Norway follows the boundary line that was established between Sweden—which ruled Norway up to 1905—and Russia in the early nineteenth century. The Finnish-Soviet border, for its part, and to a lesser extent the existing Finnish-Russian border, still make obvious the exclusive power of boundaries. This exclusiveness has a long history and as such is one part of the state- and nation-building process.

Finland became an institutionalised territory in 1917 when it gained its independence. Before that the country was a part of Sweden up to 1809 and, following the Napoleonic Wars, an autonomous Grand Duchy within the Russian Empire from 1809 to 1917. Finland was a state with its own economy and administration during the Russian period but lacked any foreign relations and many other features and symbols of an independent state. During the autonomous period Russian strategic thinking viewed Finland as a military continuation of Russian territory, for there were Russian troops in the country throughout this period, and Finland's own army played a largely symbolic role (Klinge 1980). The official language of administration continued to be Swedish, even though the speakers of that language were in a clear minority. The slowly emerging image of a 'national culture' was thus a hybrid of heterogeneous cultural and social elements—partly 'national', partly 'international'.

The nationalist awakening took place slowly in Finland, and mostly through the activity of the Swedish-speaking elite who governed the country. Some scholars maintain that a national consciousness became widespread among the ordinary people only with the intensifying of the Russification campaign at the turn of the nineteenth century (Jussila 1979). A small group of key actors, recognised as 'Great Men' of their age, were important in this process before the end of the nineteenth century, but as in many European states, identity building still could not have taken place without the numerous institutions and organisations that formed the major foundation of the nation-building effort after the mid-nineteenth century: the elementary school system; the freely formed and operating associations and societies; the press; and the entire physical, social, and cultural infrastructure that was necessary for the formation of a common public opinion (Paasi 1996, 1997). These social and cultural features had their own territorial manifestations, starting from the local level and proceeding beyond the regional level to the national level. These mechanisms were also associated with the creation and reproduction of local, regional, and national consciousness, that is, Finland as a context of nested spatial identities (Herb and Kaplan 1999). National consciousness and the forms of nationalistic behaviour that were aimed at maintaining these functions of creation and reproduction were not associated exclusively with national icons and symbols but were constructed in a broad-based manner on the practices of numerous institutions, practices through which the 'national culture' became a part of people's everyday lives (Paasi 1996, 1999b). In this way the conditions necessary to produce a national identity, as listed by Smith (1991:14), gradually came about: ideas of the historical territory or homeland, common myths and historical recollections, a unified national culture, recognition of mutual rights and duties, and a single economy with associated mobility of its members. In a word, this created the basis for practices and narratives through which the territory became identified as a place, a centre of meanings. This 'place' was ultimately a contested one, as dramatically illustrated in the Civil War in spring 1918.

DISCOURSES ON FINLAND AS A BOUNDED PLACE

National historiography and 'geo-ideology' in Finland, as in other countries, has been prepared to furnish Finland as a territory and experienced place with narratives of continuity and history that extend back far into the past. The wildest rhetorical flights of fancy represented by school history books treat Finland as an entity recognisable as it emerged from beneath the ice of the last glaciation! The main problem would seem to be representation of the relationships between space and time, that is, between territory as a place of 'us' and history (Paasi 1996).

The emerging identity of a localised social community requires the identification of boundaries of the place and community: People become aware of 'their' culture when they stand at its boundaries (Cohen 1982). For centuries the boundary between (Sweden-)Finland and Russia, which was indeed more of a frontier than a boundary, ran through an area occupied on both sides by a Finnish-speaking population, and when Finland became a Grand Duchy of Russia, this line became a more or less formal customs border that signified the aspirations of Finland to control its territory rather than any explicit act of delimitation or exclusion; no clearly defined boundary yet existed between Finland and Russia in the nineteenth century. Under Swedish rule the Finns had been loyal to the crown of Sweden and had had very little contact with their 'ethnic brothers' beyond the boundary in the east.

With the altered political situation in the early nineteenth century and the simultaneous emergence of a romantic admiration for peoples living 'close to nature'—again an international trend—the question of relations with the people living behind the border in Eastern Karelia in Russia came to the fore. The fact that the *Kalevala* ballads that formed the Finnish national epic had been collected mainly on the Russian side of the border inspired a further sense of identification, and it was indeed in the spirit of Romanticism that the history of a people and its contemporary political significance should be regarded as all the greater the older, more numerous, and more primitive that people was (Tiitta 1994: 150). In this respect, however, culture and nature pointed to opposite strategies for the production of territoriality, for where the former emphasised the historical connection between peoples, the latter provided an ideologically timeless argument frequently in the deterministic tones of 'natural law' (Voionmaa 1919: 34).

In effect the former eastern boundary of Sweden-Finland lost much of its significance when Finland became part of Russia, and the Finns and Eastern Karelians became in principle fellow citizens (Jääskeläinen 1961: 22). In practice, however, it was not long before the idea began to spread in Finland that the formal border with Russia was an *artificial*, not a natural, construct. This is a fitting illustration of the fact that state boundaries may be contested because the boundaries of territory and the social identities of inhabitants do not coincide. The compiler of the *Kalevala* ballad collection, Elias Lönnrot, wrote that the areas settled by Finns extended deep into Russian territory. Similarly, J. L. Runeberg, when outlining the chief elements of the national landscape, evidently had in mind the entire Finnish–Eastern Karelian ethnic group (Jääskeläinen 1961: 29–31). These cultural persons, in a way, represented effectively formal geopolitical reasoning: They adopted a self-declared role in defining the cultural structures and boundaries of the national space (O'Tuathail 1996: 60).

The question of Eastern Karelia became particularly relevant when Finland gained independence in 1917, whereupon the areas of Finnish-speaking settlement left beyond the border in Soviet Russia became an object of interest for some groups of Finns. This fascination with the East is evident in the book by Voionmaa (1919), in which he considered at length the essential quality of 'Greater Finland' and its foundations in the natural sciences. Appealing to the geopolitical ideas of Rudolf Kjellen, he noted that 'Finland without Russian Karelia or the Kola Peninsula is like a loaf without a crust' (p. 32). Admittedly he also named the Finnish-speaking area of Northern Sweden and the Finnmark area of Northern Norway as 'irredenta' territories of Finland, showing that the limits of his geopolitical imagination did not fit into the existing territorial framework.

The question of Finland's eastern boundary was a critical one in the Peace of Tartu, concluded in 1920, which left the Finnish-speaking areas lying beyond this boundary as part of Soviet Russia. This in turn inspired a revival of the notion of 'Greater Finland' during the interwar years. Finnish-Soviet relations between the wars were characterised by mistrust, which was reflected in Finland in the form of a sharp demarcation made in all matters linked with the Soviet Union; the gaze was more than before turned to the West. On a local scale this meant the nationalisation of peripheries, that is, efforts to integrate the people living in border areas, first of all on the eastern border, with the broader nation. This took place in many forms and often integrative practices were full of national symbolism (Paasi 1996).

The principal works of Kjellen, who had an immense background influence on geopolitics, were published in Finnish translation around 1920, and his inspiration provided a crucial background for the concept of Greater Finland and efforts to join Eastern Karelia in Finland after gaining independence (Klinge 1972). The most extensive treatise on political geography was written by Leiviskä (1938), who included state boundaries following features of nationality, culture, economics, and transport among the 'natural boundaries' or 'structural boundaries', and attributed the problems of Finland's eastern boundary to 'the danger attached to it' (p. 68). Leiviskä's text portrayed the Soviet Union as the 'other', categorically deviant from 'us', a reminder that symbolic boundaries and identity are two parts of the same coin (Bauman 1990). During the 1920s and 1930s the ideas of 'us' and the 'other' dominated the social action and diverging discourses in Finland: foreign policy, church, national defence, and so forth. Trade with the Soviet Union also collapsed after Finland gained its independence, which indicates the poor relations between the two states (Paasi 1999a).

The Finland painted in the representations of the Finnish scientists after 1917 was firmly located in the West, the justifications for this being mainly cultural, that is, connections with Europe and Scandinavia. Thus Voionmaa (1933), a historian and economic geographer, saw Finland as an area of 'contact' or 'conflict' between East and West, and he also distinguished Scandinavia as a more extensive object of identification. The location of Finland in the West was particularly typical of the approach of geography textbooks between the wars, and applied equally to books on political geography produced in other countries (Paasi 1996).

WORLD WAR II AND THE CONSTRUCTION
OF THE NEW EASTERN BOUNDARY

The most dramatic expression of the deepening mistrust between the two states was that, on the eve of the Second World War, the Soviet Union demanded that Finland relinquish certain areas on the Karelian Isthmus, in the interests of the defence of Leningrad, located only some thirty kilometres from the existing border. Admittedly, in the arena of large-scale geopolitics, Finland and the Baltic states had already been included in the Soviet sphere of influence in August 1939. Finland's refusal to comply with these demands led to the Winter War of 1939–1940, as a consequence of which Finland was forced to relinquish the whole of the Karelian Isthmus to the Soviet Union. In the course of the Continuation War of 1941–1944 Finnish troops regained these areas and occupied extensive parts of Eastern Karelia, thereby coming close to implementing in practice the notion of 'Greater Finland', which was widely espoused by the political leadership of that time (Paasi 1996).

The final outcome of the war was nevertheless that the boundary areas were transformed dramatically: Finland was obliged to cede to the Soviet Union not only the areas lost in 1940 but also the Petsamo area of Lapland (see figure 10.1). More than 420,000 inhabitants of the ceded areas had to be resettled in the remaining parts of Finland, which was a serious challenge for their regional and social identities. Meanwhile, on the larger scale, the declared aim of the new Finnish foreign policy became adjustment to the 'geographically' dictated constraints of living next door to a major world power. The self-defined neutrality, cautious foreign policy, and carefully nurtured connections with the Soviet Union that existed throughout the 1960s and 1970s did not convince all circles outside Finland; these acts became widely interpreted in the West as 'Finlandisation'. The major background for this perception was obviously the Treaty of Friendship, Cooperation, and Mutual Assistance that Finnish political elites were forced to sign in 1948 (Paasi 1999a). And, as far as the postwar geopolitical representations of the state are concerned, in Anglo-American political geography textbooks Finland was simply represented as part of Eastern Europe, a fact that the Finns themselves could hardly admit. This renders intelligible the fact that the territorial area of a state is always absolute from the viewpoint of its sovereignty, whereas the representations of this geopolitical space may differ dramatically depending on where and by whom these representations are created. This means that there are always ideological and political considerations attached to the definition of a territory and its boundaries.

Whereas the term *natural boundary* was often used in connection with

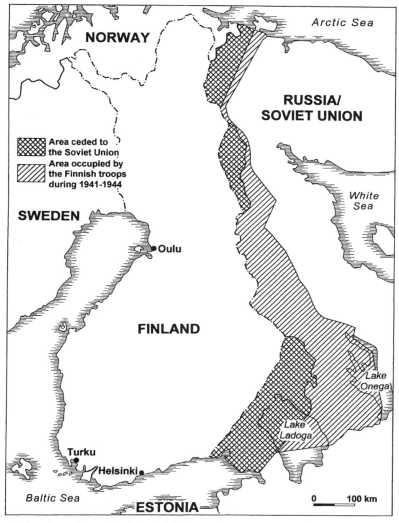

Figure 10.1. Areas Occupied by Finnish Troops in 1941–1944 and Areas Ceded to the Soviet Union in 1944

the Finnish-Soviet border before World War II, after the war the border was portrayed—as were Finnish-Soviet relations in general—by using a much more realistic and neutral terminology. After the war the Control Commission of the Allied Forces—controlled by the Soviet Union—censored textbooks and literature so that anti-Soviet attitudes had to be removed. The Finnish-Russian border, in a way, disappeared from political discourse. Both the ceded areas and the new border became taboos that were rarely discussed in public. The border was closed, and Finland established in 1947 a frontier zone on the border area, which varied from five hundred to three thousand metres in width. The zone was under strict control during the Soviet era and is so even today. Numerous families were still living in this area after the war, but all others needed permission to visit the zone, and this was exceptionally complicated for foreigners, who needed to apply for permission to the Security Police. People living in the zone may well be labelled 'prisoners of space' because the zone effectively controlled their social relations (Paasi 1996). After the collapse of the Soviet Union, the zone was cut to 'move' the homes of residents outside it.

The closed border was open to some timber transport and joint projects with the Soviet Union, such as the construction of the Kostomuksha mining combine during the 1970s. Strictly controlled tourism of Finnish travellers to Leningrad and Vyborg (the former Finnish city in Karelia) made possible a rather embryonic cross-border operation. All forms of co-operation were, in any case, established and controlled formally at the level of the two states. This was very much the case up to the collapse of the socialist bloc of Eastern Europe (Paasi 1999a).

THE EUROPEAN UNION AND THE POST-SOVIET BOUNDARY DISCOURSES

The new formal, neutral Finnish state ideology after World War II overshadowed the bitter feelings prevailing in the civil society, for example, among the evacuated Karelians. One major discourse of the 1990s brought together many ongoing tendencies and strategies as far as the boundary was concerned: the question of the ceded (Karelian) areas and implicitly the question of the correct location of the boundary (Paasi 1999a, 1999c). This debate had been going on in civil society since the war, but official foreign policy was, and still is, on another track. Statesmen have been perpetually of the opinion that these debates are not in the 'sphere of national interest' and not part of the foreign policy agenda. One reason for this attitude has been the fact that a major criterion for new members in the EU is that the candidate state cannot have boundary disputes with its neighbours. The debate on the ceded areas, maintained by both moderate (Union of Karelia) and hard-line associations (Tarto Peace Movement, the Great Finland Association), continues particularly in letters-to-the-editor sections of newspapers. In extreme cases arguments reflect the tunes of old Ratzelian organistic thinking, representing Finland as a wounded body that can be heeled only by joining the ceded areas into the territorial whole.

Surveys carried out in Finland (and Russia also) during the 1990s indicate that the majority of ordinary people do not support any reopening of negotiations with Russia on border questions (Paasi 1999a). These attitudes may partly reflect the fact that the history of the border has been a history of conflicts, and partly—at least among the Finns—that the former Finnish areas behind the border are in very poor shape and their restoration would demand huge investments from the state. Furthermore, the size of the present-day Russian population in the ceded Karelia, some 400,000 inhabitants, also has cooled down the most heated claims. This population, divided between two larger administrative areas, Leningrad Oblast and the Republic of Karelia, is equal to almost one-tenth of Finland's population. This population is mainly Russian speaking, Finnish speakers being a small minority (Paasi 1996: 284). This means that cultural identities in border areas are divided by the border, even if the Finnish evacuated Karelians still miss the lost territory.

No wonder, then, that in spite of the opinions of official foreign policy makers and the complicated situation in the area, the question of the restoration of the area seems to emerge in the media every summer, when the associations of the people from ceded Karelian areas have their annual meetings. The most recent survey (1999) of fourteen- to fifteen-year-old school children shows that one-third of them would like to have these areas back in Finland. One can question the motives of those who posed the questions more than the attitudes of the school children. Asking young, innocent children questions that include geopolitical dynamite but do not belong to their 'place (and time) experience', then 'objectifying' these as results, constructs rather than measures opinions.

FORMS OF CO-OPERATION

As elsewhere in Europe, the disintegration of the Soviet Union has finally led to the relative de-territorialisation of the Finnish-Russian boundary, and numerous cross-border projects are now taking place. The roles of this border have varied historically, reflecting both Finnish-Soviet/Russian relations and transformations in global and European geopolitics. Finland's entry into the EU in 1995 modified the territorial context most dramatically, and the Finnish-Russian boundary is now also concomitantly a boundary between the EU and Russia, not merely an ordinary boundary between two states.

Whereas the public debate after the Soviet demise but before 1995 often looked at the border in terms of potential threats (mass migration of illegal people, crime, nuclear power station risks, pollution), these discourses have been gradually pushed aside as EU-based economic practices and discourses strive to open up the border and permit freer movement of capital, goods, and people. Local meanings of the border have also varied crucially over time, and changes are now taking place in the everyday lives of people living in border areas. Territorial transformations provide a major challenge for the territorial identities that existed for almost fifty years and were formally ended with the existing borderline, cutting the territorial identities of people who had to leave their homes behind the new border. It is obvious, however, that informally the memories associated with the ceded areas have been an important part of the spatial identities of elderly people (Paasi 1996).

On a broader scale, the regional structures between Scandinavia and Russia are now changing dramatically, at least on paper. Many efforts to territorialise or regionalise the Nordic space in ways that cross the existing boundaries are in fact discursive constructions that are currently being created in Northern Europe as part of broader discourses in the European Union. They are examples of a new 'space of dependencies'. I have defined the latter as the spatial sets of constellations in which a state acts, which consist of images, discourses, strategies, and other social (cultural, economic, administrative, political) practices that are impregnated with power relations. This space is structured on divergent spatial scales. In the Finnish case this space is increasingly linked with the Western (European) space. Such expressions as 'Barents region', 'Baltic sea region', and 'Northern Dimension', which are now appearing in several states within the EU, are also examples of this (Paasi 1999c). Although they all are 'regions in discourses' and 'regions in text and maps' rather than tangible entities, nevertheless they may gradually turn out to be significant elements in social practices that can define, and ultimately have a concrete effect on, people's everyday lives.

Concrete cross-border co-operation is to an increasing degree taking place on the Finnish-Russian border. New actors have also emerged on the stage; it is no longer only the two states that mediate contacts, but increasingly enterprises, local communes, and municipalities that participate in co-operation. Twenty-five Finnish communes and municipalities have a common border with Russia. With the exception of the Imatra and Lappeenranta in southeastern Finland, the communes have remained peripheral net emigration areas since the 1960s. The opening of the border has been viewed as a potential Lotto prize in the struggle against the deprivation of the local economy. The actors of Imatra and Lappeenranta use the gateway location effectively in marketing in their tourist brochures and accentuate their local expertise in business and trade.

The 1990s witnessed the opening of several international and national crossing points that now number more than twenty (see figure 10.2). The number of international crossing points—where non-Finnish and non-Russian people can cross the border—is growing; there are currently six, with two new points under construction. The opening of new border stations has its origin in many cases in more general EU policies and programs (Tacis, INTERREG) that provide a possibility for funding these projects. The status of 'international crossing point' would mean that people could cross the border without special permission, using normal visas. This allows new degrees of freedom for cross-border activities. In Salla commune, for example, expectations regarding the opening of Kelloselkä crossing point are high, based on a rise in both future tourism and goods transport traffic (Välimaa 1999). The commune has lost 700 jobs during the last decade, which is a lot for a place with less than 5,500 inhabitants. One problem in co-ordinating the cross-border activities is that the Russian area beyond the border is divided among three larger territories (Leningrad region, the Republic of Karelia, and the Murmansk region), and these areas are perceived by the Finns as offering varying opportunities (Paasi 1999c; see figure 10.3). Hundreds of enterprises have been established in the neighbouring Russian areas by foreign capital.

The Finns have been more suspicious than Russians about the opening of the border (Kinnunen 1995). Attitudes are changing, however. At least the entrepreneurs in southeastern Finland have adopted a much more optimistic and active position, mainly due to the fact that the Russian guests spend a lot of money (Räikkönen 1999). The Russian language has not been popular among Finnish students, but it is now understood that it is a vital instrument for local business life, for example, when Russians come to shop on the Finnish side of the border (Käyhty 1995). Administrative bodies also actively recommend that people study the language. Russian is also part of the 'commercial landscape' of the cities in southeast Finland. Although negative signs—such as 'only one Russian customer at a time'—were typical at the beginning of the 1990s, many southeast Finnish shops now have at least small signs in Russian that welcome those customers (Räikkönen 1999).

Even if Helsinki is still the most common destination, visited by more than half of all tourists, Russian shoppers are increasingly one-day visitors, which means that they visit mainly the cities near the border (Pihlaja 1999). On the other hand, visitors clearly represent economic elites in the ongoing, harsh economic situation in Russian areas. The Finnish-Russian border has often been compared with the U.S.-Mexico border because of the deep gap in the prevailing standards of living. The situation has been exceptionally poor in border villages that are located far from Moscow.

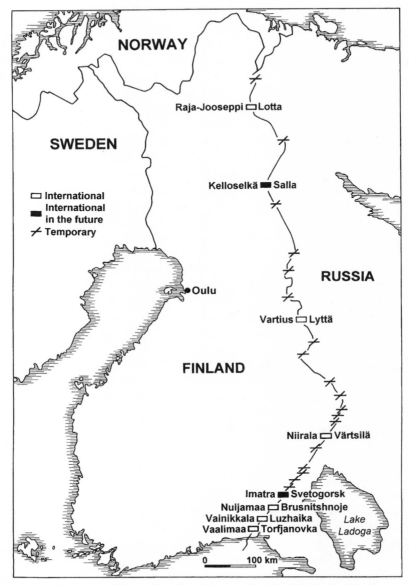

Figure 10.2.   Current and Future Crossing Points on the Finnish-Russian Border

Figure 10.3.   Division of Northwest Russia into Administrative Regions

Finland's Red Cross and Ministry of Foreign Affairs have supported hospitals in the Karelian Republic and Murmansk areas (Käyhty 1998).

Diverse forms of co-operation are now emerging in many fields, varying from humanitarian aid to tourism, from economic co-operation to local and regional spatial planning projects. In spite of various forms of integration, cross-border co-operation, and regionalisation, the border is still strictly controlled, because it is also the only border between the European Union and Russia (Paasi 1999a). In terms of foreign policy and security discourses, territorial control of the border is particularly closed.

There are, in fact, several overlapping discourses in which the roles of the boundary are understood and defined in diverse ways: in foreign policy, border guarding, economic co-operation, attitudes towards the ceded areas, and attitudes towards the Russians themselves.

THE BORDER AND CHANGING FORMS OF TERRITORIALITY

The present Finnish-Russian border is a telling illustration of the tendencies that Taylor (1994) has addressed in his deconstruction of the state as territorial container (Paasi 1999a). Although the assumption of clear territorial demarcation has been a major feature of the idea of state sovereignty, Taylor argues that a state has multifaceted territorial functions in various spheres of social action. Hence, as a power container the state tends to preserve the existing territorial boundaries, and in terms of security policy the principle of territoriality as a form of control still dominates power relations. As a wealth container the state strives towards larger territories, trying to render a more effective capital accumulation possible within the borders of the state. As a cultural container the state tends towards smaller territories—even if the representations of the existence of a homogeneous 'national culture' are pivotal in most narratives of nationhood. 'Cultural nations' can also extend well beyond the territorial borders of a nation-state. Environmental problems are not deliberated in Taylor's framework, but—as some representatives of political geography and international relations theory have pointed out—the border lines that divide the present-day geopolitical realm into separate sovereign territorial states are porous (Kuehls 1996; cf. Johnston 1996).

The modern state is a territory, which only partly remains within its territorial boundaries; the borders are actually sets of shifting discourses and social practices that mediate the links between inside and outside (Paasi 1999c). These conclusions hold up well in the case of the practices and discourses regarding the Finnish-Russian border. This border is an apt illustration of overlapping territorialities where the 'outlines' of different activity spaces do not always coincide. On the one hand, the border is still closed as far as the free movement of individuals is concerned. The number of people crossing the border is growing, but who crosses is strictly controlled. Illegal traffic is effectively prohibited, but the pressure is intense and the situation is unstable, particularly in the southwestern areas. Although borders have become lower and lower inside the EU, the external boundaries of this area are strictly controlled. Crime, such as smuggling, illegal border crossing, or use of false identification papers, strains border controls today. Finnish border guard detachments control the border effectively and also co-operate to some extent with Russian authorities to prevent border violations (Paasi 1999a). More than the crimes occurring in the immediate context of the border area, authorities are worried about the larger scale 'white-collar' crimes that have their origin particularly in Russia and that manifest themselves in 'money-laundering', managing tax-haven companies from Finland, and so on (Arolainen and Virtanen 1998; Naulapää 1998).

Finland's entry into the EU and resulting responsibility for its only border with Russia actually point towards organising a more effective patrolling system, since customs operations are now carried out on behalf of the entire EU. Border surveillance is more and more technical in nature—with cameras and electronic monitoring systems adopted during the 1990s—which makes control over the boundaries of the national space more effective and less visible. The nature of the patrolling operations has also changed. Whereas this action was very formal in Soviet times, it is now characterised by increasing co-operation and exchange of information with the Russians, for example, about criminal activities (Tuorila 1999). On the other hand, border controls are very strict, and the number of refugees who have entered Finland by crossing this boundary has been very low, only a few per year. The number of people turned back from the border has been increasing, but the total number, less than one thousand per year, is still very low relative to the intensity of passenger traffic, some 4 million crossings annually (Paasi 1999a).

I have argued elsewhere that the spaces of activities have altered so that, in some spheres of social action, control of the forms of this action has increased while in some others it has loosened (Paasi 1999b). The most fascinating sphere is the complex consisting of foreign and security policy. The Finnish-Russian boundary is itself very seldom the object of these debates, but rather is hidden in more general discourses on Finnish-Russian relations. Since the Soviet collapse 'neighbour area co-operation' has aimed at lowering the potential tensions between the two states. The most recent element in this effort is the so-called Northern Dimension that Finland has strongly suggested for a policy in the context of the EU. What the Northern Dimension should in fact include is not that clear, but basically the point is, again, to lower the boundaries between the states within the EU and Russia. As the label 'Northern' would imply, the real context is Northern Europe. A deeper analysis of the discourse on this topic reveals that the Northern Dimension would include such elements as cross-border operation towards northeastern Russian and the Kola peninsula, with the aim of integrating Russia into European co-operation and bringing the natural resources of the Kola peninsula area within the reach of the EU (Paasi 1999c).

One further element changing the discursive space of dependencies in the Finnish case has been the continual speculations of politicians and members of the security policy elite about possible NATO membership. Already the EU membership and observer membership in the Western European Union (WEU) has converted Finland's location in geopolitical self-imagination, but the question of NATO is much more radical. Official foreign policy has until recent years preferred independent defence rather than a NATO connection, but it has been pointed out that, while this is not mooted in publicity, links with NATO are nevertheless strengthening. Membership in WEU and buying 'NATO-consistent' Hornet fighters from the United States at the beginning of the 1990s, for example, have been interpreted as indications of this (Paasi 1999c).

LOCAL IDENTITY SPACES AT BORDER AREAS

We have seen how the meanings of the border between Finland and Soviet Union were constructed after Finland gained its independence and how the boundary became a critical constituent of the national identity (Campbell 1992). The exclusive border became, in a way, the symbol of the mistrust between the two states. When the new border was established after World War II, according to the interviews that were carried out at the end of the 1980s, people were at first afraid of the new situation (Paasi 1996). More than 400,000 people had lost their homes and had to construct new territorial identities in the shadow of the emerging socialist superpower. Further, national socialisation had effectively created images of the Soviet system as the enemy. New generations born after the war grew up in a formally incongruous situation: According to the new doctrine, 'good relations' between the two states prevailed, and this was also the key message in national socialisation. No wonder then that according to the same interviews, younger generations accepted the new geopolitical situation without any major problems (Paasi 1996).

The collapse of the Soviet Union, the subsequent shifts in the 'permeability' of the border, entry into the EU, and the reforms in regional governance have modified dramatically the links between 'identity' and 'place'. Whereas the Finnish-Russian border was during the Soviet time a telling illustration of what Martinez (1994) has labelled an 'alienated borderland' where the forms of cross-border interaction were decided at the state level, the local geographies generated by border practices are now much more versatile, perhaps illustrating a remodelling of the area to what Martinez has labelled 'interdependent borderlands'. The first alterations were a dramatic decline in economic flows and a dramatic increase of 'human flows'; that is, the bilateral trade between the two states collapsed but simultaneously enabled the Finns to visit their old home areas that had been behind the border for almost fifty years. On the other hand, the national narrative of Finland as a culturally 'pure' and homogeneous place is concomitantly called into question because more than 125,000 inhabitants born abroad currently live in the state. More than 31,000 immigrants have moved to Finland from the former Soviet Union and Russia. The pressure to reorder Finland to a more cosmopolitan place by opening its boundaries is no longer a question of purely internal affairs but part of broader European policy (Entrikin 1999).

The Finnish media depicted the opening process of the Russian border very emotionally, and the pages of newspapers and magazines, as well as television, depicted the new situation and the visits of single people visibly. The first visits were made by elderly people, often war veterans and evacu- ated Karelians, who still identified themselves with the areas behind the border; younger generations have not been particularly involved in this phenomenon (Paasi 1996). The number of 'wistful travels', as they were labelled in Finland, soon decreased, because old Karelian refugees rapidly found out that the Karelia of golden dreams that they left behind fifty years before no longer existed—if it ever had. On the other hand, the Soviet population that was moved into the area from distant places remained ignorant of the history of the ceded area, where identity is cur- rently only beginning to take shape (Susiluoto 1999). Many of the golden dreams of the evacuees were based not on personal experience but on the efforts of associations of Karelians that have been active in maintaining their identity. In fact, it was discovered that one source of motivation for these visits was a chance to be together with people who belonged to the same lost community (Hakala 1996).

As far as future visits to Russia are concerned, new optimism in the field of tourism is based on a rather exotic nature-based tourism directed to northwestern Russia and the Republic of Karelia. One pilot project of an INTERREG programme was recently started to promote this activity.

The opening of the border has had a significant effect on local mobility. Because the border is between two very dissimilar economic systems, the Finns began to visit the Russian areas frequently to buy gas, cigarettes, and alcohol, which were much cheaper than in Finland. This created conflicts with the customs organisations, which actively tried to formulate legisla- tion to control these activities. The opening of the border has also trans- muted the personal and moral boundaries in local communities (Paasi 1999a). It has led at some crossing points to the rise of prostitution on both sides of the border, again in somewhat spatially multifaceted forms. On the Russian side in Värtsilä, for instance, which is the only real community in Russian Karelia located in the immediate border area, child prostitution has evolved into an acute problem. Russian prostitutes entering on the Finnish side have moved farther inland, away from the immediate border area (Parkkonen 1999a, 1999b). The same Russian community has also come to terms with a serious drug problem among local school children. One new social consequence following the opening of the border has been the rise of 'cross-border marriages'; several local couples on the Finnish side have separated because of new Russian spouses. Värtsilä has traditionally been a rural community, and these tendencies have been shaking the accustomed social order (Paasi 1999a). Prostitution and drug problems certainly reflect the deep gap between the two states in their standards of living.

CONCLUSION

The established conceptual tools of political geographers in boundary studies are under reconsideration to capture the changing roles of territoriality, the meanings of boundaries in daily life, and national narratives. Boundaries are no longer understood merely as lines that divide states as power structures but rather as symbols and institutions that mediate and generate interaction and meanings. Boundaries are not located merely in border areas but everywhere in society, in different social and cultural practices and discourses. Further, instead of one form of territoriality that a state follows—the basic assumption of political geography that for a long time operated in 'territorial trap'—it is necessary to realise that the deepening international spatial and social division of labour, all kinds of flows, and inherent complicated spaces of interdependencies create several overlapping forms of territoriality and spatial identities.

The concept of place as a coherent, bounded unit is also in question. Massey (1995) argues that the processes of spatial movement, interaction, influence, and communication challenge the practices and processes through which borderlands and boundaries have been maintained by tradition. She notes that places do have boundaries around them, but she also has some reservations about the quality of their nature. First, boundaries do not embody any eternal truths of places. Rather, they are socially constructed, and power relations are decisive for their constitution. Second, boundaries inevitably cross some other social relations that may be momentous in the construction of social space. Spatial scales are fused in places, and boundaries become more flexible. Although boundaries are often effectively used in the 'purification of space' (Sibley 1995), places that boundaries enclose are never pure. Third, boundaries matter because they are means of organising social space—they are, in fact, part of place making. This is significant because we cannot forget that boundaries have always been of vital importance in nation-building processes. We cannot ignore the fact that nationalism and national identity discourses often exploit boundaries effectively. Finally, the drawing of boundaries is an act of power.

This chapter shows that the meanings of boundaries are linked with the spatialised history of each border and with its role in nation building. In the case of the Finnish-Russian border, the reshaping of foreign policy and the international political and economic environment have been particularly important in shaping these meanings. These meanings are also related to certain 'peak experiences', such as gaining independence, World War II, the collapse of the Soviet Union, and entry into the European Union. Finland is once more faced with a new situation, as the disintegration of the Soviet Union, the laying aside of the agreements that had regulated Finnish-Soviet relations since the Second World War, membership in the European Union, debates on and links with the WEU and NATO, and other related events have altered the country's position in the geopolitical imagination and on maps and linked it more firmly with Western Europe. Even so, we are still inclined to define the country's boundaries in a highly abstract manner; now it is a question of 'the boundaries of Europe' and Finland's relation to these. The expansion of the EU placed Finland inside the boundaries of 'official Europe', creating one more dimension in the narrative of national identity and context.

At the same time, both economic and cultural cross-border links with Russia have increased. These developments mean that the Finnish-Russian boundary, so long virtually closed, is now an object of attention for various actors. It has also opened up for wide-scale cultural, economic, and political research into its historical construction and rhetorical meanings on a national scale and in the everyday lives of ordinary people. The evaluation of the changing meanings of this border make obvious that boundaries are deeply contextual phenomena, while the methods and theoretical frameworks to be used in their evaluation may provide a common ground for comparative border studies.

REFERENCES

Arolainen, T., and M. Virtanen. 1998. Itärikollisuus on vaihtanut kasvoja. *Helsingin Sanomat,* 25 January.
Bauman, Z. 1990. *Thinking Sociologically.* Oxford: Blackwell.
Campbell, D. 1992. *Writing Security.* Manchester, England: Manchester University Press.

Cohen, A., ed. 1982. *Belonging: Identity and Social Organization in British Rural Cultures.* Manchester, England: Manchester University Press.

———. 1985. *The Symbolic Construction of Community.* Chichester, England: Ellis Horwood.

Conversi, D. 1995. Reassessing current theories of nationalism: Nationalism as boundary maintenance and creation. *Nationalism and Ethnic Politics* 1: 73–85.

Entrikin, J. N. 1999. Political community, identity and cosmopolitan place. *International Sociology* 14: 269–82.

Hakala, P. 1996. Kotiseutumatkailuja kunnostaa nyt hautausmaita ja kirkkoja. *Helsingin Sanomat,* 20 July.

Herb, G., and D. Kaplan, eds. 1999. *Nested Identities.* Boston: Rowman & Littlefield.

Jääskeläinen, M. 1961. *Itä-Karjalan kysymys.* Porvoo, Finland: WSOY.

Johnston, R. J. 1996. *Nature, State and Economy.* Chichester, England: John Wiley.

Jussila, O. 1979. Nationalismi ja vallankumous venäläis-suomalaisissa suhteissa, 1899–1914. *Historiallisia tutkimuksia.* 110.

Käyhty, A. 1995. Itärajalla palvellaan jo Venäjäksi. *Helsingin Sanomat,* 11 November.

———. 1998. Elämä nilkuttaa Suomen tuliaisten varassa. *Helsingin Sanomat,* 20 October.

Kinnunen, P. 1995. A look across the border: The views and expectations of the people in Northern Finland and Northwest Russia. In M. Dahlström et al., eds. *The East-West Interface in the European North,* 45–56. Stockholm: NST.

Kjellen, R. 1919. *Valtio elinmuotona* (orig. *Staten som livsforsm*). Hämeenlinna, Finland: Karisto.

Klinge, M. 1972. *Vihan veljistä valtiososialismiin.* Porvoo, Finland: WSOY.

———. 1980. Poliittisen ja kulttuurisen Suomen muotoutuminen. In P. Tommila, A. Reitala, and V. Kallio, eds. *Suomen kulttuurihistoria II,* 11–41. Porvoo, Finland: WSOY.

Kuehls, T. 1996. *Beyond Sovereign Territory.* Minneapolis: University of Minnesota Press.

Leiviskä, I. 1938. *Poliittinen maantiede (Geopolitiikka).* Porvoo, Finland: WSOY.

Martinez, O. 1994. The dynamics of border interaction: New approaches to border analysis. In C. H. Schofield, ed. *Global Boundaries,* 1–15. London: Routledge.

Massey, D. 1995. The conceptualization of place. In D. Massey and P. Jess, eds. *A Place in the World?* 46–85. Oxford: Open University.

Naulapää, R. 1998. Itärikollisuuden uhka on torjuttavissa. *Helsingin Sanomat,* 13 February.

Newman, D., and A. Paasi. 1998. Fences and neighbours in the postmodern world: Boundary narratives in political geography. *Progress in Human Geography* 22: 186–207.

O'Tuathail, G. 1996. *Critical Geopolitics.* London: Routledge.

Paasi, A. 1991. Deconstructing regions: Notes on scales of spatial life. *Environment and Planning A* 21: 239–56.

———. 1996. *Territories, Boundaries and Consciousness: The Changing Geographies of the Finnish-Russian Border.* Chichester, England: John Wiley.

———. 1997. Geographical perspectives on Finnish national identity. *Geojournal* 43: 41–50.

———. 1998. Boundaries as social processes: Territoriality in the world of flows. *Geopolitics* 3: 69–88.

———. 1999a. Boundaries as social practice and discourse: The Finnish-Russian border. *Regional Studies* 33: 669–80.

———. 1999b. The Finnish-Russian border in the world of de-territorialization. In L. Hedegaard and B. Lindström, eds. *The NEBI (North European and Baltic Sea Integration) Yearbook 1999*, 215–28. Berlin: Springer.

———. 1999c. Nationalizing the everyday life: Individual and collective identities as practice and discourse. *Geography Research Forum* 19: 4–21.

———. 2002. Boundaries in a globalizing world. In K. Anderson, M. Domosh, S. Pile, and N. Thrift, eds. *Handbook of Cultural Geography*. London: Sage.

Parkkonen, M. 1999a. Rajan pahimmat ongelmat heroiini ja lapsiprostituutio. *Helsingin Sanomat*, 23 October.

———. 1999b. Värtsilän salakauppa levinnyt Kiteelle. *Helsingin Sanomat*, 24 October.

Pihlaja, J. 1999. Venäläisturistien kiinnostus ostosmatkoihin säilynyt. *Helsingin Sanomat*, 18 June.

Räikkönen, H. 1999. Venäläisyys Lappeenrannan toiminnallisissa yhteyksissä ja maisemassa. Mc.S. thesis, University of Helsinki, Department of Geography.

Shapiro, M. J., and H. R. Alker, eds. 1996. *Challenging Boundaries*. Minneapolis: University of Minnesota Press.

Sibley, D. 1995. *Geographies of Exclusion*. London: Routledge.

Smith, A. D. 1991. *National Identity*. Reno: University of Nevada Press.

———. 1996. Culture, community and territory: The politics of ethnicity and nationalism. *International Affairs* 72: 445–58.

Susiluoto, I. 1999. *Pieni Karjalakirja*. Helsinki: Ajatus.

Taylor, P. J. 1994. The state as container: Territoriality in the modern world-system. *Progress in Human Geography* 18: 151–62.

Tiitta, A. 1994. Harmaakiven maa. Zacharias Topelius ja Suomen maantiede. *Bidrag till kännedom av Finlands natur och folk* 147.

Tuorila, L. 1999. Nykyaika puree rajavartioinnissa. *Hallinto* 6: 6–9.

Välimaa, S. 1999. Itärajasta lisää sykettä Sallaan. *Kaleva*, 10 August.

Voionmaa, V. 1919. *Suomen uusi asema. Maantieteellisiä ja historiallisia peruspiirteitä*. Porvoo, Finland: WSOY.

———. 1933. Suomen historian maantieteellinen pohja. In G. Suolahti et al., eds. *Suomen kulttuurihistoria*, 13–25. Jyväskylä-Helsinki: Gummerus.

Chapter Eleven

An Emerging Borderland in Eastern Slavonia?

Mladen Klemencic and Clive Schofield

It is perhaps axiomatic to observe that nowhere in Europe have borders and borderlands undergone such a profound transformation in recent years as in the geographical space that, before 1991, constituted 'Yugoslavia'. Where internal limits existed, international boundaries (re)emerged. The functions of these boundaries have also, inevitably, changed radically, and this has had fundamental implications for the borderland communities in question, the compositions of which have also frequently been substantially altered.

Eastern Slavonia emerged as a distinct politico-geographical entity following the breakup of the former Yugoslav federal state. In 1991 the region formed the front line in the armed conflict between Croatian and Serbian/Yugoslav forces and as a result experienced considerable material destruction and human suffering. Between 1991 and 1995, the region was subject to international intervention in the form of a United Nations peacekeeping force that served to maintain the status quo.

In late 1995, in parallel with the Dayton peace negotiations relating to Bosnia-Hercegovina, agreement was reached on the reintegration of the region into Croatia. As a result, a two-year process was undertaken by the parties to the conflict, which formally reached its conclusion in early 1998. During this period, Eastern Slavonia was governed by the United Nations Transitional Authority in Eastern Slavonia (UNTAES). Although the UN has now relinquished its authority in Eastern Slavonia and the region is internationally recognised as an integral part of the Republic of Croatia, the consequences of the conflict are still significant and painful. The process of reintegration is an ongoing one, with the return of refugees and displaced persons and reconciliation between the Croat, Serbian, and Hungarian communities the focal issues in the normalisation of everyday life.

This chapter traces events in Eastern Slavonia between 1991 and the present and assesses the success of UN efforts at dispute resolution. Events in the region in the aftermath of the UN's withdrawal are also subject to scrutiny, with a view to exploring the prospects for the region and analysing whether and how new borderland regional identities are being forged in Eastern Slavonia.

WHAT AND WHERE IS EASTERN SLAVONIA?

The Croatian territory occupied by Serb forces in 1991, during the early stages of the disintegration of Yugoslavia, is commonly referred to as 'Eastern Slavonia'. The region in question is defined by the limit of Serbian control rather than coinciding with a distinct, pre-existing administrative area. In fact, 'Eastern Slavonia' is composed of parts of three larger historical regions: Slavonia, Syrmium (Srijem), and Baranja (see figure 11.1).

That part of eastern Croatia that was occupied by Serb forces in 1991 comprised almost the entirety of non-Hungarian Baranja, the easternmost part of Slavonia, and the Croatian part of Syrmium. The area in question can therefore be accurately referred to as 'Baranja, eastern Slavonia, and western Syrmium'. Given this rather cumbersome title, it is perhaps not surprising that the shorthand term 'Eastern Slavonia' came into use. The terms 'Croatia's Danube Region' and 'Croatian Danubeland' (*Hrvatsko Podunavlje*) have also been used, particularly by Croatian sources, as alternative, concise names for the region. These terms emphasise Croatian sovereignty as well as the pivotal role of the Danube in the area. As far as the local Serb authorities controlling the region in the 1991–1995 period were concerned, however, the area was simply part of the internationally unrecognised 'Republic of Krajina'. United Nations peacekeepers officially referred to the region as UN Protected Area, Sector East.

The boundary between the Yugoslav federal republics of Croatia and Serbia (Vojvodina) was delimited in detail in 1945–1946 and could be said to be well established by the time it was elevated to the status of an international boundary with the breakup of Yugoslavia. The only boundary dispute as such between the two sides can be termed a positional one relating to pockets of territory belonging to either state that have ended up on the 'wrong' side of the river as a result of the meanderings of the Danube.

Eastern Slavonia, comprising the easternmost part of Croatia along the Danube river, has an area of 2,580 square kilometres amounting to 4.6

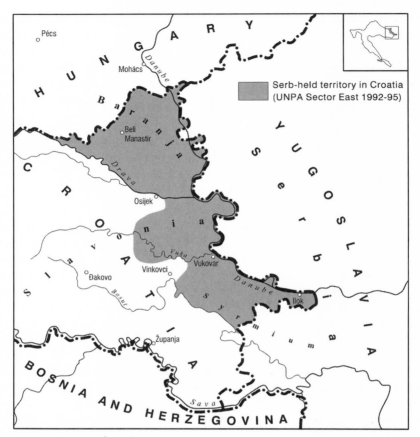

Figure 11.1.   Eastern Slavonia

percent of Croatia's state territory. According to the last census prior to the conflict that engulfed the region, that of 1991, the territory constituting Eastern Slavonia had a population of 193,513. Of this total Croats were the most numerous inhabitants, numbering 86,086 (44.5 percent), but the population was clearly a mixed one. Serbs represented the second most numerous ethnic group in the region, accounting for 67,676 inhabitants (35 percent). Other nationalities (including Hungarians, Ruthenians, and those who opted to define themselves as 'Yugoslavs') and those who chose not to declare a particular nationality amounted to 39,751 people (20.5 percent). The Hungarian community was concentrated in Baranja, while a small Ruthenian population was settled in the villages of Petrovci and Mikluševci near Vukovar.

In economic terms the Danubian portion of Croatia undoubtedly represented the most significant 'gain' the Serbs made in the course of the 1991 Serbo-Croat war. In contrast to the sparsely inhabited and economically peripheral nature of the Krajina uplands, low-lying eastern Croatia was heavily populated and developed, boasting light industry and the most productive agricultural land in the country on the floodplains of the Danube. The area also provides the eastern hinterland for Croatia's fourth largest city, Osijek. Moreover, in Syrmium, near Djeletovci, Serbian forces occupied the largest oil-producing region in the former Yugoslavia. In the late 1980s the production of oil from these fields was approximately 5,200 barrels per day.

Strategically, the Serb-occupied area provided Serbia (Yugoslavia) with a buffer zone and bridgehead on the western side of the major physical obstacle to a Serb offensive against Croatia, the Danube. The Serb occupation also amputated Croatia's Danubian character (through the port at Vukovar) and thus access to Europe's largest inland waterway system. In addition, as the site of the heaviest fighting of the 1991 conflict, the reintegration of Eastern Slavonia, and the town of Vukovar in particular, acquired great symbolic importance for Croatia.

THE OCCUPATION OF EASTERN SLAVONIA AND INTERNATIONAL INTERVENTION

Eastern Croatia is the only part of Croatia that shares a border with Serbia (Vojvodina). Because of this proximity to Serbia proper, this region suffered the brunt of the Serbian offensive of July 1991 and experienced some of the most intense fighting of the Croat-Serb conflict.

Prior to the conflict Serbs were a minority in all five border municipalities. This soon changed. As a result of what is now commonly termed 'ethnic cleansing', the vast majority of the non-Serb population, in excess of 100,000 people, fled or were forced out. This campaign of ethnic cleansing was somewhat less severe in Baranja than in Slavonia and Syrmium; nevertheless, the impact was significant.

The collapse of the former Yugoslavia in 1991 seemed to take the international community by surprise (Almond 1994). Nevertheless, mediation was attempted, starting with the dispatch of a fact-finding mission of observers to the scene of the crisis by the European Community in mid-1991. As the conflict developed, the international community's involvement increased.

A UN peace-keeping operation, officially named the UN Protection Force (UNPROFOR), was intended as an interim arrangement with the main aim of creating conditions for political negotiations and the overall solution of the post-Yugoslav crises through those negotiations. As part of the so-called Vance Plan, UN troops were stationed in parts of Croatia designated as UN Protected Areas (UNPAs), which were to be demilitarised; the role of UNPROFOR was to ensure that the areas remained demilitarised. UNPROFOR, together with the humanitarian agencies of the UN, would also ensure safe and peaceful return of displaced persons to their homes within the UNPAs. The entire area under UN protection was divided for operational purposes into four 'sectors' (East, West, North, South). Eastern Slavonia was designated UNPA Sector East.

CONSOLIDATION BY FORCE AND PEACEFUL REINTEGRATION OF EASTERN SLAVONIA

The ambiguous nature of the Vance Plan concerning the role of the UN peacekeepers and the future of the UNPAs was at least partially responsible for the perceived failure of the international community's intervention. UNPROFOR was caught between the Croatian interpretation of the plan—that the UN's role should be to assist the Croatian authorities to reassert their control over the Serb-occupied areas, to disarm the Serbs, and to assist in the return of Croatian refugees to the UNPAs—and the Serb view, that the UN force was there to protect the Serb-held areas and ensure their separation from Croatia. UNPROFOR therefore suffered from the unenviable position of attempting to supervise an agreement that it had neither the mandate nor the resources to enforce, and ultimately was even unable to extend its own authority throughout the UNPAs, which remained under the control of the local Serb authorities.

For more than three years UNPROFOR maintained a traditional peacekeeping role, fulfilling a 'disengagement' mission by patrolling lines of confrontation and reporting incidents between opposing forces (Boutros-Ghali 1992). However, the UNPAs were by no means demilitarised, no discernible progress was seen on the return of refugees in the Serb-occupied areas, and no sincere talks on reintegration of the UNPAs into Croatia proper took place. This lack of progress gave rise to Croatian fears that the UN peacekeepers were merely helping to preserve an unsatisfactory de facto situation analogous to the UN operation in divided Cyprus, with the prospect of a permanent institutionalised partition of Croatia. As a result of these frustrations, coupled with a very significant enhancement in the capabilities of Croatia's armed forces after 1991, Zagreb changed tack, essentially taking the matter into its own hands. By August 1995 military offensives had resulted in the Croatian authorities regaining control over the Serb-controlled parts of Western Slavonia and former UN sectors

North and South (the Krajina). As a result, the Serb-held proportion of Croatian state territory was slashed from around one-quarter to less than 5 percent: Eastern Slavonia (UNPA Sector East).

These events, coupled with the successes of Bosnian and Croatian forces in western and central Bosnia, strengthened Zagreb's negotiating position over Eastern Slavonia considerably. The international diplomatic climate also favoured the resolution of the Eastern Slavonian 'problem', which was viewed by U.S. authorities as a necessary precondition for the Dayton negotiations and peace in Bosnia (Ó'Tuathail 1996). A definitive and peaceful resolution to the Eastern Slavonia dispute was perceived as removing an obstacle to peace in Bosnia, leaving the road to Dayton open and paved.

The peaceful reintegration of Eastern Slavonia is based on the Basic Agreement on the Region of Eastern Slavonia, Baranja, and Western Syrmium of 12 November 1995. This agreement, consisting of fourteen points, proposed a staged peaceful reintegration of the region into Croatia within one year, with the possibility of an extension of not more than an additional year. All refugees from the region would be allowed to return, while the pre-existing Serb population would be able to remain. The agreement was accepted and confirmed by UN Security Council Resolution (UNSCR) 1025 of 30 November 1995, and on 15 January 1996 UNTAES was established for an initial twelve-month period.

The UNTAES mission can be readily divided into several stages. The first stage, lasting roughly up to September 1996, involved initial meetings of 'executive committees' tasked with addressing various infrastructural problems in fields such as telecommunications, road and rail traffic, agriculture, and municipal and health services. These committees consisted of Croatian and Serbian technical experts, assisted by international mediators. Although these negotiations were by no means always harmonious, they did take place as scheduled, and this step-by-step approach ultimately yielded significant results.

Plans for the demilitarisation of the region met with qualified success; the concentration of weapons in the region certainly decreased significantly, but the collection of small arms remained incomplete. The demilitarisation campaign was followed by the deployment of a Transitional Police Force (TPF) starting in July 1996. The TPF was a mixed Croat and Serb force trained at a U.S. police academy in Budapest. Initially the TPF consisted mainly of Serbian members, but over time the number of Croats increased. Croatian government payments to the region's pensioners, whatever their nationality, were also introduced, paid in Croatian kuna.

The second phase of UNTAES's activities lasted roughly from September to the end of 1996. The main actions undertaken in this period related to the full reintegration of public services. The Croatian government opened offices in the region so that Croatian documents could be issued to the local inhabitants. However, this process was not without hitches, as on several occasions such offices were closed as a result of Serb protests over the fate of Eastern Slavonia and Serb rights once reintegration with Croatia was completed. The autumn of 1996 also saw the start of de-mining efforts, initially concentrated on villages close to the former division line.

Tensions ran high in Eastern Slavonia in early 1997 preceding local elections scheduled for 16 March, as the Serb population prepared itself for the region's reintegration into Croatia, scheduled for 17 July 1997. There were also widespread fears of a Serbian exodus from the region on transfer to Croatian control. In an effort to reassure the Serb population and persuade the UN that any such exodus would not be their fault, on 13 January the Croatian government presented a *Memorandum on the Completion of Peaceful Reintegration* to UNTAES, outlining the Serbs' future rights. The proposals, which went significantly beyond existing agreements, guaranteed that ethnic Serbs would be exempt from military service with the Croatian army for two years after reintegration; reserved two seats for Serbs in Croatia's upper house of government; promised advisory positions for Serbs in the interior, justice, education, and culture ministries; promised cultural and educational autonomy; and promised full voting rights to all Serbs who obtained Croatian papers. Agreement was also reached in March between senior Croatian and UN officials on co-operation towards the 'two-way' return of an estimated 150,000 people displaced by the war in Croatia. This would allow some 80,000 Croats to return to their homes in Eastern Slavonia and 60,000 Serb refugees to return home to western Croatia.

Eventually, as a result of the efforts of all sides, voting took place in Eastern Slavonia on 13–14 April as part of Croatia's local elections, with the local Serbian leadership deciding at the last minute that their parties would participate. The UN transitional administrator (retired U.S. general Jacques Klein) pronounced the voting 'free and fair', despite irregularities resulting in the polls being open longer than planned, and stated that this represented 'a victory for reconciliation [refugees'] return, and a better future' (*RFE/RL Newsline* 23 April 1997: part ii).

Eastern Slavonia's population voted along clear ethnic lines. The Serbs voted for the only Serbian party, the SDSS, and the Croats primarily, but not exclusively, voted for President Tudjman's ruling Croatian Democratic Union (HDZ). The elections were held within the framework of the Croatian counties of Vukovar-Syrmium and Osijek-Baranja, both of which stretch beyond the UNTAES-controlled zone.[1] Displaced persons were also able to cast their votes at polling stations outside Eastern Slavonia. As a result, Croatian parties secured sixteen out of Eastern Slavonia's twenty-seven districts, leaving the SSDS eleven.

In July 1997 the UN Security Council voted in favour of a final six-month extension of the UNTAES mandate, to 15 January 1998. General Klein took the opportunity to claim a large measure of success for the mission, pointing out that Eastern Slavonia had been reintegrated into the Croatian electricity and telephone networks, local elections had been completed successfully, 98 percent of the region's population had now accepted Croatian identity papers, and a mixed Croat-Serb joint police force had been set up in the region, with seven hundred Serbs involved.

The key event related to Eastern Slavonia that took place in late 1997 was the negotiation of a soft border regime between Croatia and Yugoslavia. The two sides signed six agreements in Belgrade on 15 September dealing with transportation, border regions, social insurance, and legal aid. This was represented as the most significant step towards normalisation that the parties had taken. The hardest agreement to reach was that on cross-border traffic. Under the accord, citizens of both countries living in the border area are able to cross the border with a special pass and do not need a visa.

Implementing the agreement proved problematic and was repeatedly delayed. Eventually, however, on 14 December 1997, the Small Border Regime, as it was called, came into effect. At the time it went into operation it was reported that eight thousand Eastern Slavonian residents had been issued with the special passes (*Tanjug* 1997). This 'soft border' regime worked effectively and proved to be an important component in the overall reintegration process. Indeed, the opportunity for the local population, and in particular Eastern Slavonia's Serbs, to cross the border with relative ease was especially significant given the context of Yugoslavia's international isolation, including sanctions and border restrictions.

Finally, on 15 January 1998, Eastern Slavonia returned to full Croatian control, although a UN police force stayed on for a further six months at the request of both the Croatian and local Serb authorities.

BEYOND REINTEGRATION

The key challenges faced by the region in the aftermath of reintegration into Croatia were and remain the implementation of the refugee return program, encompassing the return of displaced persons, predominantly Croatians and Hungarians, to the region; the corresponding return of Croatian Serbs resident in Eastern Slavonia to other parts of Croatia (notably the Krajina); and the return of Croatian Serb refugees in Bosnia and Yugoslavia to Eastern Slavonia and other parts of Croatia. Fundamentally linked to this process was the vital issue of securing the retention of the local Serb population who had resided in the Danube region throughout the 1990s, in order to preserve (or re-create) the multiethnic character of the region.

Although ominous predictions of a massive flight of Eastern Slavonia's Serbian population to Yugoslavia proved to be unfounded, a gradual exodus of ethnic Serbs from the region was observed in the immediate post-reintegration period. Although the Organization for Security and Co-operation in Europe (OSCE) and UN representatives in Croatia acknowledged that the situation in Eastern Slavonia was generally stable, significant concerns were raised in early 1998 about the fact that Serbs were continuing to leave the region, often under direct pressure from spontaneously returning Croatian refugees keen to retake possession of property occupied by Serbian families. OSCE and UN sources cited growing feelings of insecurity on the part of the Serbs and a conviction that the government in Zagreb was not committed to seeing them stay as the chief reasons for the population movement. The latter perception is reinforced by the fact that although Serbs formed a substantial minority in Croatia prior to 1991, amounting to approximately 12 percent of the total population, in 1999 that figure was closer to 6 percent.

Substantial and sustained international diplomatic pressure was therefore subsequently brought to bear on Croatia to facilitate the return of Croatian Serb refugees to their homes and to prevent the Serb population of Eastern Slavonia from fleeing to Yugoslavia. Indeed, Germany's chief of refugee affairs on 23 April 1998 went so far as to raise the prospect of sanctions against Zagreb if the situation persisted. In this context, the Croatian government's initial program, which was designed to facilitate the return of refugees to Eastern Slavonia and which linked the right of return to provision of housing and international aid, was greeted with protests. The apparently ambivalent nature of the Croatian government's policy towards its minorities did little to reassure the ethnic Serbs of Eastern Slavonia, whose leaders complained of discrimination and harassment of Serbs in the region, particularly on the part of Croat returnees. A spokesman for the OSCE meanwhile commented that 'return is an individual right and . . . cannot be made dependent on other conditions' (*RFE/RL Newsline* 2 April 1998).

In May 1998, however, the U.S. ambassador to Zagreb stated that Croatia had yielded to all the criticisms made by the international community related to the return of Serbian refugees. Croatia's revised plans for the return of refugees, guaranteeing 'all citizens' the right to return home, was approved by the Croatian parliament on 26 June. The plan envisaged as many as 220,000 people returning to their homes inside and outside Croatia by 2003, with 24,000 ethnic Serbs expected to return to Croatia in 1998 alone. The new plan was welcomed by the leader of the Serb community in Croatia, Vojislav Stanimirovic, in early July 1998.

Nevertheless, the essentially nationalist character of the Croatian regime, President Tudjman's leanings towards authoritarianism, the limitations on the democratisation of political life in Croatia (emphasised by the ruling party's dominance of access to the printed and particularly electronic media), and persistent allegations of cronyism and corruption at high levels severely hampered Croatia's professed aspirations for integration into Euro-Atlantic institutions. These factors served to undermine Croatia's economy as a whole and encourage a gradual Serb exodus from Eastern Slavonia.

In this context, the most significant post-reintegration development in Croatia was the demise of President Tudjman in December 1999 and the change of government in January 2000, when Tudjman's ruling HDZ party was swept from power.[2] The first priority of the new Croatian government has been to improve the economic lot of its citizens.[3] To achieve this goal and end Croatia's international isolation, a policy of positive engagement with Western states has been adopted. Alongside efforts towards enhancing democratisation, freedom of the press, and anti-corruption efforts, a key component of this process has been to guarantee minority and refugee rights.

Thus, on 11 May 2000, the Croatian parliament passed a minority rights law guaranteeing minority rights and freedoms in line with European standards. The new law deals with minorities' cultural, educational, and linguistic rights and restored an earlier law guaranteeing proportional representation in parliament for minorities constituting more than 8 percent of the population. As previously noted, the Serbian portion of Croatia's population fell drastically in the wake of Croatia's military actions of 1995. However, many Serbs have returned, and should they constitute 8 percent or more of the population by the time of the next census, they could secure 19 of the 151 legislative seats. Additionally, just under US$3 million of the government's new budget was reported to have been earmarked for minority affairs, the largest part of which is destined for the Serbs (*RFE/RL Newsline* 12 May 2000).

Such moves accompanied the ongoing and successful execution of the so-called two-way return process. According to figures provided by Croatia's Office for Displaced Persons and Refugees (ODPR), the official body charged with conducting the program, by 1 May 2000, the total number of formerly displaced persons who had returned to the region (former refugees, mainly Croats and other non-Serbs) stood at 48,995. The number waiting to return (predominantly awaiting the completion of reconstruction activities) was 32,429. Complementing this movement of population, the ODPR had also assisted in the return of 31,717 people (mainly Serbs temporarily settled in Eastern Slavonia) from the Danube region to other parts of Croatia. In addition, some 4,500 people were still waiting to return: 2,600 to other parts of Croatia and 1,900 internally displaced within the region and awaiting return to their homes.

It is worth observing that the dynamics of the population makeup of Eastern Slavonia are also closely related to the success of efforts in the fields of reconstruction and economic revitalisation in the region. According to Croatian officials, the international community has exhibited a notable lack of enthusiasm for underpinning the reintegration of Eastern Slavonia into Croatia economically, where ultimately it may be most significant. Although the Croatian government has initiated a significant number of projects in the region, Eastern Slavonia remains economically depressed, and this has promoted substantial population shifts. Although economic stagnation can be partially blamed on over-concentration on housing and infrastructure projects rather than economic restructuring, privatisation, and facilitating business start-ups, this situation can be to a large extent attributed to donor fatigue (*RFE/RL Newsline* 10 November 1999). Aid, attention, and resources have been diverted to other, more pressing, crises such as Kosova, to Eastern Slavonia's detriment.

The multiethnic character of Eastern Slavonia has, for the present at least, been retained. In addition, the new Croatian administration has secured some notable foreign policy successes as a result of its more liberal policies, notably Croatia's May 2000 admission into NATO's Partnership for Peace (something denied to the previous regime). Furthermore, at the time of writing, negotiations are under way on Croatia's membership in the World Trade Organization (WTO), and Brussels has agreed to begin negotiations towards admitting Croatia to various EU-related programs. As Croatian Foreign Minister Tonino Picula noted on 31 May 2000, however, these positive steps are dependent on the development of democracy, human and minority rights, and freedom of the press (*RFE/RL Newsline* 20 June 2000).

BORDERLAND IDENTITIES

In many ways Croatia as a whole can be viewed as a borderland state. This is certainly the case in terms of the Croatian nationalist perception of the country's historical role. The Croatian national identity was suppressed for most of the twentieth century, as a consequence of incorporation within the Serbian-dominated Kingdom of Yugoslavia and later communist Yugoslavia. Following the demise of communism and the breakup of Yugoslavia, however, Croatia finally re-emerged and established its place on the political map of Europe. Having secured its sovereign space in 1991, President Tudjman's government embarked on a program of nation building. The aim of reforging the Croatian national identity was to promote solidarity and national security and, ultimately, to ensure that nation and state become spatially congruent.

Following independence many Croats regarded themselves as finally being 'on their own land'. Tudjman's policies in the first decade of the 'new' state's existence reflected this, promoting the concept of an ethnically Croatian nation-state and a desire to match ethnic to political boundaries. For Tudjman's government, boundaries and territory—the key issues at stake in Eastern Slavonia—were fundamental to establishing or reinforcing a distinctive Croatian national identity, a means of defining the distinction between 'us' and 'them' (Paasi 1996: 10). In this case the 'us' were perceived as Croatians and 'them' as other nationalities, but particularly the Serbs. Indeed, the traditional Croatian nationalist view is one of Croatia as a barrier, with Serbs and Serbia portrayed as the primary threat to Croatia and ultimately the West as a whole, in their role as representatives of the 'hostile' East.

The prevailing national narratives of the Tudjman regime drew on a definition of Croatia as a borderland poised on the West-East division line, but one oriented towards the West throughout its history—a role that Croatia played in particular in the course of the Ottoman conquest of southeastern Europe. The term applied to Croatia in the Ottoman period, when Croatia formed the bulwark of Austro-Hungary's military frontier, was *antemurale christianitatis,* or the 'defender of Christianity.' If Croatia can be regarded as a borderland state, then Eastern Slavonia, positioned as it is in direct contact with Serbia and thus viewed as representing the 'front line', can be regarded as the critical borderland within that state.

Similarly, if Croats in general are seen as *antemurale christianitatis,* then Croats from Eastern Slavonia have been viewed as some sort of *antemurale Croatiae*—a view promoting a radically nationalised community, hostile to the 'others' represented by the Serbs and re-created and reinforced by the Serb-Croatian conflict of 1991. This has provided the Croatian community of Eastern Slavonia, often focused through groups representing displaced people, with a distinctive borderland identity that has proved itself to be highly sensitive to any moves towards an increase in transboundary cooperation between Croatia and Serbia. Many Eastern Slavonian Croats opposed the Small Border Regime on this basis, and the Croatian nationalist lobby has repeatedly blocked the new government's reconstruction bill, which would make funds available to Serbian as well as Croatian refugees on the basis that this would 'give the [Serbian] aggressors rights equal to those of the [Croatian] victims' (*RFE/RL Newsline* 22 May 2000).

Croats, and those from Eastern Slavonia in particular, are perhaps best characterised as 'national borderlanders' (Martinez 1994: 6). That is, although they may be subject to transboundary economic and cultural influences, they have

> 'low-level or superficial contact with the opposite side of the border owing to their indifference to their next-door neighbours or their unwillingness or inability to function in any substantive way in another society'—in this case Serbia. In contrast, Serbs may be regarded as 'transnational borderlanders': 'individuals who maintain significant ties with the neighbouring nation; they seek to overcome obstacles that impede such contact and they take advantage of every opportunity to visit, shop, work, study or live intermittently on the "other" side'. (Martinez 1994: 6)

Although the Serbian community of Eastern Slavonia has had to come to terms with the reality of the existence of the Croatia-Yugoslavia international boundary, many remain dependent on Serbia as their 'mental homeland'. Many therefore accept Croatia only formally while maintaining a distinctive Serbian identity. It is therefore of crucial importance to them that the international border remain permeable. Many have relatives and friends across the border, and some maintain properties or take advantage of educational and employment opportunities in Yugoslavia. The Small Border Regime is therefore of great significance to Eastern Slavonia's Serbs because it provides the legal framework to develop transboundary activities. The region's geographical proximity to Serbia proper, coupled with ease of access across the international boundary, provided a sense of security that was probably decisive in the majority of the Serbian community's decision to remain in Croatia.

Besides the Croats and Serbs, other ethnic groups, such as Hungarians and Ruthenians, live in the region in smaller numbers. Clearly the Croat-Serb conflict has overshadowed developments for these communities in the last decade. While many Hungarians left Eastern Slavonia for nearby Hungary proper as a consequence of the conflict, many Ruthenians, far from their psychological ethnic homeland of Transcarpathia (part of Ukraine), were displaced within Croatia. Both communities appear to accept Eastern Slavonia's existence within the Croatian political-geographical framework. Furthermore, Croatia's legal provisions regarding minority rights, particularly in the post-Tudjman period, seem to provide an acceptable framework for their continued existence in the region.

Their ethnic identity is recognised by law, and support is provided for cultural and educational activities, together with the possibility of representation in parliament.

CONCLUSION: PROSPECTS FOR EASTERN SLAVONIA

The peaceful reintegration of Eastern Slavonia into Croatia has rightly been viewed as a significant success. Indeed, when set against the dismal record of failure of other international peace-keeping and peace-building efforts elsewhere in the former Yugoslavia, UNTAES's achievements in Eastern Slavonia take on an added lustre. Although Eastern Slavonia saw extensive ethnic cleansing and a radical change in the region's ethnic composition, the 'final' outcome under UN guidance has been a gradual return to the prewar situation.

The UN's success in Eastern Slavonia can in large part be traced to the clear, achievable mandate of the UN mission in the region. In contrast to the general framework and vagueness of UNPROFOR's mandate, UNTAES had clear-cut goals and forceful leadership in the shape, primarily, of General Jacques Klein.

The UN's performance in Eastern Slavonia should, however, be seen in the context of former Yugoslavia and its disputes as a whole—particularly the course of the war in Bosnia. The peaceful reintegration of the region was only possible in the wake of the profound military reversals suffered by Serbian forces elsewhere in Croatia and in Bosnia in 1995, coupled with a sea change in the international community's, and especially the United States's, approach to the problems of the region. Ultimately, despite the fact that it appeared in 1995 that Croatian forces were poised to retake the region by force, all the actors concerned had an interest in the resolution of the Eastern Slavonia issue because a peaceful compromise there provided the potential for trade-offs elsewhere. The apparent success of UNTAES has, however, been called into question by events in Eastern Slavonia following its full reintegration into the Croatian state. In particular, concerns were raised over a gradual exodus of the Serb population from the region and continuing intercommunity tension.

In the immediate aftermath of reintegration, although Eastern Slavonia remained multiethnic, the atmosphere in the region resembled more a cessation of hostilities than a real peace. Ethnic tensions were pronounced, and intercommunity relations were characterised by suspicion—Serbs, for example, fearing Croatian actions in relation to education as attempts to promote ethnic assimilation and complaining of discrimination and intimidation. These attitudes were allied to a perception that Tudjman's nationalist-oriented government lacked the political will to rebuild a multiethnic Croatian society, a situation exacerbated by economic difficulties. Meanwhile, Tudjman's government exhibited suspicion bordering on paranoia with regard to international mediation efforts, fearing an international conspiracy to somehow resurrect Yugoslavia. Indeed, this was one of the chief factors believed to have been behind the stalling of the soft border regime for Eastern Slavonia.

Although at present there seems to be little indication that Eastern Slavonia and Serb-Croat relations in general are entering a post-nationalist era, the end of the Tudjman era in Croatian politics provides considerable hope for the prospects of Eastern Slavonia evolving into a peaceful multiethnic borderland. The new government's commitment to minority and refugee rights as a central pillar in its drive towards integration with Euro-Atlantic institutions and economic recovery bodes well for Eastern Slavonia's minorities. Similarly, the new Croatian government's willingness to engage in regional co-operation (while simultaneously rejecting any new 'Balkan or neo-Yugoslav' state) represents another positive sign (*RFE/RL Newsline* 12 January 2000). It is therefore possible to envisage (and hope for) the eventual emergence of a unique and sustainable multiethnic borderland identity in Eastern Slavonia.

Nevertheless, at present the inhabitants of Eastern Slavonia still tend to define themselves on the basis of their ethnic backgrounds, and there is little indication that a distinctive identity linked to the emergence of Eastern Slavonia as a separate borderland region is being formulated. Croats and Serbs from the region may be aware of their special position within their respective communities but clearly continue to identify themselves first and foremost as Croats or Serbs.

An Eastern Slavonian borderland identity will take a considerable period of time to develop, and it seems clear that at present no unified regional identity exists. However, distinct regional identities may emerge and eventually interrelate or even merge. From a Croatian perspective, returnees to the region will in time have to come to accept their Serbian neighbours as equal citizens, and there are positive signs that this is taking place. The geographical proximity of Serbia, viewed as a threat and geopolitical disadvantage, may in future be perceived as an opportunity and even advantage, particularly in economic terms. From the Serbian perspective, a transboundary identity may well be forged, with easy access to Serbia across a soft border representing a key component. In this regard the fact that the Small Border Regime is in place and operating successfully is significant. Indeed, it has been observed that the special passes allowing easy access to Yugoslavia have been taken up by some Croat residents of Eastern Slavonia so that they can take advantage of price differentials across the border. The fact that for some at least the border is beginning to be perceived as an opportunity rather than a constraint is an encouraging sign—even if the scale of the transactions is limited.[4]

It is therefore conceivable that the present alienated Croatia-Yugoslavia border will in time shift towards one that is coexistent or even interdependent (Martinez 1994: 1–5). The importance of this process, and the progress of interethnic relations in Eastern Slavonia, should not be underestimated, as it has the potential to profoundly influence bilateral relations. On the one hand, progress in Eastern Slavonia may serve to stimulate a normalisation in contacts between Croatia and Serbia; on the other, a deterioration in relations could have a correspondingly negative influence on the two states—ultimately with the potential to generate renewed conflict.

NOTES

1. In that part of Eastern Slavonia within Vukovar-Syrmium county, there were 37,125 votes: 34,402 for SDSS candidates, 2,077 for the HDZ, and 646 for other Croatian parties. In the part within Osijek-Baranja county, there were 29,777 votes: 24,406 for the SDSS and 5,231 for the HDZ and other 'Croatian' parties.

2. In parliamentary elections on 3 January the Social Democratic–Liberal coalition won seventy-one seats, while its allied coalition of four smaller centrist parties won twenty-four seats. The HDZ, in power since 1990, was reduced to forty seats. Iviva Racan became Croatian prime minister. Subsequently, on 7 February Stipe Mesic of the four centrist parties in government defeated the challenge of Drazen Budisa of the Social Democrat–Liberal coalition to become the successor to President Tudjman (*RFE/RL Newsline* 12 January 2000, 8 February 2000).

3. In January 2000 it was reported that the unemployment rate in Croatia was in excess of 20 percent and monthly per capita income was approximately US$400 (*RFE/ RL Newsline* 4 January 2000).

4. It is worth noting here that transboundary trade and interaction have been severely hampered by the fact that the bridges across the Danube between Croatia and Yugoslavia were either destroyed or severely damaged in the Kosova NATO air campaign.

REFERENCES

Almond, M. 1994. *Europe's Backyard War*. London: Heinemann.
Baletic, Z., et al. 1994. *Croatia between Aggression and Peace*. Zagreb: AGM.
Boban, L. 1992. *Hrvatske granice [Croatian Borders], 1918–1991*. Zagreb: Skolska knjiga.
Boundary and Security Bulletin. 1993–2000. Durham, England: International Boundaries
    Research Unit.
Boutros-Ghali, B. 1992. *An Agenda for Peace*. New York: United Nations.

Cohen, B., and G. Stamkoski, eds. 1995. *With No Peace to Keep: United Nations Peacekeeping and the War in the Former Yugoslavia.* London: Grainpress.

Fontes: Izvori za hrvatsku povijest [Sources for Croatian History]. 1995. Vol. 1. Zagreb: Croatian State Archives.

Hill, R. 1993. Preventive diplomacy, peace-making and peace-keeping. In *SIPRI Yearbook 1993,* 45–65. Stockholm: SIPRI.

Hooson, D., ed. 1994. *Geography and National Identity.* Oxford: Blackwell.

Kicošev, S. 1993. Promene broja i etnicke strukture stanovništva Baranje tokom 20 veka [Changes of numbers and ethnic structure of the population of Baranja during the 20th century]. In *Srbi u Hrvatskoj, naseljavanje, broj i teritorijalni razmještaj,* 225–40, Beograd, Yugoslavia: Geografski fakultet, Univerziteta u Beogradu.

Klemencic, M. 1993. Causes and dynamic of the war in Croatia. *Acta Geographica Croatica* 28: 187–94.

Klemencic, M., and C. H. Schofield. 1995a. An UNhappy birthday in former Yugoslavia: A Croatian border war. *Boundary and Security Bulletin* 2, no. 3: 47–54.

———. 1995b. Summer storms over the Balkans. *Boundary and Security Bulletin* 3, no. 3: 34–40.

———. 1995c. After the storm. *Jane's Intelligence Review* 7, no. 12: 542–44.

Martinez, O. J. 1994. The dynamics of border interaction. In C. H. Schofield, ed. *Global Boundaries,* 1–15. London: Routledge.

Ó'Tuathail, G. 1996. *Critical Geopolitics.* Minneapolis: University of Minnesota Press.

Paasi, A. 1996. Inclusion, exclusion and territorial identities. *Nordisk Samhallsgeografik Tidskrift* 23, October: 3–17.

RFE/RL Newsline. 1997–2000 (Radio Free Europe/Radio Liberty, Prague).

Smith, G., et al. 1998. *Nation-Building in Post-Soviet Borderlands: The Politics of National Identities.* Cambridge: Cambridge University Press.

Szajkowski, B. 1993. *Encyclopaedia of Conflicts, Disputes and Flashpoints in Eastern Europe, Russia and the Successor States.* Harlow, England: Longman.

Tanjug. 1997. 14 December (Yugoslav news agency, Belgrade, Yugoslavia).

UNPROFOR. 1994. Working for peace together. Leaflet. Zagreb: UNPROFOR Division of Information.

Vego, M. 1993. The army of Serbian Krajina. *Jane's Intelligence Review* 10, no. 5: 438–45.

Chapter Twelve

Galician Identities and Political Cartographies on the Polish-Ukrainian Border

Luiza Bialasiewicz and John O'Loughlin

With the removal of the Iron Curtain, dramatic geopolitical changes have reshaped the daily lives of eastern Europeans, especially those living near the borders of the former Soviet Union. The final delimitation of the border of Europe (here, defined as countries sharing membership in the European Union and other Western political/military institutions such as NATO) is, as yet, unfinished, with the possibility of a new geopolitical divide along the former Soviet border further encouraged by the differential rates of political and economic transitions amongst the countries of the region. This new border geography is being formed, however, against a historical backdrop that places current border regions not as peripheries but as centres of long-standing regional entities. Galicia, straddling the Polish-Ukrainian border, remains not just a regional memory as a former autonomous Habsburg province but is rapidly being re-created as a post-1989 spatial-historical imagination and an entry card into Europe.

As the ex-Eastern Bloc states shake off the spatial-symbolic stigmata of the Cold War order, their relationship to the broader European whole—the perennial question 'Will we qualify as European?'—has come to dominate debates from Bialystok to Budapest. The question is certainly not new for, over time, the cardinal problem in defining Europe has centred precisely on the inclusion or exclusion of its eastern borderlands. The designation of a European West has, in fact, long been predicated on the notion of Europe as 'not Russia' (O'Loughlin and Kolossov 2002). The search for Europe's 'natural' boundary, which would, somehow, separate the civilised, modern West from the premodern East, has always been crucial to this process of signification: a 'civilisational' divide that has fluctuated according to prevailing political as well as intellectual requisites (Delanty 1995; Heffernan 1999; Wolff 1994).

The momentous changes of 1989 have come to signify what was, above all, a 'return to Europe', a 'reunion with European civilization from which the countries of Central and Eastern Europe were "unnaturally" wrenched by years of Communist domination' (Shaw 1998: 124; Kundera 1983). Countries such as the Czech Republic, Hungary, and Poland have progressively drifted into what is now often termed Central or East Central Europe, with the term 'Eastern Europe' most often relegated to the ostensibly less-Western successor states to the USSR. The 1998 expansion of the North Atlantic Treaty Organization (NATO) to encompass the Czech Republic, Hungary, and Poland has served only to accentuate what is the primary geopolitical divide emergent in the region today: the growing chasm between those states anointed as bona fide Europeans, slated for fast-track incorporation into Western security and economic structures, and 'the others', relegated to the margins of Europe, if not entirely denied the right to symbolic membership in the European family of nations. The process of geographical myth-making continues—only now carried out by self-appointed Central Europeans (Geremek 1999) as well as by Brussels bureaucrats and Washington policymakers. More than a liberation—a return to some idealised, unbounded Europe of years past—the opening of the Iron Curtain has thus given birth to a whole new set of territorialisations, marking 'some remarkably persistent geopolitical instincts of the European idea through the ages' (Heffernan 1999: 239).

Geographical designations are of no small consequence, however. Testimony to the enormous power vested within spatial narratives, Europeanness has come to denote a 'way in' (Dahrendorf 1999a, 1999b), the *étoile polaire* for the ex-communist states. The processes of national construction (or, perhaps more accurately, re-construction) in the new European democracies post-1989 and their crafting of bounded territorialised communities have been indelibly marked by questions of these same communities' past and present relationship to the broader European whole. In this chapter we focus on the representational struggle occurring at what is (at least in the short term) the probable future boundary of the European space, the Polish-Ukrainian border. We locate our examination within the emerging tension between the concurrent opening of state boundaries and the accompanying idealisation of shared spaces and multiple identities that contrast with the progressive re-bounding of rigid civilisational, strategic, and economic divides. Our attention focuses on the contrast between post-1989 local re-imaginations of Galicia as a space of civilised multinational coexistence and the geopolitical and civilisational boundary-drawing exercises that cut through the region's heart. In exploring this contradiction, we examine the spatial ideology and iconography of the Galician representation, querying the ways in which its vision as a historical ethnocultural *oikumene* is being proposed as an antidote to the new walls as a novel means of articulating territories and inhabitants in the European cosmos (O'Loughlin 2000). We analyse the ways in which the re-signification of the border as a space—as Galicia—is being used to subvert the borderline and, by extension, other borders that are symbolically coterminous with the confines of Central Europe, of Europe, and of the West.

GALICIAN DREAMS AND GEOPOLITICAL CARTOGRAPHIES

The 'new geopolitics' is characterised, above all, by the multiscalar processes of territorial control and strategic reconsiderations in the era of American hegemony. Rapid political change in the form of democratisation and economic change consequent on globalisation have rendered Cold War lineups anachronistic. Few regions have been altered as much as the 'crush zone' between Europe and Russia. Rather than the coincidence of state borders with strategic zones and a world of division and order, we have entered an era of geopolitical transition that, at least for the short term, will continue to produce numerous territorial alternatives, regional posturings, ideological machinations, and vivid recall of historical antecedents. While geopolitical strategists try to influence the nature and location of new dividing lines, local groups on the divide may not toe the strategic line or fulfil their assigned roles. Existing de jure (political or administrative) borders often overlap with de facto (ethnic, linguistic, cultural, or civilisational) territories, and in a time of evolving political and cultural identities, cartographic claims abound. Earlier ethnic hatreds in 1918–1921 and 1944–1946 resulted tragically in the forced relocation (or ethnic cleansing) of millions in the territories of the former Austro-Hungarian, Russian, and Ottoman empires. The winners, advised by political geographers such as Isaiah Bowman (Martin 1980), tried to reduce rival claims and ethnic mixing by imposing a cartographic order matching political and cultural territories using the principle of exclusivity. Though relatively few ethnically mixed territories remain in the former communist states of Europe, the geopolitical sea change of the end of the Cold War has opened up opportunities for a return to the multiethnic local worlds of the early twentieth century, in which groups shared spaces while maintaining their own linguistic and religious traditions. In such a post-nationalist world, a search for pre-existing regional identities is under way, from the large-scale construction of a *Mitteleuropa* to the regional scale, characterised by cross-border economic development zones like Euro-Bug (along the Bug River, which separates Poland and Belarus) and local regional enterprises like Galicia. If such cross-border and inter-territorial enterprises are successful, then a new geopolitics that is not state dominated will have emerged from the ashes of the European civil wars and subsequent Cold War.

A glance at the 'fragments of Europe' in Foucher's 1993 book offers convincing evidence of the frequent changes of borders of Poland and its neighbours. The maps in this chapter illustrate only some of the historical changes since 966, the traditional date of the establishment of a Polish state. Borders mark the territorial edges of identities, either from above (state formed), from outside (delimited by war victors), or internally (national claims). Although national identities can adapt to new state borders, there is usually a time lag, and historical claims persist long after geopolitical realities have redefined national borders. Further, because identities are constantly made and re-made, so too borders are claimed, counterclaimed, and reclaimed. Borders can be lines of separation (like the Iron Curtain) or contact (as inside the European Union); every geographical boundary combines these functions to some extent. Borders thus structure the opportunities for conflict (rival territorial claims) or co-operation (trade). More than anything else, the nature of the border (guarded, open, strictly or poorly demarcated, partially open, etc.) reflects the nature of the relations between the respective states. Borderlands, the zones of mixture, contact, and conflict, have their own geographies that distinguish them from their states and render them uncomfortable categories to cultural cartographers concerned with heartlands, domains, and cores. Our examination in this chapter highlights but one portion of the vast border zone stretching from Kaliningrad on the Baltic to Odessa on the Black Sea, a vast borderland which, as Applebaum (1994) among others has noted, has been a terrain of struggle for over a thousand years, its cultural, ethnic, and religious diversity only extinguished by the force of post-1945 frontiers.

Paasi (1986, 1996), in his examination of the institutionalisation of regions, argues that one of the first steps in the formation of the conceptual shape of any regional entity/identity is precisely the establishment of a distinct set of territorial symbols, the most important of these being the name. Naming creates a togetherness, a shared representation of belonging, and joins personal histories to a collective history. As representations of space, regions are mythical constructions, often later legalised with state symbols, governmental agency making, borders, and other symbols of political control. As a regional 'entity', Galicia too was born of myth—and from myth would rise again. And in the post-communist era, with myths debunked and historical antecedents in short supply, that of *Galicia Felix* (Happy Galicia) would prove particularly attractive, for a number of reasons. Most visibly, the years after 1989 witnessed 'Galicia' cropping up on store signs and adorning a variety of products in southeastern Poland. Yet beyond its role as a marketing tool, the use of the 'Galician' denominative also began to proliferate among a variety of public and private institutions, as well as countless historical preservation associations and literary and cultural groups, while portraits of the emperor (re)appeared on the walls of numerous provincial bars, offices, restaurants, and coffee houses from Krakow to Nowy Sacz to L'viv/Lwów.

Naming, however, also acts to situate territories and their inhabitants in geopolitical, civilisational, historical, and cultural space. Galicia's name thus not only evokes a series of nostalgic associations of home and tradition but also offers other spatial cues recalling a broader set of geographical containers and wider geopolitical representations. Galicia, as Austro-Hungarian, as European, as not-Eastern, certainly as not Russian, is thus located within the Western (or, more accurately, European) 'cosmos'. In contrast to the chaos and backwardness of the Eastern steppes beyond it, Galicia is firmly located within the European tradition, 'before and beyond' the communist occupation, 1945–1991. As always, the names that we grant to our social world, to ourselves, and to the institutions to which we belong are hardly accidental but emerge, rather, from a complex negotiation of meanings that attempts to make sense of the local, national, and international spaces in which we are located.

The Galician resurgence has not limited itself to nominative acts, in fact, and in recent years has begun to take on an increasingly political tone in opposition to the formal politics of the Polish state. What of the political or cultural identity uses of Galicia? The emergence and consolidation of new sets of local-global economic networks and their associated place-selling strategies are hardly a novel phenomenon, though rare in eastern Europe. Turning to Paasi (1986, 1996) again, we stress here the importance of making a distinction between 'regional identity' as the identity of the region itself (in our case, the identity of Galicia) and the potentially endless identities of the regional actors/inhabitants that may or may not coincide with the regional identity. Regional identity is best conceived, in fact, as a shared or dominant territorial idea or representation of the region, and thus irreducible to the singular identities of regional actors/inhabitants. It is a shared geographical representation that induces coherent behaviour and, over time, acts to consolidate the region (Dematteis 1989). And one thing is certain about the Galician ideal: Lots of people seem to believe in it. Galicia is a powerful, still-living myth in the culture of two nations, the Polish and the Ukrainian. Certainly, it is not a unitary or homogeneous myth, yet in both cultures it is viewed, overwhelmingly, as an ideal past, as a lost Arcadia and, by extension, 'as the path towards their future' (Sowa 1994: 6).

Sowa (1994) identifies two guiding elements of the present-day Galician myth. The first is the idealisation of the lost time/space of the local—of the familiar Galician village or *shtetl* (small Jewish settlement) but also of the urban magnificence of turn-of-the-century Cracow and L'viv (Lwów). The second lies with the ideal of social and ethnic peace and the pacific coexistence of the 'many peoples, many nations' inhabiting these lands since time immemorial. Both, however, are predicated on a unitary/unified Galicia and thus on a negation of the border that now cuts through it (Sowa 1994; Wiegandt 1988; Wyrozumski 1994). To reclaim the past, Galicia must thus be reconceptualised as a border *space*, a limen of coexistence.

Proponents of nostalgia for Habsburg Galicia do not see their yearnings running counter to the respective contemporary national aspirations, just as the Galician conservatives' love of Austria during the period of provincial autonomy in 1869–1918 was never conceived in opposition to Polish, Jewish, or Ruthenian national aspirations (Szul 1996). The role assigned to Galicia in the post-1989 period draws heavily, in fact, on the spatial-representational equation, Galician = Austrian = European. Adopting one shared geographical/territorial representation, Galicia thus grants its believers access to another, highly valued, shared geographical representation that is the European one. And it is by re-imagining Galicia as a historical, cultural, and traditional liminal *borderland* that its proponents attempt to usurp the power of the *borderline*. This distinction closely recalls Michel de Certeau's (1984) differentiation between spatial imaginaries that are cartographic and those that are narrative, emerging from practices and stories and thus, fundamentally, subversive. Unlike the cartographic, bounded spatial imaginaries of nation-states, narrative identities (such as the Galician one) do not rely on binding actors in(to) space; they do not rely on the setting up of boundaries of inclusion/exclusion. Rather, to quote de Certeau, such forms of identity 'establish an itinerary', 'guide', 'pass through', and 'transgress', establishing a space that is '*topological*, concerning the deformation [and combination] of figures, rather than *topical*, defining places' (de Certeau 1984: 129). Such topological spaces oppose the unitary metric of the borderline; within them 'diverse scales are brought together through networks of "internal" and "external" ties in defining geographical variation in social phenomena' (Agnew 1993: 264).

Making the Galicia Myth

The image of the Galician borderlands as an outpost of 'Western civilisation'—the boundary of Europe beyond which lay the chaos of the East—had begun to be elaborated in the sixteenth century. It was then that the multiethnic, multireligious, and multilingual 'melting pot' first became codified as a distinct political project, with the evolution of the Polish state from a medieval monarchy into the Polish-Lithuanian ('Jagiellonian') Commonwealth (see figure 12.1) While Polish nationalism grew ever more prominent during the eighteenth and nineteenth centuries, there remained a place where Polish national feeling would be channelled into the idealisation of another institutionalised multinational coexistence; where the multiethnic *koinè* of the Eastern borderlands would be preserved as ideal and practice, only now with better postal service; it would be the home of the emperor's peoples, Habsburg Galicia (see figure 12.2).

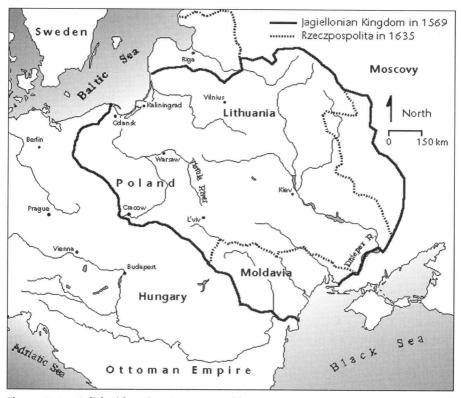

Figure 12.1. Polish-Lithuanian Commonwealth

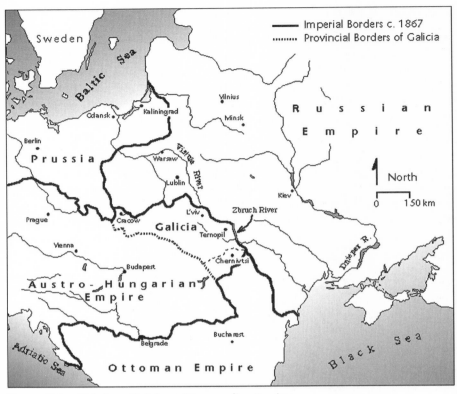

Figure 12.2.   Habsburg Galicia and Surrounding Empires

Although during the early decades of the partitions Polish cultural life and national(ist) organising efforts in the Habsburg territories were relatively underdeveloped, following Austria's defeat by Prussia and the subsequent *Ausgleich* with Hungary in 1867, a significant shift occurred in the Austro-Polish relationship (Estreicher 1951; Kann 1977; Shedel 1983; Wandycz 1982). For the first time, Polish interests were acknowledged by Vienna in administrative fashion, with the granting of virtual autonomy to the Poles of Galicia. In the post-1866 period, this crownland was granted more privileges than any other province in the Austrian half of the Dual Monarchy (Kann 1977; Shedel 1983). A Polish-dominated school board was added to an already Polish-controlled provincial Diet, 'thus giving Poles the means of ending the former policy of Germanisation and setting up a Polonised school system' (Wandycz 1982: 85). In 1869, an imperial decree established Polish as the language of the bureaucracy and of the courts within Galician provincial boundaries and, in 1870–1871, Polish was restored as the official language of instruction in the crownland's two universities in Cracow and L'viv/Lwów. Politically, the viceroyalty was made a Polish monopoly and, in 1871, a Polish *Landesminister* for Galicia was made a permanent fixture of every Austrian cabinet. Poles began to be appointed to important ministerial posts in subsequent Habsburg cabinets, including prime minister. As Poles rose in the ranks of the imperial bureaucracy, the Galician elite became a vital incubator of Polish national feeling, understandably so, as Poles' status within the Habsburg realm stood in increasingly sharper contrast to the condition of their co-nationals in the Russian and Prussian empires.

It was 'simple pragmatism' that proved most important in effecting a reconciliation between Galician Polish elites and the Empire (Wandycz 1982), with the failure of the 1863 insurrection seen as the convincing factor that turned the Polish leadership towards a settlement with Austria. 'Austria threatened the Polish element far less than did Russia and Prussia and if the Poles were to breathe, they must form a kind of lung, some area relatively free for the development of their national culture, and in Russia and Prussia this was impossible' (Estreicher 1951: 444). It was this recognition that would lead to the famous declaration of loyalty to the Habsburg emperor, issued by the Galician Diet on 10 December 1866, which described Austria as the defender of Polish national interest and the guardian of Western civilisation in the Polish tradition: 'Without fear of deserting our national ideal, believing in the mission of Austria and trusting in the durability of the changes announced by the monarch as his firm purpose, we declare from the bottom of our hearts that with thee, most illustrious lord, we stand and we will stand' (Wandycz 1982).

But allegiance to the emperor as good Austrians also placed Galician Poles on an equal footing with the other peoples of the Empire and located them firmly within the Austro-German (and thus European) politico-cultural sphere. Perhaps even more important, however, such self-identification marked the difference of Galician Poles from the Slavic world that lay across the imperial boundary. Habsburg officials were well aware of the Poles' anti-Russian sentiments. As Count Friedrich Beust, a Habsburg prime minister, remarked, 'By holding out the prospect for the reconstitution of the Polish state under Habsburg protection, hatred for Russia can become a pragmatic love for Austria' (cited in Wandycz 1982). In subsequent years, many Polish national leaders, such as the head of the Austrian Polish Social Democratic Party, Ignacy Daszynski, painted Galicia as a 'Polish Piedmont', aiming to achieve Polish unity under the benevolent Habsburg umbrella (Buszko 1989). The distinct Galician conservatism was, moreover, the product of a very particular vision of the Polish past and Poland's future interests. This vision was elaborated in the late

1860s by the so-called Cracow Historical School (Orton 1982; Buszko 1989). Arguing that the blame for the dismemberment of the Polish state lay primarily with the Poles themselves, as their political institutions and policies had bred anarchy, the historians of the Cracow School (led by Jozef Szujski, the first chair of Polish history at the Jagiellonian University) rejected previous insurrections as disastrous for Polish interests and became the leading Polish proponents of loyalty to the emperor, influencing a generation of political leaders and tracing the outlines of a distinct Galician conservatism guided by 'sober deliberation', recourse only to legal means, 'adherence to traditional verities', and loyalty to Austria as the rightful legal heir to the crown of the old Polish Commonwealth. It is thus due to the rights conferred by the Empire that the Polish elite under Habsburg occupation would fast become Polish-speaking 'Austrians', with Galician loyalty to the imperial project translating the Polish nobility and political leaders into fully fledged Europeans (Wiegandt 1988). (Benedict Anderson [1983: 56], among others, has noted the 'togetherness' inadvertently created by the bureaucracy of the Austro-Hungarian Empire: a transnational 'imagined community' based in the 'interchangeability' of imperial subjects.)

More important to understanding the distinct place and time that was Habsburg Galicia, however, is its self-representation as an Arcadian space of felicitous coexistence of peoples, cultures, and languages at the borders of the Empire: *Galicia Felix.* Galicia was, then, both a mirror, a reduced representation of the multilingual, multicultural Habsburg coexistence—a part reflecting the unity of the greater whole—and also a vital, emblematic 'piece' necessary to the construction of the vision of the Empire and the emperor's 'peoples'. Certainly the Galician adhesion to the Habsburg ideal was not unique. Numerous observers, from Kann (1974) to Le Rider (1995) to Magris (1963, 1986), have, in fact, stressed that the most fervent 'Austrians' were to be found precisely at the peripheries of the Empire, on the shores of the Adriatic, in Bohemia, or in Galicia.

The Habsburg Empire itself was an ideal beyond time. As the rightful heir to the spirit of the Holy Roman Empire, it embodied both the universalism of European culture and the role of mediator between East and West, with its paternalistic myth of the 'peoples' running counter to the national ideal heir to the French Revolution. It was a supranational ethnocultural *oikumene* that strove to transcend the nation both as an exclusive territorial ideal and as the exclusive claimant of identity. This ideal was ensured by the Habsburg imperial bureaucracy that reached out into the corners of its territories. The laws of the Empire, similarly, guaranteed individual and local freedoms, albeit under the emperor's watchful eyes.

Habsburg Galicia was the quintessential liminal community, characterised by unstable belongings and identities combined and recombined daily in an endless tangle of shifting configurations (Chlebowczyk 1975), reconfigurations, and re-representations that could take place from one conversation to the next, depending on the interlocutor. Belonging, when delimited, was traced along class and religious divides—peasant, noble, Uniate, Jewish—but it was the attribute of *tutejszy* that traced the sharpest confines, with only those 'not from here' considered as 'others', although, if imperial subjects, they were still envisioned as part of a broader commonality that included all the emperor's 'peoples'. Jews made up a vital part of Galicia's multinational, multicultural *koinè*, making up 30 percent of the population of both Cracow and L'viv/Lwów and over 50 percent in a number of key Galician towns. The Habsburg *koinè*, in fact, is inconceivable without the Jewish cultural elite, who were the first to raise the cry of alarm at the dismemberment of the Galician Babel, as the Habsburg dream slid into a nightmare of language laws, ethnic registers, and violent national revindications (Prager 1995; Wrobel 1994).

Borders and Geopolitical Games

The institutional attempts at the delimitation of the Galician space along national and ethnic lines—and the beginnings of the slow death of the Habsburg ideal of 'unity in diversity'—date to the 1896–1897 Austrian electoral reform, which would, for the first time ever, demarcate constituencies along ethnic lines, through the construction of ethnically or linguistically separate voters' registers (the famed *Nationale Kataster*). The primacy of ethnic divides tended not only to de-emphasise (and, to some extent, delegitimise) the traditional role afforded to the provinces and to the imperial government but also, perhaps even more important, 'reduced the position of the individual as citizen of the state, stressing, instead, the individual's role as a member of an ethnic group' (Stourzh 1991: 19). As Jacques Le Rider (1995) notes, from the emperor's *Meine Völker*, a historical, organic pluri-cultural unity cemented together by dynastic right, the citizens of Austria would now become 'nationals', with the structuration of public bodies along ethnic lines producing the entirely new need to attribute ethnic membership to individuals, 'constrained by the nationalism of others to become a nation', as Joseph Roth (1985) would note of the period in his collection of essays *Juden auf Wandershaft*.

Individuals were now supposed to delimit their belonging to one collectivity, the *Volkstamm*, with the imperial state now able to 'objectively' attribute ethnic membership to persons on the basis of evidence gathered through official questionnaires (the venerable Habsburg census began to include a linguistic questionnaire only in 1880). According to the 1880 census, Poles made up 51 percent of the Galician population, while Ukrainians/Ruthenians accounted for 43 percent. As Wereszycki (1990: 141) notes, however, the Polish figure included the bulk of Galicia's significant Jewish population who, for the purposes of the census (in which nationality was determined by language: Polish, German, or Ukrainian) were identified as Poles. The modern ideal of a nation bound to a distinct territorial base thus slowly supplanted previously dominant Austro-Marxist conceptions of freely chosen nationality within which nationality could attach to persons, wherever they lived and whoever they lived with, at any rate if they chose to claim it (Hobsbawn 1990).

The shape of the newly independent Poland was determined at the Paris Peace Conference in 1919. The final settlement of Poland's eastern boundary proved most problematic, particularly in Galicia, where Polish leaders disputed Ukrainian claims to territories east of the San River. With the collapse of Habsburg rule on 1 November 1918, local Ukrainian leaders proclaimed the birth of the West Ukrainian People's Republic, which claimed all Galician lands east of the San as well as northern Bukovina and Carpathian Rus. The Republic encountered stiff opposition from Galician Poles, and conflict soon precipitated into a Polish-Ukrainian war that lasted until the summer of 1919, when the Ukrainian forces were driven out of Galicia (Kozlowski 1990). As Magocsi (1993: 127) notes, the Allied powers were concerned above all with the threat of Bolshevik revolution from the East and thus acquiesced to Polish demands to occupy Eastern Galicia in temporary fashion. The Treaty of St. Germain in September 1919 granted only those territories west of the San to Poland, leaving the final disposition of Eastern Galicia unresolved. In December 1919, British statesman Lord Curzon suggested two possible boundaries through Galicia, one of which served as the southernmost extension of what he proposed should be Poland's eastern frontier along the so-called Curzon Line. Should Eastern Galicia become an independent Ukrainian republic, then the first Curzon variant would be accepted; should such a republic not be recognised, then the second variant, which was farther east and included L'viv/Lwów, would serve as Poland's border. In fact, neither of these variants or any subsequent proposals were accepted by Poland, whose annexation of all of East Galicia was recognised in March 1923 (Magosci 1993: 127) (see figure 12.3). The Curzon Line thus came to identify the maximum territorial reach of Soviet political influence in Europe, and in the years to come provided 'both a reference in the discussion on state boundaries in Eastern Europe and a political rationale for the new Soviet boundary' (Kordan 1997: 705).

Although the interwar Polish state vociferously asserted its claims to what it pronounced as its national territories (and despite the increasingly

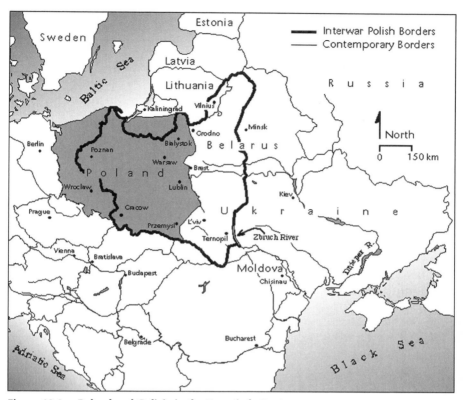

Figure 12.3.   Poland and Galicia in the Twentieth Century

national[istic] attacks of certain political forces such as Roman Dmowski's National Democrats), Poland remained a multiethnic, multicultural state; in 1931, ethnic Poles made up only 69 percent of the population. The violent national struggles from 1914 to 1920 and the subsequent national repartitioning of the Habsburg lands did not succeed in fully purifying the East Central European spaces—and certainly not those of Galicia.

That task was to be accomplished by Nazi Germany first and completed by postwar planners later. By 1945, the 'Final Solution' had eliminated 5.4 million Eastern and Central European Jews, erasing almost all traces of the vibrant Aszkenazic communities in Galicia and the Pale (Himka 1999). Another 9 million to 10 million people—Roma, Poles, Ukrainians, Belorussians, and Russians—were killed in the Nazi sweep. The multinational dream of the Habsburgs—Karl Renner's ideal of 'freely chosen nationalisms', barely alive after the strife of World War I and the interwar years—died at Auschwitz.

The Allied postwar project for the reordering of the Eastern border-lands of Europe, although clothed in the rhetoric of peace and political stability, in epistemological terms lay perfectly in line with the 'pure cartography' of politics put into practice by Nazi geopoliticians (Raffestin, Lopreno, and Pasteur 1995). By the war's end, it became common dogma to assert that the presence of large numbers of ethnolinguistic minorities within the states of East Central Europe had been one of the major factors contributing to political instability during the interwar years (Magosci 1993). The apparent solution would lie in '*bringing some logic* to the map of Europe' (Kordan 1997; emphasis added) and although substantial tensions existed on the specific details, there was little fundamental disagreement among the members of the victorious Grand Alliance on the necessity of sorting out the demographic mixture of the East. To clean up the Eastern European space, populations must be realigned to conform to the new state borders: Between 1944 and 1948, no less than 31 million people were uprooted and moved from their homes as part of organised population transfers and forced resettlement (Magosci 1993: 164). The new boundary between Poland and the Soviet Union—designated by the Curzon Line—cut clear across Galicia, and its 'enforcement' necessitated a massive population exchange between as well as within the two countries. The new border, as Kordan notes, was considered 'diplomatically convenient', most importantly since it 'satisfied Soviet geostrategic demands' but also since it 'resolved once and for all the vexing Polish Question which for so long threatened the victorious Grand Alliance and promised to compromise Allied post-war relations' (1997: 705). Simply put, the line was 'just and right', as Winston Churchill proclaimed following the Yalta Conference.

From the Soviet perspective, however, for the new border to be 'just and right', certain complicating demographic issues had to settled. First, there was the problem of the large Polish population that now found itself on the 'wrong' side of the border, in the USSR; similarly, a sizeable Ukrainian population was 'separated' from its now-ordained 'ethnolinguistic homeland' in the Ukrainian SSR. The solution was to be found in a program of forced population transfer that swept through communities on both sides of the new border, uprooting and resettling more than 1.4 million individuals, including 810,000 Polish inhabitants of former Eastern Galicia and Volhynia and 630,000 individuals identified with the Ukrainian ethnolinguistic community coming primarily from the borderlands of Podlachia, Chelm, Jaroslaw, and the Lemko region (Kordan 1997). In the Soviet Union, ethnic Poles and Jews who were citizens of Poland prior to 1939 and wished to leave were allowed to register for resettlement along with members of their immediate families: 882,000 registered for the patriation (Kordan 1997: 707; Kozlowski 1990). Those fleeing were predominantly Polish urban dwellers from the key historical centres of Polish settlement in Eastern Galicia: L'viv (Lwów), Ternopil (Tarnopol), Ivano-Frankivsk (Stanislawòw), and Drohobych. Although the Polish anticommunist underground, the *Armia Krajowa* (Home Army), appealed to the Galician Poles to oppose resettlement efforts and attempted to organise local resistance, such resistance was limited and sporadic (Albert 1989; Magosci 1993; Kordan 1997). On the Polish side of the border, between October 1944 and September 1946, 497,680 Ukrainians registered for patriation, settling primarily in the Ternopil, Ivano-Frankivsk, and L'viv *oblasts* (Kordan 1997). Hoping to conclude the operation rapidly, by 31 December 1945 Polish and Soviet authorities had abandoned the relatively passive character of the resettlement efforts, engaging the aid of special Polish and Soviet internal security forces. Within the course of a single year (July 1945 to July 1946) some 400,000 were uprooted and deported (Kordan 1997). The violence of the campaign spurred on popular resistance—channelled into support for the Ukrainian nationalist insurgency—the *Ukrains'ka Povstan'ska Armiia* (UPA), which had been operating underground in Galicia since 1943 against both German and Soviet forces. To extirpate resistance, a definitive solution took the form of a concerted operation of the Polish, Soviet, and Czechoslovak military forces aimed at relocating the entire remaining population; the *Akcja Wisla*, carried out between 29 April and 31 July 1947. Villages throughout the borderlands were emptied, and 139,467 persons were deported in the two-month period and dispersed throughout the newly acquired territories in western and northeastern Poland. The Habsburg dream of mixed populations living under the benevolent gaze of the emperor was finally put to flight.

GALICIA AND CONTEMPORARY GEOSTRATEGIC ORDERS

Previously we alluded to the ways in which the dreams of Galicians and the present re-territorialisations of these 'lands between' meld into a much broader reconfiguration of Europe after the demise of the Cold War geopolitical order. It is here, in fact, at the Polish-Ukrainian borderlands, that a new geopolitical 'crush zone'—a new 'iron curtain' of belonging—is fast taking form (for preliminary theorisations of this emergent divide, see Huntington 1996; Kolossov and O'Loughlin 1999; O'Loughlin 2000). Ukraine is increasingly finding itself on the eastern side of the new divide. In spring 1999, Poland announced a new, highly restrictive visa regime for Ukrainian (and other ex-Soviet) citizens, 'to conform with future EU norms.' As the Polish Foreign Ministry stated: 'These measures are being implemented only to stop criminal flows, and are certainly not meant to regiment the flows of goods and law-abiding people. We have a very good relationship with the Ukraine' (Rzeczpospolita 1999: 3). As expected, Ukrainians, both government and citizen groups, reacted vociferously. The Ukrainian National Committee for the Defense of National Borders recently declared a new set of rules regimenting foreigners' stay and movements in border areas. According to the new ordinance, the term 'border area' would no longer apply merely to the five-kilometre strip of territory along Ukraine's national boundary but would now comprise the entire territory of all border *rayons* (counties). All foreigners present in or passing through these areas should, at all times, be in possession of a legal document attesting 'their necessity to be in that particular place'. Such documents could be obtained only with the permission of the Ukrainian Ministry of the Interior in Kiev (Rzeczpospolita 1999).

Although Poland is, in many senses, on the 'right side' of the new divide, the international community's—as well as the Polish state's— recent boundary-drawing exercises are not passing uncontested. To the tune of 'Huntington go home!', numerous Polish commentators have, in fact, assailed the tracing of a civilisational watershed along the country's eastern borderlands. Popular commentator Ludwik Stomma (whose 1997 editorial coined the above battle cry), for one, labelled Huntington a fanatic and a fascist, 'severing the world into pieces', and called upon Polish national leaders to restrain themselves from facile enthusiasm for a Western 'club' that operates on the principle of exclusion. 'I want no part of a West that ends somewhere before Lwów and Nowogrodek'. . . . no part of a West . . . based on the principle of division: proposing a world view based solely in fear. And fear—fear of the other—always breeds hate' (Stomma 1997: 89).

Back in Galicia, the Cracow City Council (*Rada Miasta Krakowa*) (as well as a number of other local/regional actors and institutions) have also become increasingly vocal on matters that are usually the province of national policy-making bodies, most visibly foreign policy. In particular, since 1990 Galician actors have taken an increasingly active role in shaping Polish state policy towards Ukraine, while also cultivating a broad dialogue and exchange program with cities in western Ukraine and organising trips and exchanges. In fact, a number of associations active in promoting dialogue with 'the lands of Eastern Galicia' (now in western Ukraine) operate in Cracow, from the *Fundacja Sw. Wlodzimierza Chrzciciela Rusi Kijowskiej* (promoting Ukrainian culture in Poland and publishing an almanac entitled *Between Neighbours* under the auspices of the Jagiellonian University) to the *Zwiazek Wysiedlonych* (disseminating historical documents and raising awareness about the post–World War II resettlement activities on both sides of the border as well as organising exchanges and trips for those resettled and their families to 'home places' such as Belz, Sokol, and Krystynopol).

Such local 'scale-jumping strategies' (Smith 1993) of empowerment had been put into practice quite successfully by Galician economic actors ever since the Iron Curtain came down, with local entrepreneurs and chamber of commerce leaders rapidly launching themselves and their regions into international trade and capital investment networks, long before national bodies regulating this activity had been set up. Trade and traffic across Poland's eastern borders, however, continue to be severely hindered by lengthy delays, and Ukrainian leaders have consistently appealed to Poland to keep the border open, allowing the 6 million Ukrainians, most of whom are *chelnoki* (shuttle traders), to continue to have access to Polish marketplaces and kiosks (Turek 1998). Although a key element of Ukrainian foreign policy is the future acquisition of associate membership in the EU, and thus a progressive opening of its border to the European space, the Ukrainian-Polish border is, at present, an almost impenetrable barrier. Traders often have to wait up to four days travelling east at the Ukrainian border crossings, and the zones around crossing points have become a deregulated space where anything and everything can be bought and sold and all rules (national or international) are off; the roadside ditches each summer breed epidemics of diphtheria or even cholera. Although the Cold War–era Soviet border is no more, the barbed-wire fences and restrictions on the free movement of goods and people remain, now more than ever. L'viv, sixty kilometres from the Polish border, received only twenty thousand foreign tourists in 1998 (Gorchinskaya 1999) despite the city's designation as a UNESCO world heritage site and its wealth of Habsburg-era buildings, streetscapes, and low prices, reminiscent of Prague in 1989 before mass tourism invaded that other imperial jewel.

Although the geopolitical imaginations of—and policy prescriptions for—the 'New Europe' embrace the iconography of unbounded spaces, 'free of past dividing lines', the reality on the ground is vastly different. Post-Soviet fears have, in fact, made the Polish-Ukrainian border highly contested, the NATO expansion process being a case in point. Alongside a variety of discourses of 'righting past wrongs' and admitting 'worthy' and 'historically democratic' nations under the alliance's umbrella, the prevalent thrust of the expansion rhetoric centred precisely on the importance of re-instituting a proper/just/moral European order: a 'one Europe for all', a Europe without divides, without the rigid frontier lines assigned by Cold War geopolitics (or, as NATO pundits claim, the EU's increasingly exclusionary 'Euro-curtain'). In fact, alliance leaders would stress on numerous occasions the open and 'unaccomplished' nature of the NATO expansion process, noting that the enlargement 'would not be a one-time event, but a process that will continue after the first round' (Bialasiewicz 1999).

United States secretary of State Madeline Albright was busy singing the praises of the demise of 'a system of interstate relations in which everyone had to choose a side': With the collapse of the bipolar order, states (like Poland and the Ukraine) would finally be 'free' to pursue a 'multi-vectored' foreign policy, oriented towards both the East and the West. In a March 1998 speech in Kyiv, Albright declared: 'I think that the most important feature of our new era is that we are trying very hard to erase the dividing lines in Europe. We believe that the era of the zero sum—where if one side wins, the other side loses—is over' (cited in Clover 1999). Just weeks later, agreements codifying NATO's new walls began to be drafted.

CONCLUSION

The story of the Polish-Ukrainian borderlands cannot be reduced to a dichotomy between dreams of pacific coexistence and rigid civilisational or security watersheds. At the same time that the U.S. foreign policy community lauds the open spaces of the New Europe, it busies itself in constructing new walls; so too are Galician dreams being seized upon by the Polish state to promote and justify a series of geopolitical positionings that are anything but inclusive. Polish *Ostpolitik* has, in fact, been assailed by many Ukrainian leaders as replicating the worst of the past, with Foreign Minister Bronislaw Geremek's (1999) recent statements regarding Poland's role in guiding the Ukraine to a free market economy and liberal democracy—and thus 'into the west'—sounding to some Ukrainian commentators like 'the sound of the returning *pany*' (Polish nobility or landed gentry).

The Galician ideal of the multicultural border space—what Le Rider (1995) characterises as the secret of its 'always unaccomplished identity'—is precisely the cartographic chaos of East Central Europe that so frightens policymakers and amateur geopoliticians alike. The tracing of borderlines is always an inherently violent act—operating both a material and a symbolic violence—enforcing a simplification of territory, of identity, and of belonging, as well as of the ways to represent these elements (Ara and Magris 1982; Zanini 1997). The foremost scholar of the Habsburg myth, Claudio Magris (1986, 1999), in fact, takes de Certeau's (1984) distinction a step further. There are endless stories possible about border spaces, he notes; the borderline, however, has—and can only have—but one story: a singular, undisputed narrative determined by sheer force. There are many stories of Galicia, some certainly more relevant than others ('relevant' as shared geographical representations/territorial ideologies that organise action—see Dematteis 1989). All exist, however, in opposition to the cartographic reality of the Polish-Ukrainian border.

One such narrative is the project for the Carpathian Euroregion, promoted by the Council of Europe and the Soros Foundation with the aim of 'promoting cross-border cooperation and harmonization, especially in the fields of cultural and educational matters, among the border territories of the Ukraine, Poland, Slovakia and Hungary' (Carpathian Euroregion 1995). The Euroregion, first proposed in 1992, brings together the Polish border provinces of Przemysl and Krosno and the Ukrainian oblasts of Chernovtsy, Ivano-Frankivsk, L'viv, and Zakarpatska, along with a number of Slovakian and Hungarian border counties, and specifies a whole series of co-operation agreements in fields as varied as environmental protection, economic development and trade, tourism, and cultural and historical preservation. It is precisely the fluidity of this budding Euroregion's border space that is represented by its promoters as a sign of Europeanisation—of progress towards (or perhaps a return to) its 'natural state' (Suli-Zakar and Czimre 2000) as a multicultural, multiethnic *koinè*. The success of this initiative will mark, at least in part, the continuing relevance of the Habsburg ideal in post–Cold War East Central Europe.

NOTE

This research was supported by a doctoral fellowship from the National Science Foundation Graduate Training Program to Luiza Bialasiewicz and a research grant from the Geography and Regional Science Program of the National Science Foundation to John O'Loughlin.

REFERENCES

Agnew, J. 1993. Representing space: Space, scale and culture in social science. In J. Duncan and D. Ley, eds. *Place/Culture/Representation*, 251–71. London: Routledge.
Albert, A. 1989. *Najnowsza Historia Polski*. London: Polonia Book Fund.
Anderson, B. 1983. *Imagined Communities: Reflections on the Origins and Spread of Nationalism*. London: Verso.
Applebaum, A. 1994. *Between East and West: Across the Borderlands of Europe*. New York: Pantheon.
Ara, A., and C. Magris. 1982. *Trieste: Un identità di frontiera*. Turin: Einaudi.
Bialasiewicz, L. 1999. Through America into Europe? Representational games in the

lands between. Paper presented at the Challenging the American Century Conference, Loughborough University, 1–4 July.

Buszko, J. 1989. *Galicja, 1859–1914: Polski Piemont?* Warsaw: PWN.

Calimani, R., ed. 1998. *Le vie del mondo Berlino, Budapest, Praga, Vienna e Trieste: Intelletuali ebrei e cultura Europea dal 1880 al 1930.* Milan: Electa.

Carpathian Euroregion. 1995. Mission statement. Debrecen, Hungary: Carpathian Euroregion.

Chlebowczyk, J. 1975. *Procesy narodotworcze we wschodniej Europie srodkowej w dobie kapitalizmu.* Warsaw: PWN.

Chlopecki, J. 1995. Galicja: Skrzyzowanie Drog. In *Galicja i Jej Dziedzictwo,* vol. 2. Rzeszow, Poland: Uniwersytet Rzeszowski.

Clover, C. 1999. Kosovo swings Ukraine's political pendulum further east. *Financial Times,* 29 April.

Dahrendorf, R. 1999a. Le parole per dire 'Europa'. *La Repubblica,* 30 July: 17.

———. 1999b. Postscript. In *Reflections on the Revolution in Europe.* London: Chatto and Windus.

de Certeau, M. 1984. *The Practice of Everyday Life.* Berkeley: University of California Press.

Delanty, G. 1995. *Inventing Europe: Idea, Identity, Reality.* New York: St. Martin's Press.

Dematteis, G. 1989. *Le metafore della terra.* Milan: Feltrinelli.

Estreicher, S. 1951. Galicja in the period of autonomy and self-government, 1848–1917. In *The Cambridge History of Poland: From Augustus II to Pilsudski, 1697–1935,* 435–58. Cambridge: Cambridge University Press.

Foucher, M. 1993. *Fragments d'Europe: Atlas de l'Europe mediane et orientale.* Paris: Fayard.

Geremek, B. 1999. Poland and East-Central Europe: The case of new geopolitics. Presentation to the School of International and Public Affairs, Columbia University, 1 October.

Gorchinskaya, K. 1999. Lviv still waiting for boom times: City turns to tourism to lure investment, rescue economy. *Kiev Post,* 27 May.

Hann, C. 1998. Postsocialist nationalism: Rediscovering the past in Southeast Poland. *Slavic Review* 58: 840–63.

Heffernan, M. 1999. *The Meaning of Europe: Geography and Geopolitics.* London: Arnold.

Himka, J.-P. 1999. Ukrainian collaboration in the extermination of the Jews during World War II: Sorting out the long-term and conjunctural factors. *Zwoje-Internetowy Periodyk Kulturalny* no. 3/6.

Hobsbawm, E. 1987. *The Age of Empire, 1875–1914.* London: Penguin.

———. 1990. *Nations and Nationalism since 1780.* Cambridge: Cambridge University Press.

Huntington, S. 1996. *The Clash of Civilizations and the Remaking of World Order.* New York: Simon & Schuster.

Kann, R. A. 1974. *A History of the Habsburg Empire, 1526–1918.* Berkeley: University of California Press.

———. 1977. *The Multi-national Empire: Nationalism and National Reform in the Habsburg Monarchy, 1848–1918.* New York: Octagon Books.

Kolossov, V., and J. O'Loughlin. 1998. New borders for New World orders: Territorialities at the *fin-de-siecle. Geojournal* 43: 259–73.

———. 1999. Pseudo-states as harbingers of a new geopolitics: The example of the Trans-Dniester Moldovan Republic (TMR). *Geopolitics* 3: 151–76.

Kordan, B. 1997. Making borders stick: Population transfer and resettlement in the trans-Curzon territories, 1944–1949. *International Migration Review* 31: 704–20.

Korshak, S. 1998. Used car dealers brave risky run for the border. *Kiev Post*, 13 January.

Kozlowski, M. 1990. *Miedzy Sanem a Zbruczem: Walki o Lwow i Galicje Wschodnia, 1918–1919.* Krakow: ZNAK.

Kundera, M. 1983. Un occident kidnappé, ou la tragédie de l'Europe centrale. *Le Débat* 27, November: 2–24.

Le Rider, J. 1995. *Mitteleuropa: Storia di un mito.* Bologna: Il Mulino.

Magocsi, P. R. 1993. *Historical Atlas of East-Central Europe.* Seattle: University of Washington Press.

Magris, C. 1963. *Il mito absburgico nella letteratura austriaca moderna.* Torino: Einaudi.

———. 1986. *Danubio.* Milan: Garzanti.

———. 1999. *Utopia e disincanto: Storie, speranze, illusioni del moderno.* Milan: Garzanti.

Martin, G. 1980. *The Life and Thought of Isaiah Bowman.* Hamden, CT: Archon Books.

Newman, D., and A. Paasi. 1998. Fences and neighbours in the postmodern world: Boundary narratives in political geography. *Progress in Human Geography* 22: 186–207.

O'Loughlin, J. 2000. Ordering the 'Crush Zone': Geopolitical games in post–Cold War Eastern Europe. In N. Kliot and D. Newman, eds. *Geopolitics and Globalization: The Changing World Political Map,* 34–55. London: Frank Cass.

O'Loughlin, J., and V. Kolossov. 2002. Still 'not worth the bones of a single Pomeranian grenadier': What the geopolitics of the Kosovo war of 1999 revealed about NATO expansionism and Russian insecurities. *Political Geography* 21.

Orton, L. 1982. The Stanczyk portfolio and the politics of Galicjan Loyalism. *Polish Review* 2, nos. 1–2: 55–64.

———. 1983. The formation of modern Cracow, 1866–1914. *Austrian History Yearbook* 19/20: 105–17.

Paasi, A. 1986. The institutionalisation of regions: A theoretical framework for understanding the emergence of regions and the constitution of regional identity. *Fennia* 164: 106–46.

———. 1996. *Territories, Boundaries and Consciousness: The Changing Geographies of the Finnish-Russian Border.* London: John Wiley.

Prager, L. 1995. Galicyjsko-zydowska historia w zwierciadle trzech biografii: Mordechaj Gebirtig, Ignacy Schipper i Dow Saddan. In J. Chlopecki and H. Madurowicz-Urbanska, eds. *Galicja i jej Dziedzictwo,* vol. 2. Rzeszow, Poland: WSP.

Raffestin, C., D. Lopreno, and Y. Pasteur. 1995. *Géopolitique et histoire.* Lausanne: Payot.

Roth, J. 1985. *Ebrei erranti.* Milan: Adelphi.

Rzeczpospolita. 1999. *Do Jalty z zezwoleniem.* 7 August: 3.

Shaw, D. 1998. The chickens of Versailles: The new central and eastern Europe. In B. Graham, ed. *Modern Europe: Place, Culture and Identity,* 121–42. London: Arnold.

Shedel, J. 1983. Austria and its Polish subjects, 1866–1914: A relationship of interests. *Austrian History Yearbook* 19/20: 23–41.

Smith, N. 1993. Homeless/global: Scaling places. In J. Bird et al., eds. *Mapping the Futures,* 57–79. London: Routledge.

Sowa, K. 1994. Slowo wstepne. In J. Chlopecki and H. Madurowicz-Urbanska, eds. *Galicja i jej Dziedzictwo,* vol. 1. Rzeszow, Poland: WSP.

Stomma, L. 1997. Huntington go home! *Polityka* 4, no. 2073: 89.

Stourzh, G. 1991. The multinational empire revisited: Reflections on late Imperial Austria. *Austrian History Yearbook* 22: 1–22.

Suli-Zakar, I., and K. Czimre. 2000. The political geography and geopolitical role of the Carpathian Region. In M. P. Pagnini, V. Kolossov, and M. Antonsich, eds. *Europe between Political Geography and Geopolitics: On the Centenary of Ratzel's 'Politische Geographie'.* Trieste: University of Trieste.

Szul, R. 1996. Galicja: Teatr czy rzeczywistosc? In B. Jalowiecki, ed. *Oblicza Polskich Regionow,* 224–37. Warsaw: Europejski Instytut Rozwoju Regionalnego i Lokalnego.

Turek, B. 1998. Ukraine: Diplomat appeals to Poland to keep border open. *RFE/RL Daily Digest* 12 May (available at www.rferl.org).

Wandycz, P. 1982. The Poles in the Habsburg monarchy. In A. Markovits and F. Sysyn, eds. *Nationbuilding and the Politics of Nationalism: Essays on Austrian Galicia.* Cambridge, MA: Harvard University Press.

Wereszycki, H. 1990. *Historia Polityczna Polski, 1864–1918.* Wroclaw: Ossolineum.

Wiegandt, E. 1988. *Austria Felix czyli o Micie Galicji w Polskiej Prozie Wspolczesnej.* Poznan: UAM.

Wolff, L. 1994. *Inventing Eastern Europe: The Map of Civilisation on the Mind of the Enlightenment.* Stanford, CA: Stanford University Press.

Wrobel, P. 1994. The Jews of Galicja under Austrian-Polish rule, 1869–1918. *Austrian History Yearbook* 25: 97–138.

Wyrozumski, J. 1994. Przedmowa. In J. Chlopecki and H. Madurowicz-Urbanska, eds. *Galicja i jej Dziedzictwo,* vol. 1, 9–10. Rzeszow, Poland: WSP.

Zanini, P. 1997. *Significati del confine: I limiti naturali, storici, mentali.* Milan: Bruno Mondadori.

Chapter Thirteen

Place and Discourse in the Formation of the Northeast Estonian Borderland

Joni Virkkunen

There has been extensive change in the European political map during the last few years. The fading barriers of the international economic market and deepening European integration have created an illusion of a less territorial world. A borderless Europe can, however, be contrasted with the creation of new nation-states and an awareness of ethno-territorial conflicts, which increasingly have become part of our everyday lives through national and international media. The post-Soviet Estonian concerns of national security and Northeast Estonian borderland identity exemplify the continuous significance and manifold character of border constructions.

The newly established territorial border between Estonia and Russia was celebrated as a national victory by Estonians. The border has a strong symbolic meaning to a nation that for fifty years considered itself oppressed by the Soviet Union. The significance of the border has been explicitly articulated, both in practical policy formulations by the Estonian government—the constitution, legislation, and so on—and through formal geopolitics of the Estonian strategic planners and institutions. Border politics is historically embedded and takes place on diverse geographical scales. In Estonia, the post-Soviet 'nationalisation' of Estonian administration (Brubaker 1996; Smith, Aasland, and Mole 1994) formed a new contextual frame for both international and local geopolitical discourse. That has also become one of the most disputed elements of post-Soviet Estonian politics, both expressing the hegemonic position of Estonian nationals and creating a very sensitive context for alternative politics.

239

This chapter focuses on the Estonian and non-Estonian views of post-Soviet Estonian territorial politics. Three case studies are presented, all of which, from their particular viewpoints, describe the role of discourse in the formation of Northeast Estonian borderlands. First, the representations of the Baltic News Service illustrate an Estonian-speaking discourse, which is closely related to Estonian 'nationalisation' but yet is emerging in a media-related context. Second, the Estonian viewpoint is contrasted with an analysis of the political and territorial images in the election campaign of the non-Estonian political parties prior to the 1999 parliamentary elections. This expresses the number of formalised, non-Estonian views on post-Soviet Estonian politics and sets an interesting, strategy-oriented, interethnic, and territorial argumentation. Third, the structure and argumentation of locally based social movements bring specific local concerns and the meaning of place into contemporary Estonian territorial politics. Social movements illustrate an institutionalised grassroots attitude and interpretation of locally significant problems. The three discourses and spaces of border politics in this study are discussed within the context of the Northeast Estonian borderland and the city of Narva.

NARVA—THE NORTHEAST ESTONIAN BORDERLAND

Narva is a unique town in Estonia. It is an old Estonian border town originating from the mid-thirteenth century. Narva's geographical location, between St. Petersburg (130 kilometres away) and Tallinn (240 kilometres away) as well as between Pskov and the Gulf of Finland (see figure 13.1), has affected its development for centuries. On the one hand, the geographical position has provided Narva with good opportunities for trade and subsequent economic benefits, but on the other hand, Narva's strategic location has made it vulnerable: Narva has been the scene of almost continuous battles between the great powers of the East (Moscow, Novgorod, Russia, and the Soviet Union) and the West (Denmark, Sweden, and Germany) (Eilart et al. 1965; Süvalep 1995; Pahtma and Tamman 1997, 1998). Narva is still 'in between' two competing states and cultures. It has become a cultural and political border zone between Estonia and Russia.

The border zone character of Narva extends far back in history. The contemporary Estonian borderland cannot, however, be understood without placing it in the specific context of Soviet state-building practices on the one hand and the extraordinary changes of the 'nationalised' Estonian state on the other. In the Soviet centrally planned system, Narva was to serve the political and ideological goals of Sovietisation, socialism, and

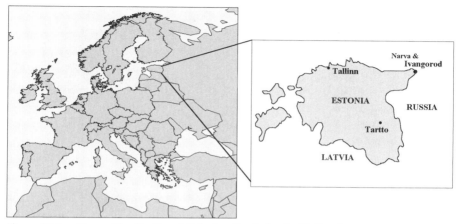

Figure 13.1. Narva: The Northeast Estonian Borderland with Russia

economic growth (Misiunas and Taagepera 1993: 282; Hallik and Vseviov 1996: 25). Most of the town was destroyed during World War II, and the majority of the population was forced to leave for personal safety or forcibly relocated by the authorities. The relocation policy of Soviet authorities was part of Soviet state building and aimed at replacing the 'non-reliable' Estonians with trustworthy Soviet-minded workers (Hallik and Vseviov 1996: 25; see also Smith 1990; Katus 1992: 325). Narva and the surrounding region of Ida-Virumaa had a strategic importance to the entire Northwest region of the Soviet Union because of the large oil shale deposits and related industries such as electricity production (Hallik and Vseviov 1995: 10–11). Still today, the robust industrial output combined with historical value make both Narva and the region essential parts of Estonian territory. Tables 13.1 and 13.2, which show contemporary demographic structure and citizenship, however, exemplify the sensitive social context in which the contemporary Estonian border is embedded. Not only residing at the strategically significant border region, Narva is dominated by Russian culture and non-Estonian citizens.

The border zone character of Narva and the very contradictory interpretation of history between the Estonian and immigrant population have given the post-Soviet Estonian border discourse very sensitive and rather conflicting overtones (Saarikoski 1993; Silva 1998; Liikanen and Virkkunen 1999). The non-Estonian national discourse has taken a directly contradictory position in relation to the Estonian national discourse. Both the contemporary 'nationalisation' project (Brubaker 1996) and the territorial history of the Estonian (and Soviet Estonian) state are conceived and

Table 13.1.   Population by Ethnicity in Narva, 1989 Census

Nationality	Number	Percentage
Russian	64,819	86.9
Estonian	2,901	3.9
Ukrainian	2,285	3.1
Belorussian	1,813	2.4
Finn	525	0.7
Tatar	439	0.6
Other	1,790	2.4
All	74,572	100.0

Source: Estonian Statistics Office 1998.

represented in opposition. The territorial representations of the Baltic News Service (Estonian view) and the political advertisements of Russian parties (non-Estonian view), as well as the local politics of social movements, each express particular forms and positions in overall post-Soviet politics. News from the Baltic News Service, an internationally owned Estonian news agency, illustrates one of the dominant Estonian discourses on interethnic and territorial development.

BOUNDARIES IN THE NEWS OF THE BALTIC NEWS SERVICE

The Estonian discourse about interethnic relations and Northeast Estonian development can be characterised by three concepts: loyalty, security, and integration. From the Estonian viewpoint, the extensive non-Estonian presence, especially in the Northeast Estonian industrial regions, is frightening. This reflects the Estonian conception of the past and also a

Table 13.2.   Share of Estonians, Russians, and Non-citizens in Narva

Document	Number	Percentage
Estonian passport	21,070	32.1
Estonian alien passport	19,790	30.2
Russian passport	18,230	27.8
Birth certificate	6,213	9.5
Soviet passport	282	0.4
All	65,585	100.0

Source: Narva City Council 1998.

fear of possible disloyalty and potential territorial demands. The post-Soviet Estonian 'nationalisation' reflects this Estonian conception of 'the Russian other' and territorial (in)security.

The rather rapid and complete demographic change (Katus 1992), the total destruction of Estonian social structures, and the expanded use of Russian as a language of 'internal communication' in Soviet Estonia created an existential fear and a feeling of cultural inferiority among Estonians (Helemäe and Saar 1995; Virkkunen 1999). From the Estonian viewpoint, these were aspects of national state-building initiatives of the Soviet state, as well as state-introduced catastrophes for national dignity and succession. Consequently, Soviet rule was personalised by the large number of Soviet-era immigrants who, in everyday parlance, appeared as 'Russians' or 'occupants', a rather homogenous group with either Soviet or Russian territorial identity (Volkonski 1996). This 'Russian other' became a source of possible conflict and instability for Estonians, especially in the Russian-speaking Northeast.

How would the 'Russians' in Estonia react in a situation in which Estonia was attacked by foreign military forces? Would they remain loyal to the Estonian state in all circumstances, or would they easily be manipulated to support anti-Estonian activity? To what extent is it safe to grant the 'Russians' access to citizenship and political decision making? To what extent would straightforward access to citizenship and political decision making integrate the 'Russian' population into the Estonian society and thereby create an increased sense of territorial stability? These questions have influenced the direction of the Estonian political discourse and the formation of post-Soviet Estonian boundaries (Järve 1997; Kirch 1997; Pettai 1997; Heidmets 1998). From the Estonian viewpoint, liberal citizenship regulations and the wide inclusion of 'possibly disloyal' non-Estonians would, over the long term, pose serious threats for national and territorial security (Park 1995a, 1995b; Raitviir 1996; Silva 1998; Aalto 2000). Moreover, territorial security-related issues have extended the border discourse beyond the area of political issues to concerns of integrating non-Estonian society and citizenship (Pettai 1997; Kruusvall 1998). The Baltic News Service (BNS) mediates images for the use of media, which is why the BNS can be considered one of the most significant players in post-Soviet Estonian media publicity and geopolitical image production.

On its Internet home page (http://www.bns.ee), the BNS represents itself as the largest news agency of the Baltic states, holding a market share that ranges from 60 to 80 percent of the total respective news market. The BNS distributes approximately a thousand daily news items in five languages (Estonian, Latvian, Lithuanian, Russian, and English), mainly for Baltic mass media and financial institutions as well as government institutions and industrial companies. The BNS has its roots in civil initiatives for freedom of the press in the late Soviet period but has transformed itself over a ten-year period into a relatively large, internationally owned media company. It is co-owned by the leading Finnish and Swedish business dailies *Kauppalehti* and *Dagens Industri,* respectively, as well as by the Direkt news agency of Sweden and the Bridge Telerate of the United States. Because it is not sufficient to discuss Northeast Estonia merely in geographical terms, as a territorial borderland, the regional viewpoint (Narva as a specific town in the Northeast) in the following analysis of BNS representations is complemented with cultural images of the Russian-speaking population as an 'internal other'. This gives a more complete view of geopolitical images mediated by the BNS.

By utilising a very broad categorisation of social representations, the BNS can be said to provide the public with interethnic and territorial discourses with supposedly objective, integrative, and disintegrative images. The news service attempts to play a relatively neutral role as news mediator. However, it frequently ends up confirming the already-existing stereotypes (see table 13.3, items II and III) that many Estonians hold about Narva: that it is a dangerous and ideologically distant borderland in the Russian-speaking Northeast. Narva is commonly viewed as a left-wing, Soviet-minded town, dominated by monolingual Russian-speaking Soviet activists, mafia, and other sources of instability. Without a doubt, this view reinforces existing barriers between ethnic groups in Estonia and between the Northeast Estonian borderland and other parts of the country.

If we look at the BNS news images in greater detail, it becomes evident that both the choice of subject matter and the way in which news is reported are aspects of border politics. This is expressed in the choice of issues and social concerns selected for coverage: Instead of covering everyday incidents and positive events in the Northeast border region (see items I and II in table 13.3), the majority of news assigns Narva a specific territorial and political character (see item III in table 13.3). In relation to the Northeast Estonian territorial discourse, the general interethnic discourse of the BNS about the Russian-speaking 'other' is more optimistic but still problematic. Non-Estonian integration and formation of interethnic relations are not viewed as prior problems but rather as challenging aspects of the post-Soviet Estonian state. Although the BNS presents positive and optimistic views on ethnic integration, the very politicised images of the few radical activists colour the rather ambivalent attitude towards the contemporary Estonian borders and fill them with negative content. In a sense, the Russian-speaking population is represented through a few radical activists such as Nikolai Rook, Oleg Morozov, and Juri Mišin (leading figures of the Russian Citizens' Association of Estonia), who often

Table 13.3. Types of Images Mediated by the Baltic News Service

I Objective News Images

"The city council of Narva is led by Elisa Suikkanen from Central Party" (3 Nov)
"The first language examination of new kind was arranged in Narva" (23 Nov)
"An Estonian language Russian school will be established in Narva" (14 Nov)

II Integrative News Images

"The integration program of aliens was completed with new initiatives" (12 Nov)
"The Roundtable of National Minorities negotiates the integration schedule of aliens" (12 Nov)
"Estonia got 270 new citizens in October" (4 Nov)
"Riigikogu ensures also individuals with no citizenship an access to the autumn elections" (16 June)

III Disintegrative News Images

"Only three principals of the 32 Narva schools know Estonian" (2 Nov)
"A man attempted to load a bomb in Narva but was hurt" (2 July)
"The director of Narva Electric Plants Anatoli Paal was murdered" (29 June)
"The largest demonstration during the history of Estonia took place in Narva" (26 May)
"The Narva border is being crossed with illegal documents" (15 May)
"Narva residents do not give up celebrating the October Revolution" (1 Nov)
"A KGB officer strives for power in Narva with an assistance of the Central Party" (8 Oct)
"Mišin does not consider himself as law breaker" (3 May)
"Morozov and Šaumjan to the court in June" (20 May)
"The leader of Russian Citizens' Association, Oleg Morozov, was arrested" (2 Aug)
"Police do not acknowledge Morozov as political prisoner" (2 Aug)
"A representative in Russian Duma ready to protect Morozov" (6 Aug)
"Morozov spreads rumors about an outlined mass deportation" (25 Aug)

Source: Baltic News Service 1999.

appear as pro-Slavic activists with very close contacts to 'motherland Russia'. For these activists, the ends tend to justify all the means in non-Estonian politics. They are even more radical in argumentation than non-Estonian parties. The BNS may downplay territorial and interethnic boundaries, but it also reproduces them through such radicalised ethnic imagery.

BORDERS IN THE PARLIAMENTARY ELECTION CAMPAIGN OF NON-ESTONIAN PARTIES

When comparing the non-Estonian discourse on post-Soviet territorial or interethnic boundaries with that of the Baltic News Service, it becomes evident that history and contemporary political realities are significant for emerging political discourse. Despite the popularised character of the

1999 parliamentary election campaign, the public representations of electoral advertising clearly illustrate the manifold identity-related character of the non-Estonian border discourse. Political advertising represents a strategy-oriented action that often utilises intentionally fabricated images in a specific political contention. In an analysis, this political character of election advertising challenges the way in which the representations are interpreted. Political advertising and its images must be interpreted within their social and political context, created for particular purposes and groups of reference.

In institutionalised non-Estonian politics, there are four major parties, all of which originate from the late and post-Soviet political conditions, agreements, and disagreements (Raitviir 1996; Laidvee 1998). The point of departure for the creation of a non-Estonian party structure was evidently the social reforms and strengthened Estonian national movement during the late 1980s and early 1990s (Raitviir 1996; Laidvee 1998). For the 1999 parliamentary election, only two non-Estonian electoral lists were established. This was due to an agreement between the three major non-Estonian parties, which, from a strategic viewpoint, recognised a need to establish a common electoral list for power and ethnic purposes to maximise the number of votes from Russian-speaking citizens. Although there is a non-Estonian party with the same name, the Estonian United People's Party (*Eestimaa Ühendatud Rahvapartei*) in the context of the 1999 parliamentary elections refers to a joint electoral list of the Estonian United People's Party (*Eestimaa Ühendatud Rahvapartei*), the Estonian Social Democratic Worker's Party (*Eesti Sotsiaaldemokraatlik Tööpartei*), and the Russian Unity Party (*Vene Ühtsuspartei*). The other ethnicity-based electoral list of non-Estonians was the Russian Party in Estonia (*Vene Erakond Eestis*), which promoted its primary goal of interethnic equality through more radical political activity.

The ethnic and territorial representations of non-Estonian parties are analysed here using two major Russian-speaking newspapers—*Estonija* (issued five times per week, with a circulation of 5,000) and *Molodezh Estonii* (issued three times per week, with a circulation of 5,300)— published during the 1999 election campaign. The newspapers provide an interesting viewpoint: the indoctrination of non-Estonian parties in the form of interviews with or articles written by candidates themselves. Explicit political advertisements were few during the campaign, but they incorporated conceptual and territorial images for electoral purposes as well as self-written articles and interviews with candidates. The major share of the campaign took place during a rather short period before the election on 7 March and, therefore, advertisements, self-written articles, and interviews with candidates from 6 February to 7 March were incorporated in the analysis (*Estonija* 1999; *Moladezh Estonii* 1999).

In general, the political campaign depicted in the two newspapers appears weak and passive. During a one-month period prior to the elections, *Molodezh Estonii* published only eighteen electoral ads or candidate interviews, most of which (fourteen) promoted the campaign of the Russian Party in Estonia. This rather narrow political commitment of the paper demonstrates that the *Estonija* newspaper was more engaged with electoral debate than its competitor. Despite its explicit support for the Estonian United People's Party, a number of primarily Estonian parties or electoral lists used the column space of *Estonija* to attract the attention and votes of enfranchised non-Estonian citizens: Of fifty-five ads and candidate interviews, twenty-eight supported the Estonian United People's Party and twenty-five supported parties or electoral lists of Estonian origin. Both Russian-speaking and Estonian parties saw the increased number of non-Estonian voters as possibilities for creating a new basis for political argumentation and power.

A great deal of the material supporting the United People's Party was merely short lists of candidates, providing the only visibility for the party (see figure 13.2). The 'People—Equal Rights to All!' slogan in the tiny ads unequivocally expresses one of the main concerns of the party: social and interethnic equality. This concern was raised in a majority of the advertisements. The head of the United People's Party, Viktor Andrejev, stressed in his only half-page advertisement in *Estonija* (6 March) the strategic importance of the non-Estonian electoral coalition in the non-Estonian politics of 'making Estonia a flourishing democratic society with no social or national discrimination'. By encouraging people to vote 'our' (non-Esto-

---

**Список кандидатов в дебутаты Рийгикогу
от Объединенной народной партии Эстонии
(Eestimaa Ühendatud Rahvapartei)
по ИЗБИРАТЕЛЬОМУ ОКРУГУ N 8**

Jõgeva maakond, Tartu maakond N 1902 Georgi Naidenkov
                                N 1903 Kalju Hermann
N 1899 Gennadi Kulkov   N 1904 Maire Lass
N 1900 Oleg Kurnossov   N 1905 Tiina Peemot
N 1901 Fjodor Savhihhin   N 1906 Valentina Karnouhhova

ЛЮДЯМ– ВСЕ ПРАВА ЛЮДЕЙ !

NB! Названние партии и список от ОНПЭ публикуется на эстонском язы-ке – как на избирательньх участках

Figure 13.2.   Political Advertisements in the Non-Estonian Press

Source: Estonija 1999: 2.

nian) representatives into parliament, Andrejev made a clear distinction between non-Estonian and Estonian interests and representatives in parliament. In a way, this ethnic division cast Andrejev's party's image as the first 'inter-ethnic party of equality' into the very contrasting light of ethnic votes, rights issues, and discrimination. The Estonian United People's Party attempted to break the boundaries between the Estonian- and Russian-speaking societies by promoting universal equality. Ironically, the actual argumentation of the 1999 election campaign reinforced the border-erecting activity between the two communities. Compared with the somewhat contradictory message of the United People's Party, the conceptual and territorial images of the Russian Party in Estonia pushed for similar issues, but with a more radical ethnic argumentation.

SOCIAL MOVEMENTS AND THE LOCAL NON-ESTONIAN BOUNDARY DISCOURSE IN NARVA

Borderland identities and geopolitical images typically reflect interstate power relations, strategies of the national political elite, and conduct of locally significant argumentation. Here, the notion of 'the political' refers to politics taking place on several scales and in various forms. To emphasise the role of place and geographical scale in the formation of Northeast Estonia, it is necessary to focus on the institutionalisation of locally based social movements in Narva. The politics of social movements represents the locally significant concerns that become articulated through less-formal social activities, providing a different angle on the ethnic and territorial discourse of the Northeast Estonian borderland.

In Narva, the socially significant issues are rather different from those represented at the national level by the Baltic News Service or the political parties. From the local perspective, the primary social concerns are issues related to neither the colour of passport (citizenship) nor to national security, the argumentation of national non-Estonian parties, and Estonian political activists. Also, political and human rights issues, which have coloured the public discussion of the post-Soviet Estonian legal boundaries, seldom arise in other political arenas outside international organisations or the Russian government. Instead, the local discourse of Narva is concrete in terms of everyday survival and personal security:

> I have a large family—four children, me and my husband—and nowadays only I am employed. The child benefit is very small, so how can we manage with my tiny salary of under 2000 crowns only . . . !? (Non-Estonian female in her forties)

This quote from one of the in-depth interviews conducted in Narva expresses well the socioeconomic fear that dominates the local sociopolitical concerns of Narva. In the post-Soviet context, low income and survival concerns reflect especially local aspects of post-Soviet socioeconomic transformation. In the Northeast Estonian context, these cannot be directly related to a 'political or cultural conflict', which is considered one of the most decisive elements of post-Soviet Estonian territorial discourse. Rather, local discourses revolve around personal and subjectively interpreted feelings of insecurity experienced in the tangible atmosphere of transformation. In this contextual sense, both Soviet history and the Northeast Estonian discursive landscape surface as essential elements of the present social situation.

When the Estonian state was able to establish nationally defined territorial boundaries, the historically functional region of Narva and Ivangorod was divided between two states. The national boundary reflected an anti-Soviet identity, which manifested itself as strict border control and a Western emphasis in Estonia's political and economic orientation on the one hand, and liberal values in institutionalised socioeconomic policies on the other. Consequently, both cross-border commuting and access to the formerly close markets of St. Petersburg were highly restricted. Formerly state-owned companies became autonomous and, most important, needed to adapt to the conditions of free economic trade and global competition. The privatised companies were no longer responsible for offering employment for nonproductive labour or providing local communities with social facilities such as housing and day-care. Over the short term, these changes in production and market relations became the most crucial elements defining the post-Soviet context in which the local interpretations of the border were being constructed.

Issues such as territorial border crossing and language as symbolic of ethnic exclusion, along with insecure employment, high unemployment, and increased influence of employers, have come to dominate the local noninstitutionally based argumentation of Narva. Despite the very passive political culture among the Russian-speaking population in the Northeast Estonian border region (Berg and Sikk 1998), low real income and purchasing power as well as social concerns such as increased alcohol abuse and drug use have become the major institutionalised initiatives in Narva. In addition to local businesses and governmental institutions (city council and town government), there are more than fifty private and public institutions that, from their particular viewpoints, participate in the 'local geopolitical discourse' and border production.

Social movements in Narva can generally be classified according to their main sphere of function: (1) initial culture and citizenship, (2) public and self-interest, and (3) integration and sustainable development (see table 13.4). The number of movements illustrates that the largest share of pri-

Table 13.4.   Types of Social Movements in Narva

I Initial Culture and Citizenship	II Public and Self-Interest	III Integration and Sustainable Development
Jewish Society	*Children:*	*Health and Crime Prevention:*
Latvian Society	Association of Children's	Association of Physical Culture
Ukrainian Society	Welfare	and Sports of Narva
Korean Society	Children's Day Centre "LAD"	Sport Association "GALLA"
Swedish Society	Own Home for All Children	Association in Favor of a
German Society	*Family:*	Healthy Lifestyle "Eluterve
Finnish Society	Association of Single Mothers	Narva"
Tatar Society	"EMME"	*Youth and Crime Prevention:*
Narvamaa	Many Children's Families	Scouts
Estonian Society	"Suur Perekond"	Youth Organisation "New
Slavic Society	*Handicapped:*	Generation"
Coordination of National	Parents of Handicapped	Union of Youth
Associations	Children "Päikene"	Red Cross
Union of Russian Citizens	Association of Blind People	People to People
	Association of Handicapped	*Sustainable Development:*
	People	Narva NGO Centre
	Association of Handicapped	Centre for Social Integration
	"EENAR"	Centre for Cross Border
	Handicapped Sport	Cooperation and
	Organisation "Ordo"	Sustainable Development
	Abuse of Alcohol and Drugs:	Centre of Industrial Ecology
	Association VMK	
	Karitas	
	Association of Alcohol and	
	Drugs Addicts	
	Fortuna	
	Women:	
	Women's Association	
	"Narvjutjanka"	
	Estonian Women's Association	
	Business Women's Association	
	Other:	
	Labour Union Centre	
	Association of Voters	
	Association of Veterans	
	Association of Pensioners	
	Association of Inventors	
	Association of Tenants	
	Humor Club "Integration"	

vate institutionalised activity in Narva takes place in the sphere of 'public or self-interest', for example, in the sphere that drives for social change and sustainability, either from the personal or the general social interest. Most of these movements have been institutionalised to advocate particular interests of specific interest groups. They are active but rather small single-issue movements, established for solving specific locally significant problems. Movements like the Labour Union Centre and Union of Russian Citizens are very different in character, not adopting specific issues or agendas but embracing general social and political development instead. Furthermore, social movements preoccupied with leisure time activities for youth (sports), territorial integration (language teaching, legal counselling), and sustainable development play a significant role in Northeast Estonian border politics, albeit a very different one from the institutionalised political parties or party-like movements such as the Labour Union Centre and Union of Russian Citizens.

The organisation of these movements expresses locally significant issues such as the socioeconomic concerns of Narva. However, these concerns do not express the way the movements tangibly act for social change but rather reflect the conceived needs of their committed activists. Here, the role of leading activists and the form of discourse become central in shaping and structuring concrete social campaigns. Initially nonpolitical issues, such as creating indigenous language courses, may in a certain political context become politicised and used in demands for change. In Narva, not only have the Labour Union Centre and the Union of Russian Citizens become more radicalised and active party-like movements, so too have sports clubs and youth societies, transformed into elements of local social politics (Balashov 1999; Sušak 1999). Like images produced by the Baltic News Service and non-Estonian political parties, these explicitly nonpolitical local movements provide young people with certain moral codes and images of the conceptual and territorial 'other'. In Northeast Estonia, such codes and images primarily make reference to a drug-free and active leisure time, belonging to a particular locally embedded identity dissimilar from Estonian traditional culture and Russian territorial imagination.

CONCLUSION

Northeast Estonia is an interesting post-Soviet borderland that has faced enormous social changes and contrasting contentions on several geographical scales of Estonian territorial politics. The news releases of the Baltic News Service not only provide major Estonian media with 'objective' news-like images from the region but also both confirm and attempt to diminish existing Estonian stereotypes of Northeast Estonia. Compared to the contradictory messages of the BNS, the political campaign of the non-Estonian parties during the 1999 election campaign represented a more politically defined construction of interethnic and territorial boundaries. The non-Estonian political campaign in 1999 was twofold and controversial: the Estonian United People's Party (*Eestimaa Ühendatud Rahvapartei*) attempted to create the image of a nonethnic electoral list of equality while still encouraging people to vote for 'our' non-Estonian candidates. The Russian Party in Estonia (*Vene Erakond Eestis*) became similar in the public eye but had more radical ethnic argumentation and leaned towards a more politicised non-Estonian identity and calculated political strategy for gaining power. This was also the case for locally based social movements, although with a very different point of departure and intention.

The locally based social movements have their roots in everyday contexts and particular social histories of the population. In Narva, they have mainly become associated with increasing socioeconomic insecurity and related issues such as indigenous cultures' rights, abuse of alcohol and drugs, or sustainable political development. These insecurities and concerns are similar to those expressed by political parties or the national media; however, locally based movements have an immediate local or even personal element. The movements represent small-scale grassroots politics. The subjective component relates the local discourse to the extraordinary changes in the local everyday context and reflects the need to adapt the *sense of place* to new everyday conditions. In this sense, place provides local discourse not only with a context for action (location) but also with a source of identity. In the news discourse of the BNS and the election discourse of non-Estonian parties, place has a similar role, but only with an indirect reference to personal history and conceptual dangers. Nonetheless, the three discourses studied here confirm that both territorial and conceptual border discourses are place related. Borders express themselves as a specific *location* in the spatial distribution of social and economic activities, as a *locale* for everyday routine social interaction, and as a *sense of place*.

NOTE

I would like to thank the Centre of Crossborder Cooperation (Narva and Tartu, Estonia) and the Academy of Finland (project number SA 40832) for making this study possible.

REFERENCES

Aalto, P. 2000. Beyond restoration: The construction of post-Soviet geopolitics in Estonia. *Cooperation and Conflict* 35, no. 1: 65–88.

Balashov, B. 1999. Youth Association 'New Generation'. Personal interview. Narva, Estonia, 4 May.

Berg, E., and A. Sikk. 1998. Poliitilsest kultuurist Eesti kirdeperifeerias. *Akadeemia* 4: 702–21.

Brubaker, R. 1996. *Nationalism Reframed: Nationhood and the National Question in the New Europe.* New York: Cambridge University Press.

Eilart, J., et al. 1965. *Kas tunned maad?—Teadmik Eesti NSV matkaile ning kodu-uurijaile.* Tallinn, Estonia: Estonian SSR Kirjandus 'Eesti Raamat'.

Estonija. 1999. 10 February–6 March.

Hallik, K., and D. Vseviov. 1995. Rahvastik ja selle kujunemine. In T. Kaasik, ed. *Ida-Virumaa: Inimene, Majandus, Loodus.* Tallinn, Estonia: Stockholmi Keskkonna Instituut.

———. 1996. Virumaa teine pool. In S. Kalju, ed. *Koguteos Virumaa.* Tallinn, Estonia: Lääneviru maavalitsus/Idaviru maavalitsus.

Heidmets, M., ed. 1998. *Vene küsimus ja Eesti valikud.* Tallinn, Estonia: Tallinna Pedagoogikaülikool Kirjandus.

Helemäe, Y., and E. Saar. 1995. National reconstruction and social re-stratification. *Nationalities Papers* 23, no. 1: 127–39.

Järve, P., ed. 1997. *Vene noored Eestis: Sotsioloogiline mosaiik—Materialide kogumik.* Tallinn, Estonia: Kirjastus Avita.

Katus, K. 1992. Demokraafiline ülevaade. In S. Õispuu, ed. *Eesti ajalugu—ärkamisajast kuni tänapäevani.* Tallinn, Estonia: Koolibri.

Kirch, A. 1997. *The Integration of Non-Estonians into Estonian Society: History, Problems and Trends.* Tallinn, Estonia: United States Institute of Peace.

Kruusvall, J. 1998. Usaldus ja usaldamatus rahvussuhetes. In M. Heidmets, ed. *Vene küsimus ja Eesti valikud.* Tallinn, Estonia: Tallinna Pedagoogikaülikool Kirjandus.

Laidvee, I. 1998. Vene parteid Eestis. Thesis, Department of Politology, University of Tartu, Estonia (available at http://www.ut.ee/ABVKeskus/eesti/vene_parteid_Eestis.html).

Liikanen, I., and J. Virkkunen. 1999. The political construction of identity in Estonia. In O. Brednikova and V. Voronkov, eds. *Nomadic Borders.* Working Papers of the Centre for Independent Social Research, no. 7. St. Petersburg: Centre for Independent Social Research.

Misiunas, R., and R. Taagepera. 1993. *The Baltic States: Years of Dependence, 1940–1990.* London: Hurst.

Molodezh Estonii. 1999. 10 February–6 March.

Narva City Council. 1998. Share of Estonian, Russian and non-citizens in Narva (unpublished statistics).

Pahtma, L., and H. Tamman. 1997. Artiklite kogumik. *Eesti ajalooarhiivi toimetused 2,* no. 9.

———. 1998. Rootsi suurriigi Vene impeeriumisse. *Eesti ajalooarhiivi toimetused 3,* no. 10.

Palang, H., and T. Tammaru. 1996. Üleandmed. In S. Kalju, ed. *Koguteos Virumaa.* Tallinn, Estonia: Lääneviru maavalitsus/Idaviru maavalitsus.

Park, A. 1995a. Ethnicity and independence: The case of Estonia in comparative perspective. *Proceedings of the Estonian Academy of Science, Humanities, and Social Sciences* 44, no. 3: 302–32.

———. 1995b. Explaining Estonian citizenship policy: A case study in post-imperial relations in comparative perspective. *Proceedings of the Estonian Academy of Science, Humanities, and Social Sciences* 44, no. 3: 354–77.

Pettai, I. 1997. Muulaste integreerumine Eesti ühiskonda: Soovid ja tegelikkus. In A. Piirimägi and A. Dusman, ed. *Rahvuste integreerumise eeldused Eesti ühiskonda Ida-Virumaal 27.–29. november 1996: Konverentsi materjalide kogumik.* Jõhvi: DISANTREK.

Raitviir, T. 1996. *Eesti Üleminekuperioodi valimiste (1989–1993) võrdlev uurimus.* Tallinn, Estonia: Institute of International and Social Studies.

Ruutsoo, R. 1993. Transitional societies and social movements in Estonia, 1987–1994. *Proceedings of the Estonian Academy of Science, Humanities, and Social Sciences* 42, no. 2: 195–214.

Saarikoski, V. 1993. Russian minorities in the Baltic states—A brief analysis of the arguments of the present political dialogue regarding Russian minorities in the Baltic states. In P. Joenniemi and P. Vares, eds. *New Actors on the International Arena—The Foreign Policies of the Baltic Countries.* Tampere Peace Research Institute, Research Report 50. Tampere, Finland: TAPRI.

Sillate J., and Ü Purga. 1995. *Economy: Present State and Potential in Ida-Virumaa: Man, Nature, Population and Its Formation.* UNDP Development Report. Tallinn, Estonia: UNDP.

Silva, E. 1998. Inimõiguste probleem Eestis 1990.-ndate aastate Eesti ajakirjanduse põhjal. Thesis, Department of Politology, University of Tartu (available at http://www.ut.ee/ABVKeskus/eesti/iea/inimoigused_eesti_ajakirjanduses.html).

Smith, G. 1990. Nationalities policy from Lenin to Gorbachev. In G. Smith, ed. *Nationalities Question in the Soviet Union.* London: Longman.

Smith, G., A. Aasland, and R. Mole. 1994. Statehood, ethnic relations and citizenship. In G. Smith, ed. *The Baltic States—The National Self-Determination of Estonia, Latvia and Lithuania.* London: Macmillan.

Statistical Office of Estonia. 1990. *Eesti Vabariigi maakondade, linnade ja alevite rahvastik. 1989 I Statistika kogumik.* Tallinn: Statistical Office of Estonia.

———. 1998. *Reference Book of Population Statistics.* Nr. 1/98. Tallinn: Statistical Office of Estonia.

Sušak, N. 1999. Association of physical culture and sports in Narva. Personal interview, Narva, Estonia, 19 April.

Süvalep, A. 1995. *Taani-aegne Narva.* Narva, Estonia: Narva Muuseum, 1995.

Tilly, C. 1993. Social movements as historically specific clusters of political performances. *Berkeley Journal of Sociology* 38: 1–30.

Virkkunen, J. 1999. The politics of identity: Ethnicity, minority and nationalism in Soviet Estonia. *GeoJournal* 48: 83–89.

Volkonski, P. 1996. Integratsioon ja erinevad mõttemistüüpid (Mõnengaid mõtteid psühholoogilisest ernevustest eestlaste ja venelaste vahel). In E. Vaikmäe-Koit, ed. *Etnilised väemused Eestis, nende tänased probleemid ja tulevik—konveretsi materiaalid 21–22. November 1995.* Tartu, Estonia: Tartu trükk.

Chapter Fourteen

Symbolic and Functional Balance on Europe's Northern Borders

Kristiina Karppi

The changing nature of the European East-West dichotomy, the growing politicisation of ethnic identities, and the increasing cross-border movement of people, goods, capital, and ideas have all contributed to the widening critical rethinking of states, sovereignty, nation, and boundaries. Simultaneously, we are compelled to reconsider the dimensions and meanings of territoriality and identity. This chapter seeks to address some of the political, economic, and cultural transformations in the European northernmost border area of Norway, Sweden, Finland, and the Murmansk *oblast* of northwestern Russia (the Kola peninsula) after the collapse of Soviet socialism roughly a decade ago. These modifications are mirrored against certain former geopolitical developments connected to the making of the national territories and history of this northern area, here referred to as 'Northern Borders'. The question debated is whether there is room for a common understanding of a region overarching the national and the slowly warming Cold War boundaries. There are still several dividing lines between the East and the West and also some emerging fields of common interest and collaboration in this, Europe's northernmost border region. These reflect the various contextual dimensions of borders, identity, and territoriality; they interact, overlap, and bear political, economic, and social overtones. Likewise, they spell the recondite intertwining of spatial scales in the reorganisation and future of a borderland.

NORTHERN BORDERS BLENDING MULTIPLE
ACTORS AND PERIPHERALITY

The geographical concept of the 'Northern Borders' is loose and flexible, without such general territorial features as controller, subjects of governance, or clearly defined map image. Instead, it seems to complement the fuzziness and multitude of different projects, initiatives (by both governmental and nongovernmental interest groups), and the existing and overlapping territorialities of the region. Although independent of any one politically constructed territorial definition, it is not a mere discursive representation but refers to a border region with its own distinct features and spatial organisation. But is it a recognisable identity shared by both those in the region (regional identity of the people) as well as those looking in from outside (identity of the region)? In this case, there are several factors at least apparently working for such an identity, including the official end of the Cold War, the peripheral status of the area for all the states involved, the rather late division of the landscape by national borders, and the increased emphasis on cross-border co-operation in Europe. In addition, the indigenous Sami are the old inhabitants of this region, thus constituting an already existing transboundary group.

The seemingly strange notion of claiming for peripherality the role of a uniting factor in the Northern Borders deserves further attention. As the Nordic states represent one European periphery (remote geographical position, small economies and populations), their northernmost areas form a periphery within a periphery. Thus, active measures have to be taken to keep them 'afloat'. The attempts to create a sense of unity in the northern area and to increase awareness of a common future work towards this aim. As odd as it may seem, peripherality and remoteness can also be seen as identity factors and be turned into strengths, or at least recognisable and useable slogans ('self-peripheralisation'; see Joenniemi 2000). This can be said to be true in the case of Finland, for example, in the form of the Northern Dimension initiative.

The European Union was a visible force in the area in the 1990s, not least because Sweden and Finland joined it in 1995. In contrast to previous decades, there are now many and varied interest groups playing increasing roles in the European North. Their agendas range from environmental protection to exploitation of natural resources of the area, from redemption of a collective cultural group, the Sami, to the expansion of the limits of traditional understanding of security, culture, and economic co-operation. These developments are feeding a civic culture that questions the constituents of the Northern Borders as divided between state and military interests. The current multitude of actors in the region and—perhaps even more important—*of* the region challenge that one-dimensional image. But as well as factors working for regional identity, there are those working against it. The key parameters seem to be the symmetry or balance of co-operation as well as the nature and depth of interdependence across borderlines.

TERRITORIALITY AND IDENTITY
AS CONTEXTUAL CATEGORIES

The difficulty of discussing boundaries, territoriality, nation, and identity without referring to the concept of (nation-)state reflects the deeply rooted state centricity of our thinking, but also the fact that the 'state is everywhere'. Indeed, the state is often cited as being the most successful export of Europe at all times. Our understanding of the state includes such notions as the Weberian monopoly of violence within its realm, the unity of a state and a nation, and national borders separating entities that are ultimately different if measured by one or more criteria. These notions legitimised the need for state-centric instruments in transboundary communication.

Agnew (1994) has captured this in his metaphor of the 'territorial trap'. The concept refers to precisely this fixation of geographical imagination in which states are seen as universal units of territorial space, the domestic and the foreign are separate categories, and societies are subordinate to states (container states). The state is simply taken for granted as the unit of sociospatial organisation, and society when defined in terms of the state is seen as 'natural'. If these dimensions were approached openly, most of them would not necessarily pass closer scrutiny.

The institutionalisation of regions, whether nation-states or other entities, is a process of production, reproduction, construction, and transformation. According to Paasi (1996: 31–38), certain key dimensions of regional transformation can be mapped. Institutionalisation refers to the process in which regions emerge and become established, not as 'organisms' but as units of the larger system. The different stages of this process are the constitution of territorial and symbolic image, institutions, and finally the establishment of the unit in the regional structure and social consciousness.

The dimensions of the state refer to the symbolic and functional existence of an 'us' in contrast to a 'them'. In this line of thinking, the territoriality of states reflects the original, or authentic, differences between groups of people. The reasoning works in reverse, also: The state borders are drawn where two nations meet. In 'realistic' state centricity and persistence of differences *between* national units, not *within* them, there is little room for the discussion of collective identities or entities *crossing* state borders. In our case, the indigenous Sami people are such a group, divided by national boundaries, thus contesting the idea of borders excluding 'the different' from 'the similar'. States and nationalism use national myths, complex mixtures of truth and falsehood, or existing and invented traditions in making the nation and sustaining the often questionable power relations between different groups (Anderson 1983; Archard 1995). The mapping of identity, whether ethnic or spatial, is always to a degree an artificial exercise, with the persistent mythical element of clear-cut differences present (Hassner 1993: 49). The state (as any region) needs production and reproduction of 'us'. Language and education have been important in producing nationhood, and the mastering of these mechanisms is crucial for the control of the state.

It is difficult to conceive of the state being replaced as the hegemonic form of sociospatial organisation. The system of supranational order and communication follows the logic of territorial states (trade relations, customs, passport control, diplomacy, international law, and governance). Furthermore, citizenship is the primary regulatory mechanism of the relations between an individual and society (or community). It constantly reproduces and maintains the originality of the state as a means for two-dimensional economic, social, and political rights and obligations of the citizen and the state. Thus, it would be safer to argue for the other spatial patterns of organisation to complement, not threaten, the states. The states, their institutions, and their practices remain an inescapable framework also for the many cross-border initiatives.

It is equally difficult to see how other regions would radically differ from states when it comes to the 'naturalness' of their various boundaries. Territoriality and identity—regardless of spatial scale—seem to be contextual categories in that there are always specific traits of space, time, contacts, and hierarchies moulding them. Moreover, they are indeed the unique building blocks in what constitutes a region. In comparison with any region making, transboundary regional processes face additional challenges. It is not sufficient for them to build on any single, nationally delineated identity. The role of borderland identities is in many cases to be additional and complementary and to unite across national dividing lines by emphasising the particular connections, contexts, and conditions of the people.

EVOLVING CONCEPTS OF THE NORTH

The northernmost European border region has many labels, and the geographical area under each of those varies. Some of the concepts are straightforwardly connected to a specific political program; some are less loaded. It is fair to say that any regional concept is 'political' in the sense that to exist it has to be defined: Someone has to see and proclaim the connection of a particular geographical and social space before it can be referred to and articulated into discourses (Karppi 2000). In so doing, the criteria by which to define the region have to be chosen. Region building or institutionalisation of regions can thus be said to be a discursive exercise (Paasi 1996: 31–38; Murphy 1991; Neumann 1992). On the other hand, to make naming a region a rational activity, a uniting factor should exist. Neither of the two extreme perspectives (empiricist and postmodernist, or realist and constructionist) on geographical concepts—either they are real or merely inventions of observers—is fruitful. As Agnew (1999) observes, the regions are neither simply out there nor all in the mind of the observer. Geographical concepts reflect differences both in the world and in our ideas of those differences. The regions with ethnonational significance in particular, but also other spatial concepts, should not be taken for granted but as part of the social dynamic (Murphy 1991: 32). The existence of a region is in this sense related to the problem of the state and nation.

Some Governmental Initiatives in the Northern Borders

There are numerous organisations and forums—small and large, governmental and nongovernmental—in which the issues of the Northern Borders are discussed. Whereas 'European Arctic' or 'North' and 'Northern Borders' represent the less-politicised concepts, 'North Calotte' and the 'Barents Euro-Arctic Region' refer to concepts with specific contexts of development, defined actors, and agendas (Heininen 1999: 69–72; Neumann 1992). Similarly, the 'Northern Dimension' of the European Union is a political concept used when referring to the Baltic Sea co-operation, the Barents Region, or initiatives simply involving the EU and (northwestern) Russia. As such, it can be understood as a loose geographical umbrella notion and, more to the point, as a counterweight to the 'Southern Dimension', the Mediterranean focus of the European Union.

The idea of 'North Calotte' was first launched in 1957 by the interstate Nordic Council, which made recommendations to the governments of Norway, Sweden, and Finland to increase economic co-operation in the area (Käkönen 1996: 9). The concept had a specific geographical content consisting of the northern (state) administrative districts of the three countries. The North Calotte Committee was founded in 1977 to co-ordinate multilateral co-operation, and during the late 1980s the leaders of the Kola Peninsula region were invited to participate. The North Calotte

Committee functioned from 1977 to 1997 and was succeeded by the North Calotte Council (Jama and Kivimäki 1997).

During the 1990s, the debate on increasing co-action in the European North initially concentrated on developing Arctic co-operation and extending North Calotte collaboration between northern parts of Norway, Sweden, Finland, and regions across the Russian border (Christiansen and Joenniemi 1999: 93). In 1992–1993, the Norwegian initiative of the Barents Euro-Arctic Region (BEAR), started by the Norwegian minister for foreign affairs, Thorvald Stoltenberg, soon became the dominant regional idea. The members of the Barents Euro-Arctic Council are the five Nordic countries, the Russian Federation, and the European Commission, but there are also decentralised, regional bodies within the BEAR framework. This enables BEAR to function at both the central and regional levels and to pursue the maximisation of opportunities for promotion of co-operation (Stoltenberg 1999). Geographically BEAR came to include the extended North Calotte, as well as the Archangel district and the Karelian Republic of Russia (Käkönen 1996: 10).

The purpose of BEAR was to counteract marginalisation by de-emphasising the meaning of national borderlines as well as to ensure these northernmost peripheries a place in the changing European order and to act—instead of waiting—to solve some of the economic and security problems in the region. The aspect of integrating Russia into European and global structures through increased co-operation was also considered of the utmost importance (Joenniemi 2000; Solana 1999). At the end of 1998 the Northern Dimension was formally accepted as an EU policy for promoting the management of the EU's external relations in Northern Europe; political stability and security are sought through co-operation and economic interdependence (Sutela 1999: 3). 'Sustainable development' and 'interdependence breeds peace' became the objectives used in the context of BEAR and the Northern Dimension (Sutela 1999: 3; Didyk and Wiberg 1998; Summa 1997: 66). As Sutela (1999) aptly puts it, more than about particular countries, the Northern Dimension is about interdependencies, links, and regional structures. In addition to these institutional co-operative frameworks, other 'top-down' transboundary initiatives of this region have included programs such as the European Union INTERREG Barents, North Calotte/Sápmi, and Kolarctic programmes.

A Nongovernmental Approach: The Sami as a Transboundary People

In addition to these northern collaboration frameworks initiated by the states, there exist several other geographical arenas of nongovernmental organisations (NGOs) and interest groups, for example, among the indigenous Sami. In the Northern Borders the Sami have been outnumbered by ethnic Norwegians, Swedes, Finns, and Russians and constitute a majority population in only a few northern local government units. Thus the Sami share their physical and social space with members of the national majorities.

The Sami area has been a subject for partition in the regional quests of the nation-states. The Petsamo area of Finland was ceded to the Soviet Union in the Continuation War in 1945. This fixed the northeastern border of Finland and denied the Finns access to the Barents Sea, also affecting the Skolt Sami population. Among them, families were divided and ethnic ties severed as many Skolts were resettled in the Finnish areas around Lake Inari. The border between Finland and the Soviet Union was closed and hindered the traditional coexistence and seasonal migration among the Sami. This had not always been the case. *The Lapp Codicil*, an amendment to the 1751 border treaty between Denmark-Norway and Sweden-Finland, granted the Sami the right to continue exploiting the natural resources on either side of the border (Pedersen 1996). Similarly, the border treaty of 1826 between Norway and Russia provided the Eastern Sami on the Russian side of the border the right to continue fishing for salmon on the Norwegian side (Nielsen 1994: 89).

The idea of Sami unity can be claimed to be a product of the nation-states and nation building, and paradoxically it uses much of the same argumentation and vocabulary. The Sami discovered the need to politicise their identity when an external threat was apparent. Along with this grew the understanding that the small and rather dispersed groups with different languages and livelihoods formed an umbrella concept of the Sami people. As a result of the gradual growth in the number of different organisations (local, national, and Pan-Sami) during the twentieth century, the Sami now proclaim themselves to be one people (Helander 1996: 296–97).

The Sami refer to the northernmost regions of the Nordic countries and Kola peninsula as 'Sápmi', Samiland, the transboundary homeland (see figure 14.1). It is a geography formed by the use of Sami languages and denotes the areas where the Sami have lived and practiced their occupations (Broderstad 1997; Eriksson 1997; Helander 1996). Thus, for the Sami there exists a geographical entity in the European northernmost area with which they identify themselves.

The territoriality of the Sami has differed from that of the states: it is based on the flexible *Siida* or Lapp Village system, in which negotiation of the territorial zones and the flexible boundaries of group membership has played an important role (Forrest 1998; Helander 1999). The heritage of

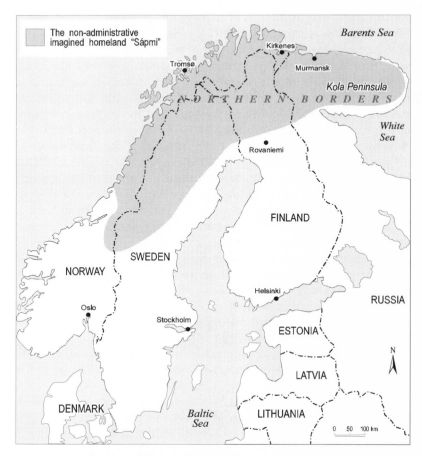

Figure 14.1.   Scandinavia and the Northern Borders

this form of territoriality has perhaps been one reason why Sami political activism has not openly resulted in ethnoregionalistic and nationalistic claims. The Sami have paid dearly for not perceiving land as property (the absence of the concept of modern ownership of land) as the states have later claimed ownership of the old Sami herding territories (*res nullius*).

   As northern co-operation has evolved in various forums and around different agendas, the Sami have become participants in some of these. They are stakeholders as local residents in the questions concerning the resources, knowledge, and future of the northernmost European areas. The Sami have been institutionally involved in the initiative of BEAR since its foundation in 1993, but their expectations were not high to start with

(Helander 1996: 299–300). BEAR reminded the Sami of the rather limited space granted to them by the states in earlier phases of history (the legacy of colonization: missionary activities, assimilation, racism, and loss of rights to land and water, but also of parts of their symbolic culture). However, the general goals of Barents co-operation, such as improvement of environmental security, regional stability, and regional networks, as well as the ability of the indigenous group to actively influence co-operation, were all well received by Sami politicians (Helander 1996: 299–300). As the institutional and socioeconomic conditions of the Russian Sami are poorer than among the Sami in the Nordic countries, BEAR was also seen as an opportunity for improving their living conditions.

STATE CENTRICITY AND REGIONAL CHALLENGES

Northern region building seems to need state as well as regional actors. As Svensson (1995) has concluded, transnational regionalisation is to a great extent dependent on the good will of national governments because it involves national interests (such as the redefinition of security) and affects several spatial scales of organisation. In short, it is too big a question to be left to regional actors alone.

Several tensions affect the balance between northern regional activity and modern state centricity. These include the fact that the EU—strongly present in the North—does not seem free of obscurity concerning the direction of spatial reorganisation. On the contrary, the development of the EU has been walking a tightrope between differing ideas of a 'common Europe', the basic tensions manifesting themselves in state centricity, growing supranationality, and the aim of increasing subnational and regional transboundary control. The paradoxical twin processes of unification and fragmentation seem inescapably simultaneous and interrelated, even within one political organisation such as the EU (Khatami and Vivekananda 1995: 35). This integration process emphasises regional and cross-border co-operation in attempts to create endogenous growth and social coherence. It pays little or no attention to national projects except when controlling and restricting, for example, the states' support of industries. Thus, although an operation of the states, the goals seem to be pursued mostly on the supra- and subnational scales. However, it is premature to proclaim the states as losers in this game, as institutional changes take place within the negotiation mechanisms with states as their kernels. Furthermore, the role of regional institutions within the EU, such as the Committee of Regions, has remained largely advisory and subordinate.

Such is also the case in northernmost Europe: Integration and regionalisation are visible as synchronous forces. The Nordic states are drawn into a tighter supranational co-operation within the EU and other state-based initiatives, but a region-building approach exists as well (Keating 1996; Schmitter 1995; Smith and Østerud 1995). In the Northern Borders, transboundary collaboration has for several decades been primarily a state-centric exercise, although local and provincial governments have been the units of significant co-operation. This situation stems from the legacy of the region. Even if the area was demarcated rather late in contrast to the national cores, the ethnically mixed northernmost areas have been seen as important in shaping the geography of the states, as well as national unity. In pursuing these goals, measures included the building of infrastructure, administrative, and legislative functions, as well as the introduction of a nationwide education system, the missionary activities already mentioned, and policies of assimilation. The existence of common resources in the North not only linked the region together but also tended to consolidate the national division of it (Nielsen 1994). For example, hunters and fishermen of the area mobilised their respective national governments to keep outsiders away, which contributed to an increased emphasis on national lines of demarcation both on land and at sea.

The Sami have not been the sole nonmajority group in the region. In the 1800s, Norway was concerned about the loyalty of the ethnically Finnish people, the Quains (*Kvens, kvener*) in the North. These nonethnic Norwegians were considered potentially unreliable in critical situations and a 'fifth column' for offensive neighbour countries (Broderstad 1997: 4). The recent Sami demands concerning land title have created tensions, especially in the local communities of the Northern Borders. Members of the national majorities, but also other ethnic groups in the northern areas (Finns in the Tornio River Valley and the Quains) have raised the Sami land rights question from the position of state versus indigenous people (Koivulehto 1999). They see themselves as legitimate stakeholders in the land rights negotiations because their families have lived in the area for generations. The claims to land title are, of course, to the greatest degree tied to the question of 'whose region'. Thus, the regional quest also has an in-built local dimension.

One of the most crucial state centricity/regionalisation dimensions in northern transboundary co-operation concerns the development of the Russian Federation. The difficult balancing between centralisation and decentralisation of power has been visible since the beginning of the 1990s, after the dissolution of the Soviet Union (Kallagher 2000; Karush and Belton 2000). The transformation and economic difficulties of Russia have eroded the economic stability of the centre-dependent regions and forced them to try to cover the losses in intergovernmental transfers and domestic markets by foreign trade (Solanko 1999). The unclear and changing relations between the national political and economic core and the regions are no help. Transboundary co-operation necessarily requires activity of the national governments but to a degree also decentralised power and resources. As Robert Bathurst (1994) has concluded, it is still difficult to foresee how the relations between Moscow and the regions will develop and to what extent the integration and opening up of, for example, the Murmansk *oblast* will be tolerated.

ON SYMMETRY AND BALANCE OF THE
CROSS-BORDER INTERDEPENDENCE

The genuine institutionalisation of a borderland region and functional development of mutual benefit seems to require balanced integration. It consists of elements such as symmetrical trade relations, equal dependency, credibility and stability of institutions, nonexistent or small social and economic disparities across the borderline and in the field of economic co-operation, and such preconditions as a legal framework securing foreign investments (Sutela 1999; Stoltenberg 1999). Similarly, cultural understanding is a valuable asset in any co-operation, not least in the transboundary context (Bathurst 1994: 55; Leitner 2000: 21; Svensson 1997). Mutual trust is an aspect of this, as are factors such as language. In his study on Swedish firms operating in Northwest Russia, Svensson (1997) found that cultural understanding often deals with anticipated differences as well as real, existing ones. In a similar vein, foreign businesspeople often bring their 'taken-for-granted' (business) culture to Russia only to be disappointed when their expectations are not met. The experiences of substantial economic and other difficulties among non-Russian partners do not encourage businesses to co-operate (Mennola et al. 1999: 18).

Today's profound social and economic disparities between the Nordic countries and Russia make equal partnership in transboundary activities virtually impossible (see Hansen 1994). An average salary in Murmansk *oblast* was US$292 in 1997 (Lausala and Valkonen 1999: 174). According to a Barents INTERREG programme evaluation by Mennola et al. (1999), many entrepreneurs in the Nordic countries consider co-operation with Russia to be humanitarian exercises rather than interesting business opportunities. Other problems of the Barents INTERREG IIA program included too large a portion of public participation in all projects (80 percent of the number of projects and 90 percent of total costs). This can be at least partially expected due to the instability of Russian society, lack of matching Russian partners, and Nordic small- and medium-sized enterprises (SMEs) avoiding financial risks. Additionally, Russian legislation, taxation, customs, tariffs, and the often-changing 'rules of the game' are considered an obstacle to co-operation (Jumppanen 1996: 61–62). On the other hand, positive factors and promises from the viewpoint of Kola peninsula development and the future integration of the Northern Borders include the relatively high quality of the educational system and the vast potential of the natural resources (Lausala and Valkonen 1999).

In previous centuries Norway and Russia maintained active local trade relations in the Pomor trade, and the Norwegian-Russian border was closed only after the Russian Revolution in 1919 (Thuen 1993; Wiberg 1996). Curiously enough, the drawing of national boundaries can be said to have been a factor behind the flourishing Pomor trade (Nielsen 1994: 94). National governments wanted to maintain the population in the northern area to consolidate their claim to it and thus granted duty-free trade relations; this made the Pomor trade profitable. Norwegian anthropologist Trond Thuen (1993) has approached the question of symmetry and asymmetry in transboundary symbiosis by using two examples of Norwegian-Russian trade relations in the Northern Borders. He has compared the trade relations in Pomor trade with the recent visiting Russian 'trader-tourists', who sold small commodities on the streets of northern Norwegian towns for a period in 1992. Thuen concludes that these cases symbolise the two different epochs of trade relations in the Northern Borders. The original Pomor period witnessed the symmetrical relationship of trading wheat and rye flour from the White Sea for the fish of coastal northern Norway, whereas the latter case featured the current asymmetry as Russian street vendors provided northern Norwegians with both legal and illegal, but cheap, goods. The only similarity between these epochs was the fact that they were both made possible by the consent of the states and also were ended by them.

Asymmetry in the economic co-operation of the Northern Borders is also visible in the official foreign trade of the Kola peninsula (Lausala and Valkonen 1999). The EU is the most important trading partner for the Murmansk *oblast*, whose structure of exports consists mainly of raw materials (fish, mining products) and electricity, whereas the imports from the EU include food, clothes, and manufactured goods. Although the privatisation of industrial enterprises in the Kola peninsula is virtually complete, the restructuring of the privatised enterprises has not proceeded very far. Often the regional authorities have been reluctant to speed up the process for fear of increasing regional unemployment (Lausala and Valkonen 1999: 151).

GENERAL DEVELOPMENT TRENDS OF STRUCTURAL IMPORTANCE

Although the European Union is expected to further unite the Western and Central European states and their economies, there are currently few positive signs of Russia integrating with the rest of Europe (Didyk and Wiberg 1998: 105; Kozyrev 1997; Mennola et al. 1999; Tiusanen 1997). The emerging economic co-operation can be undermined by the strengthening Western military integration and the expansion of NATO in the countries of the former Soviet bloc. In addition, the recent macro-scale conflicts between Russia and the Western states regarding the limits of national sovereignty in military actions in Bosnia, Kosovo, and Chechnya, as well as the occasional allegations of corruption concerning the Russian political core, have threatened the expansion of local and regional transboundary pooling of activities. However, there are now increased space and possibilities for transboundary collaboration in the field of security, as the concept is understood to cover aspects of environmental, social, and economic security in addition to 'traditional' military security.

Strategic and economic vulnerability, which may accompany asymmetric dependence, is a realistic and possible nationalistic view of Russia's European relations (Sutela 1999). If such voices gain in strength, the future of the Northern Borders development will not be particularly promising. This is one reason why proposals like the Northern Dimension have to perceive Russia as a partner, a subject of co-operation, never as an object of an outside initiative.

The Kola Peninsula region is one of the most heavily militarised areas in the world (Hønneland and Jørgensen 1999). The local legacy—the humiliation of the Russian military in the new political situation and with decaying equipment—is one major factor of uncertainty in the future of regions such as Murmansk (Bathurst 1994). The problems of this northern borderland are no longer primarily caused by state territoriality as such. As Hedegaard and Lindström (1998: 4) remind us, the entire North European and Baltic Sea area is now free of regimes bent on military aggression against their neighbours. Now, when the institutional international scene would finally seem to be open for genuine transboundary co-operation, domestic problems present obstacles.

National hinterlands such as the Northern Borders are usually dependent on the corresponding states for their development and economic opportunities, which are further intertwined with the domestic and foreign organisation of the states. In other words, the development of the Kola peninsula is far from independent of the domestic development of

Russia (its political, economic, and judicial difficulties) or of its foreign development (questions of military security, trade, and political alliances). International, national, regional, and local cannot be separated. As long as co-operation and daily activities across borders remain low, and as long as there is very little or no visible improvement in the living conditions on the eastern side of the northern border, the possibility for building *one* borderland identity seems remote. Instead, there are several separate borderland identities on each side of the border: local, (several) Sami, Quain, Norwegian, Russian, Finnish, and so on.

WHOSE NORTHERN BORDERS?

A regional borderland identity takes time to develop, and everyday communication and interaction would be its essential building blocks. For the formation of a genuine borderland, interaction and exchange on each side of the border must be in balance. However, this is not likely in the foreseeable future in the North. Asymmetrical relations are not a fertile ground for such a borderland to develop, and thus the common understanding needed for the European North seems largely to be discovered.

The same goes for the common identity of the region. The reasons for this can be sought in various spatial scales of negotiation, but also in factors such as cultural differences and the continuing asymmetrical conditions for co-operation on different sides of the old Cold War boundary. Nor is the example of the localised debate concerning land title particularly encouraging to northern region building. Instead of seeing the region as a whole, as an entity with common goals and future prospects and possibilities, the local population turns inwards and pursues policies of exclusion in seeking to secure its economic status. The atmosphere for endogenous or 'upwards' regional development initiatives could be more favourable.

Cultural coherence and cultural sensitivity would seem to be important factors of development. Perhaps the greatest obstacle to collaboration on the western side of the Russian border is that we still mistakenly expect Russia to suddenly start functioning according to Western logic. For the Russians the demand and possibility for and invitation to the decentralised cross-border collaboration are new in more ways than one. The idea of regional co-operation challenges everything in the seventy years of Soviet doctrine, or in Bathurst's words, for the Russians the 'Barents idea embodies a world turned upside down' (1994: 51). Thus, in the case of the Northern Borders, the need and the ability to interpret cultural differences and to understand their effect on and value for cross-border collaboration would be especially crucial for Westerners operating from within established and fairly predictable societies. The traditional centralisation of Russian society and all its public functions creates a real challenge for any regional transboundary initiative. Further, the difficult balance between centralisation and decentralisation is a source of a certain unpredictability in Northern Borders cross-border co-operation: Too much of the former leaves little room for regional initiatives, and too little of it creates uncertainty regarding the functioning of key institutions in society.

Considering the nature of the remaining structural obstacles to co-operation in the Northern Borders, it is fair also to emphasise the future significance of interstate relations. Regional projects require both centralised and regional action. The future of the Northern Dimension also depends on the possibility of a wider European audience to relate to the problems of the northern region. If the initiative is perceived to serve the interests of a small group of peripheral states, its potential remains low. Because perhaps the greatest difference between the traditional Nordic co-operation and the Barents co-operation is in the active participation of Russia, it is important that the agenda of BEAR remain relevant for all concerned and not focus only on the interests of the Nordic states or the EU.

Further, the 'New Divide' of a social and economic character within the Northern Borders demands time, action, and patience from all those involved. Not until the transboundary interaction is more symmetrical and balanced can a regional identity start to emerge via increased contacts. Transboundary co-operation in such concrete fields as development of infrastructure and communications is within the reach of current financial resources, but the creation of institutional stability and security remains essentially a Russian task. All in all, it seems that in the region-building approach of the North the crucial points are who defines the objectives of collaboration, who participates, on what terms, and with what resources. The future of a borderland is being written on all spatial scales and in several cabinets, the questions of symmetry and balance of interdependence being decisive.

REFERENCES

Agnew, J. 1994. The territorial trap: The geographical assumptions of international relations theory. *Review of International Political Economy* 1, no. 1: 53–80.
———. 1999. Regions on the mind does not equal regions of the mind. *Progress in Human Geography* 23, no. 1: 91–96.
Anderson, B. 1983. *Imagined Communities*. London: Verso.

Archard, D. 1995. Myths, lies and historical truth: A defense of nationalism. *Political Studies* 43, no. 3: 472–81.

Bathurst, R. 1994. Where cultures cross: Old Russia in a new north. In O. S. Stokke and O. Tunander, eds. *The Barents Region. Cooperation in Arctic Europe*, 45–56. London: Sage.

Broderstad, E. G. 1997. *Saami identity in cultural and political communities.* ARENA Working Paper 9. Oslo: University of Oslo.

Christiansen, T., and P. Joenniemi. 1999. Politics on the edge: On the restructuring of borders in the north of Europe. In H. Eskelinen, I. Liikanen, and J. Oksa, eds. *Curtains of Iron and Gold: Reconstructing Borders and Scales of Interaction*, 89–115. Aldershot, England: Ashgate.

Didyk, V., and U. Wiberg. 1998. Sustainable investment policies in the Murmansk region. In L. Hedegaard and B. Lindström, eds. 1998. *The NEBI Yearbook 1998. North European and Baltic Sea Integration*, 99–113. Berlin: Springer.

Eriksson, J. 1997. Partition and redemption. A Machiavellian analysis of *Sami* and Basque patriotism. *Umeå University, Department of Political Science. Research Report* 1.

Forrest, S. 1998. Do fences make good neighbours? The influence of territoriality in state-Sámi relations. Master's thesis, University of Northern British Columbia.

Hansen, E. 1994. Living conditions in the North: The new divide. In O. S. Stokke and O. Tunander, eds. *The Barents Region: Cooperation in Arctic Europe*, 57–70. London: Sage.

Hassner, P. 1993. Beyond nationalism and internationalism: Ethnicity and world order. *Survival* 35, no. 2: 49–65.

Hedegaard, L., and B. Lindström. 1998. The North European and Baltic opportunity. In L. Hedegaard and B. Lindström, eds. *The NEBI Yearbook 1998. North European and Baltic Sea Integration*, 3–29. Berlin: Springer.

Heininen, L. 1999. *Euroopan pohjoinen 1990-luvulla. Moniulotteisten ja ristiriitaisten intressien alue.* [*The European North in the 1990s: A region of multifunctional and conflicting interests*]. Arctic Centre Reports, no. 30. Rovaniemi, Finland: University of Lapland.

Helander, E. 1996. The status of the *Sami* people in the inter-state cooperation. In J. Käkönen, ed. *Dreaming of the Barents Region: Interpreting Cooperation in the Euro-Arctic Rim*, 296–306. Tampere Peace Research Institute, Research Report No. 73. Tampere, Finland: TAPRI.

———. 1999. *Sami* subsistence activities—Spatial aspects and structuration. *Acta Borealia* 2: 7–25.

Hønneland, G., and A.-K. Jørgensen. 1999. *Integration vs. Autonomy: Civil-Military Relations on the Kola Peninsula.* Aldershot, England: Ashgate.

Jama, J., and T. Kivimäki. 1997. Pohjoiskalottikomitea ja Pohjoiskalotin neuvosto [The North Calotte Committee and the North Calotte Council]. In T. Kivimäki and P. Väyrynen, eds. *Kansainvälinen yhteistyö Pohjoiskalotilla*, 80–133. Faculty of Social Sciences, Publications in International Relations. Rovaniemi, Finland: University of Lapland.

Joenniemi, P. 2000. At home with northernness: Finland, Russia and the Northern Dimension. *North* 11, no. 1: 19–23.

Jumppanen, P. 1996. Taloudellinen integraatio Barentsin alueella [Economic integration in the Barents Region]. In L. Heininen, ed. *Suomi uudessa Pohjois-Euroopassa*, 55–62. Arctic Centre Reports, no. 20. Rovaniemi, Finland: University of Lapland.

Käkönen, J. 1996. An introduction—Cooperation in the European circumpolar north. In J. Käkönen, ed. *Dreaming of the Barents Region: Interpreting Cooperation in the Euro-Arctic Rim,* 9–22. Tampere Peace Research Institute, Research Report No. 73. Tampere, Finland: TAPRI.

Kallagher, K. 2000. At the swearing in ceremony for Russian President Putin. *Business Central Europe* 6: 10.

Karppi, K. 2000. *Articulated Spaces. Minorities in Regional Policy.* Acta Universitatis Tamperensis, series A, vol. 721. Tampere, Finland: Tampere University.

Karush, S., and K. Belton. 2000. Putin to tighten grip on regions. *Moscow Times,* 18 May.

Keating, M. 1996. *The Invention of Regions. Political Restructuring and Territorial Government in Western Europe.* ARENA Working Paper 8. Oslo: University of Oslo.

Khatami, S., and F. Vivekananda. 1995. Ethnic nationalism, federalism and a proposal for a future European community. *Scandinavian Journal of Development Alternatives* 14, no. 3: 35–49.

Koivulehto, L. 1999. Kalotti kuohuu [North Calotte in turmoil]. *Ruijan Kaiku* 5, no. 11: 1.

Kozyrev, A. 1997. Visions of the Barents Euro-Arctic region cooperation—Past and future. In L. Heininen and R. Langlais, eds. *Europe's Northern Dimension: The BEAR Meets the South,* 45–51. Publications of the Administrative Office of the University of Lapland, no. 39. Rovaniemi, Finland: University of Lapland.

Lausala, T., and L. Valkonen, eds. 1999. *Economic Geography and Structure of the Russian Territories of the Barents Region.* Arctic Centre Reports, no. 31. Rovaniemi, Finland: University of Lapland.

Leitner, C. 2000. Walking the tightrope—Cultural diversity in the context of European integration. *EIPASCOPE* 1: 20–24.

Mennola, E., S. Skålnes, and G. Hallin. 1999. *Interreg IIA Barents- ja Pohjoiskalotti-ohjelmien väliarviointi. Väliarvioinnin loppuraportti [The final mid-term evaluation report of the Interreg IIA Barents and North Calotte programmes].* Aluekehitysosaston julkaisu 2. Helsinki, Finland: Sisäasiainministeriö.

Murphy, A. 1991. Regions as social constructs: the gap between theory and practice. *Progress in Human Geography* 15, no. 1: 22–35.

Neumann, I. B. 1992. *Regions in International Relations Theory: The Case for a Region-Building Approach.* Norwegian Institute of International Affairs, Research Report 162. Oslo, Norway: NIIA.

Nielsen, J. P. 1994. The Barents region in historical perspective: Russian-Norwegian relations 1814–1917 and the Russian commitment in the North. In O. S. Stokke and O. Tunander, eds. *The Barents Region: Cooperation in Arctic Europe,* 87–100. London: Sage.

Paasi, A. 1996. *Territories, Boundaries and Consciousness. The Changing Geographies of the Finnish-Russian Border.* Chichester: John Wiley.

Pedersen, S. 1996. Saami rights: A historical and contemporary outlook. A Nordic Saami convention and the Lapp Codicil of 1751. In I. Seurujärvi-Kari and U.-M. Kulonen, eds. *Essays on Indigenous Identity and Rights,* 66–86. Helsinki: Helsinki University Press.

Schmitter, P. C. 1995. *If the Nation-State Were to Wither Away in Europe, What Might Replace It?* ARENA Working Paper 11. Oslo: University of Oslo.

Smith, D., and Ø. Østerud. 1995. *Nation-State, Nationalism and Political Identity.* ARENA Working Paper 3. Oslo: University of Oslo.

Solana, J. 1999. Speech presented at the conference 'Russia and Europe—The Common Future', Stockholm, 13 October.

Solanko, L. 1999. *Regional Budgets and Intergovernmental Transfers in Russian North and Northwest regions.* Helsinki: Bank of Finland, Institute for Economies in Transition.

Stoltenberg, T. 1999. Regional co-operation still the only hope (interview by Lars Hedegaard). *North* 10, nos. 2/3: 42–44.

Summa, T. 1997. The Barents region from the EU's point-of-view. In L. Heininen and R. Langlais, eds. *Europe's Northern Dimension: The BEAR Meets the South,* 65–70. Publications of the Administrative Office of the University of Lapland, no. 39. Rovaniemi, Finland: University of Lapland.

Sutela, P. 1999. *The Northern Dimension: Interdependence, Specialisation and Some Popular Misconceptions.* Helsinki: Bank of Finland, Institute for Economies in Transition.

Svensson, B. 1995. *National Interests and Transnational Regionalisation. Norway, Sweden and Finland Facing Russia.* Stockholm: Swedish Institute for Regional Research (reprint).

———. 1997. *Managing Cultural Friction. Swedish Firms in Northwestern Russia.* Stockholm: Swedish Institute for Regional Research (reprint).

Thuen, T. 1993. Two epochs of Norwegian-Russian trade relations: From symmetry to asymmetry. *Acta Borealia* 2: 3–18.

Tiusanen, T. 1997. The political and economic future of Russia. In L. Heininen and R. Langlais, eds. *Europe's Northern Dimension: The BEAR Meets the South,* 117–21. Publications of the Administrative Office of the University of Lapland, no. 39. Rovaniemi, Finland: University of Lapland.

Wiberg, U. The North Calotte as an economic region. In J. Käkönen, ed. *Dreaming of the Barents Region. Interpreting Cooperation in the Euro-Arctic Rim,* 168–210. Tampere Peace Research Institute, Research Report 73. Tampere, Finland: TAPRI.

Index

About the Contributors

John Agnew is professor of geography at University of California, Los Angeles. His recent publications include *Place and Politics in Modern Italy*, *Making Political Geography*, and *American Space/American Place: Geographies of the Contemporary United States*.

Luiza Bialasiewicz is lecturer in the department of geography at the University of Durham. Her research interests center around the geopolitics of European integration and the role of Europe as a symbolic and institutional reference point in post-1989 Eastern and Central Europe.

Susanne Eder is a Ph.D. student at the Institute of Geography, University of Basel, Switzerland. Her main research interests include urban social structures and transborder interconnections.

Jouni Häkli is professor of regional studies at the University of Tampere in Finland. His recent research on territory, discourse and spatial identities has been published in such journals as *Political Geography*, *Progress in Human Geography*, *Geografiska Annaler B*. He has also published several books and monographs.

Kristiina Karppi is currently developing impact assessments at the Finnish Road Administration after receiving a Ph.D. from the University of Tampere, Finland. Recent books include *Articulated Spaces—Minorities in Regional Policy* and *Conflict and Co-operation in the North*. She is interested in administrative territoriality in the context of regional policy and regional development.

David H. Kaplan is associate professor of geography at Kent State University. He has authored several articles and books including *Nested Identities* and *Segregation in Cities*. He is coeditor of *National Identities*.

Joanna M. M. Kepka recently received her Ph.D. from the University of Oregon. Her current research interests are in interregional cross-boundary cooperation in the European Union and Central Europe.

Mladen Klemencic is lecturer in political geography in the geography department of the University of Zagreb. He has authored and edited over eighty articles and book chapters including *Atlas Europe* and *Concise Atlas of the Republic of Croatia*. He is editor-in-chief of the journal *Hrvatska revija* [Croatian Review].

Anna-Kaisa Kuusisto-Arponen is finalizing Ph.D. research at the University of Tampere in Finland. She has published in *Peace Review* and *Geografiska Annaler B* and is interested in territoriality, identity, otherness and place politics, particularly from the local point of view.

Julian Minghi is a Distinguished Professor Emeritus of the University of South Carolina. He has published numerous journal articles and book chapters including *The Structure of Political Geography* and *The Geography of Borderlands*. His contemporary research focus is on the Upper Adriatic Borderlands in an era of European Union enlargement.

Alexander B. Murphy is professor of geography at the University of Oregon. He is the author or coauthor of more than fifty articles and several books on political and cultural geographic topics, including *The Regional Dynamics of Language Differentiation in Belgium* and *Human Geography: Culture, Society, and Space,* 7th ed. He is the North American editor for *Progress in Human Geography.*

John O'Loughlin is professor of geography and faculty research associate in the Institute of Behavioral Science at the University of Colorado, Boulder. His research interests are in the political geography of post-Communism and Russian geopolitics. He is editor of *Political Geography.*

Anssi Paasi is professor of geography at the University of Oulu in Finland. He has published extensively on the history of geographical thought, on "new regional geography," region and territory building, and the socio-cultural construction of boundaries and spatial identities. His books include *Territories, Boundaries and Consciousness: The Changing Geographies of the Finnish-Russian Border* and *J. G. Granö: Pure Geography.*

Pauliina Raento is a senior lecturer of human geography at the University of Helsinki, Finland. Her research interests include Basque nationalism and identities, U.S. American gambling, and cultural geographies of Finland. Her work has appeared in *Political Geography, Geographical Review,* and several edited volumes in English and Finnish. She is the editor of *Terra,* journal of the Geographical Society of Finland.

Martin Sandtner is scientific assistant, Ph.D. student, and lecturer in statistics at the Institute of Geography, University of Basel, Switzerland. His main research interests include sustainable urban and regional development and transborder interconnections.

Clive Schofield is a research fellow at the School of Surveying and Spatial Information at the University of New South Wales in Sydney, Australia. Prior to this appointment, he was deputy director of the International Boundaries Research Unit (IBRU) at the University of Durham, UK, and his research remains focussed on international boundary issues.

Joni Virkkunen received a Ph.D. from the University of Tampere, Finland, and is a researcher and program planner at the University of Joensuu, Finland. He has published in *GeoJournal* and *Geografiska Annaler B.* Recent research deals with territory, discourse, identity politics, and crossborder interaction and co-operation.